MY 48 YEARS

AT SEA

*Congratulation Captain
Deborah Dempsey
10/13/16*

FROM DECK BOY IN DENMARK

TO CAPTAIN IN AMERICA

Georg E. Pedersen

GEORG E. PEDERSEN

DEDICATION

To my wife, NINA, for her steadfast support
throughout this writing of my memoir.

We all have a story to tell. Mine is a sea story that started in 1948 when I turn 14 and no further education was available to me. My father gave me two choices, "STAY HOME FISHING, OR SHIP OUT."

For the next 48 years I sailed the Seven Seas carrying cargo from one country to another. The ships became my home and floating workplace. Going ashore in foreign ports, I was never more than a taxi ride away from home. I learned at an early age to respect different people and their cultures, and I witnessed their struggles first hand. Being a merchant seaman is not for everybody but once it's in your blood you don't want to do anything else. I always felt I had one of the best and most exciting jobs, from Deck Boy to Captain, on 62 different ships visiting 173 ports in 73 countries, some many times over. When I began the world was busy rebuilding after WWII a great time to be young, single, and adventurous. It was a time that can never be repeated.

MY CHILDHOOD

I don't want to bore you too much with my childhood, but I feel having good parents and a good childhood is the foundation for a good life.

I was born and raised in Rodvig, a small fishing village on the Island of Zealand along the Baltic Sea, 50 miles south of Copenhagen. We all spoke the same language, "fishing," a paradise for a boy like me who was always down by the water, always daydreaming and making plans to someday have my own large ocean going fishing vessel.

My Mother was a farm girl who married my Father in 1918. Shortly thereafter they built their home where they stayed their entire lives raising their four sons. I don't remember much of my grandmother who died when I was six, but I remember my mother telling me that before she married my father, his mother told her she would never have to worry about starving because he would be a good provider, but she would have a hard time keeping his clothing clean.

I have many good memories of my grandfather Jens, who was always in a good mood and happy, and very generous to me. He lived in a house overlooking the new harbor where he sat in a chair looking out the window keeping track of the boats coming in with fish. It was my job to run down to check the daily catch and report to him.

He had a housekeeper who came daily to clean and cook for him. Since he had lived through two wars and was used to things been rationed or scarce he would often tell her before she went shopping for food or other household items, "I don't care what it costs, as long as you can get it." My father paid all his bills at the end of each month.

My father started fishing at a very early age and had his own boat by the time he was 18. He worked hard and kept expanding. He insisted that my three older brothers go to work for him right out of school and together they build a small empire in the fishing industry.

My father had very little formal education. However, that didn't stop him from becoming a very successful fisherman and businessman. He became Chairman of the Fishermen's Association, the Fish Exchange, was on the board of the harbor, road, local bank, school commission, and chairman of the conservative party in our area.

My father gave me a rowboat when I was six years old, however he also laid down the law regarding the use of the boat, how far outside the harbor I was allowed to explore, and what kind of fishing I was allowed to do. I was always to check with him or with one of my brothers before taking off. I was also told to maintain the boat and keep it clean.

During the morning hours of April 9, 1940, German troops invaded Denmark from land, air, and by sea. I was six years old and don't remember much of the beginning of WWII, but I remember a lot from the last couple years. I have also read many books and met several interesting people who were involved in the war and fought against the Germans.

It is true that Denmark is a small country without any significant military, but the Danish people are not small minded. The Germans invaded Denmark quickly, new laws went into effect, and the Danish government stayed intact during the first three years of the occupation. Problems between the two countries were settled in a business-like manner by negotiation, and the German soldiers behaved respectfully towards the Danish population. The Danish government functioned as before, and any resistance was put down by the Danish police force.

According to Hitler, the Danes were a pure Aryan race just like the Germans. The Nazis called the invaded county a "model protectorate." Winston Churchill called it "Hitler's pet canary." Later, when Hitler got mad at the Danes, he called Denmark a laughable small country without any military power.

Back In 1622, King Kristian VI invited some Jewish people from Germany and Holland to come and live in Denmark. They were welcome because they were prosperous and had connections in the international business world. Denmark gave them Citizenship, and they lived among us without any discrimination. In September, 1943 Hitler suddenly decided to arrest all the Danish Jews and transport them to concentration camps. Danes by the thousands refused to accept that fate for their fellow countrymen and resisted the Germans.

There were approximately 8000 Jews living in Denmark, and they all had to flee to safety in Sweden with the help from neighbors and other Danes and a few high ranking German officers who saw that Hitler's intention would fail. My cousin William, at age 18, rowed Jews to safety in Sweden in a small rowboat, an 18 mile round trip on a dark night with German patrol boats all around.

There were good people throughout Europe who helped the Jews during the Nazi period. But many more, when faced with the arrest and murder of their Jewish neighbors, said, "What could we do"? For the Danes one additional word made the difference, "What else can we do."

Ninety percent of the Danish Jews survived and return to Denmark after the War ended, where they found their homes and apartments had been taken care of by neighbors and friends.

During the War years the winters were very harsh with lots of snow and ice in all Danish waters. Some places further north, the ocean was completely frozen so you were able to walk across on the ice from Denmark to Sweden. In my area there was ice as far out as the eyes could see. The ice was a good minesweeper. One winter 32 German horn mines were crushed and exploded in the ice, leaving a large hole with open water and sometimes dead cod-fish, either thrown up on the ice or floating belly up, easy to scoop out before the sea gulls could grab them.

My school was two Kilometers away. In the beginning I walked, rain or shine, until I got my first and only bicycle. The school had two small buildings and offered four classes. The first two years we attended classes every other day; later it was four days a week.

The class rooms were very dull and so were the teachers, and we were scared shitless. Three of us were told by the teacher we would never learn to sing and were not allowed to sing with the class. I had no interest in the boring stuff they tried to teach us regarding what had happened hundreds of years ago. I was more interested in the future. My mind did not focus on memorizing things I was not interested in. Guess I was a dreamer looking out the window. I did okay in mathematics and reading, but lousy in everything else. I know now that I am dyslexic and therefore had a learning disability. Old-fashioned teaching methods were practiced, and I often got a slap from a big hand across my face usually around the ears. Once he hit me real hard which made me roll on the floor. Another time in geography I made a mistake naming a town in Italy. The female teacher got so upset she hit me over the head with the pointing stick which gave me a headache for the next five years. I guess I had a concussion, but I never told anybody.

With two more years of schooling to go and still in third grade, I became a little nervous. When I mentioned to my friend Ivan that we were falling behind in school and that it would look bad if we didn't get into fourth grade soon, or even worse if we had to graduate from third grade instead of fourth, Ivan laughed and said it made no difference to him as long we got out. He also pointed out that we already knew how to read, write and were fairly good in mathematic. Therefore nobody would ever be able to cheat us moneywise, and that what it's all about, money in and money out. He also pointed out that my father was on the school board so, of course, we would graduate like the rest. Otherwise that would make the teacher look bad, so we would be Okay. He was right, we all graduated out of fourth grade.

I CAME CLOSE TO DROWNING TWICE

From the ages of nine to fourteen I made good money fishing, using long lines, catching cod-fish, eels, and flounders. During the summer I had special nets for catching shrimp. I did a lot of fishing with my friend Jorgen who was four years younger than me. Or sometimes with Ivan same age as me. We were never more than two in the boat. One day Ivan and I left the harbor to pick up our long-lines we had set out the day before using herrings for bait. We no sooner started to heave in the lines, when the wind picked up. We had a lot of big codfish on our hooks. It was very exciting hauling them in, and we didn't pay much attention to the amount of water coming in the boat. We had to stop hauling in more line and fish, so we cut our line and placed a buoy as a marker.

All the fish in the boat made it very difficult to bail out the water which was coming in faster and faster. We had to make a quick decision, either dump all the fish overboard or pull a large piece of rope through the gills, lower the fish back into the water and tow them behind us. We took turns rowing and bailing out water, hoping to make it home before it got dark. We were both wet and cold, and there was quite a distance between us and the harbor.

Just before dark I recognized one of my father's boats coming toward us. It was my brother, Jens. Since he was alone in the boat and there were a lot of whitecaps around us, he was not able to spot us right away. Ivan took off his pants, tied them to an oar and started waving. Soon the boat came directly at us and alongside. We were both happy when we stepped onto the boat. Jens was mad, at first, but when we explained and showed him all the fish hanging in the water, he was impressed with our decision to save the fish. However, we would have a lot of explaining to do when we got home since we had left without telling anybody.

Sometime later I was fishing with Jorgen. We left home early in the morning on a nice calm day and found our marker before the fog set in. The day before we had set our long line with 300 hooks using worms for bate, and it would take some time to bring them all home, depending on the amount of cod-fish. Jorgen was rowing, and I was pulling in the fish when Jorgen stopped and told me to be quiet and listen.

At a distance we could hear plump, plump, a noise coming closer fast. We both knew it was the propeller from a big empty ship coming right at us and she was not using her foghorn as required by law. As the plump, plump came closer and closer, I kept my knife in my hand, ready to cut our long line as the last choice before impact.

Jorgen was ready to pull away on the oars, and within seconds we saw the bow of the ship heading right for us. I cut our line and jumped next to the oars to give him a hand getting away from the ship. The force from the ship's bow water almost capsized us but we survived. We were able to see the name which indicated it was an empty German Freighter. We yelled and called them every name in the book, but that didn't help any. I am sure they had no idea we were there.

By the time the fog lifted, we were nowhere near where we expected to be, and it took us some time to find the second marker and get the rest of the long-line and fish in. On the way home we both agreed not to mention it to anybody so we wouldn't get grounded.

When I was twelve to fourteen years old I was able to go out fishing on bigger boats, fishing for herring using gill nets in the summer. The nets would be strung out 12 feet below the water's surface. Small wooden drums painted white floated on top of the water connected to the net to keep it at the required depth. Sometime the nets would be strung out as far the eye could see. A light was on the end of the net, but that still left a lot of room for big ships to sail over our nets and damage them.

Before dark when the net was strung out, the skipper and crew would sleep for a few hours. It was my job to stay awake on lookout for big ships. If a ship approached I would turn the search light so the ship wouldn't sail over our.

Trapping minks in the wintertime was very profitable. I caught one special mink t I sold for 480 kroner which was over one hundred US dollars. I was not supposed to catch them so before I sold the skin I had to have a letter from a farmer stating that the mink was killing his chickens.

I also walked the beach early in the morning looking for amber, drift wood, or anything else from ships losing their deck load, ships which hit a mine and sank, or planes that were shot down.

The Germans took over and stayed at a hotel on the high bank overlooking the water next to the harbor which became their headquarters. The regular Army soldiers were up in age and didn't bother us, but the younger Gestapos, Hitler-Jugend and the SS were a mean bunch.

One morning the SS guard on duty saw me down on the beach and let the dogs loose to chase me away. I had no choice but to run out in the ice cold water. I guess the water was so cold the dogs decided not follow me.

April 12, 1948 was the last day of school. Riding home with Ivan and Marie, we stopped half way home, set our bikes against a tree, dumped the school books on the side of the road and burned them. Marie had forgotten she had 5 kroner (1 Dollar) in a book, so it went up in smoke. That is how much we disliked school.

Two weeks later I was working on my boat and nets when Dad came along asking what I was doing. I told him I was rigging for fishing flounders. He shook his head and said, "No you are not." You have two choices, stay home fishing with us or ship out. I told him I wanted to ship out. Unemployment for seamen at the time was high which made it very difficult to get started. My father's right hand man, Niels Pedersen, no relationship to us, had worked for my father all his life, and had a good friend who was Captain on the SS Knud, owned by United Steamship Co. Thanks to him, I managed to get a job as cabin boy on his ship right away.

Once or twice a year my father would go out on a big binge, and the party would usually last two days. The third day he would go down to the Inn and pay the bill. Whatever money he spent, my mother would take the same amount out of the bank and give to charity. Before I left home my brother, Jens, reminded me.

"As you get older and start partying out in the world, remember we have to follow our father's footsteps. Make sure when you go drinking and partying it lasts at least two days."

My brother Jens and father told me that working on the big ships was different than working on fishing boats at home. "You will be in a completely adult world, and there will be people trying to take advantage of you, so keep your mouth shut and your ears and eyes open until you learn your job. After that don't take crap from anybody. However if you don't like the big ships come on home."

Again, thanks to my mother and farther, I had the best childhood anybody could ask for. They allowed me to dream and to venture out. When I left home I felt I had a diploma in common sense and conservative thinking, knowing that there is no free lunch, always to put my money where my mouth is. I also inherited the capability of respecting and getting along with other people. I am forever grateful that I never let them down or disappointed them.

I don't think my father had any problems sending me out at 14, but I don't think he expected me to make it a life time career. My mother had mixed feelings about it, and as she stood by the train station waving goodbye she saw me as a candidate for Janteloven which was used against us small town folks by the city slickers.

The Law of Jante is taken from a book by a Danish-Norwegian Author, Aksel Sandemose. The concept suggests that the culture within Scandinavian countries discourages people from promoting their own achievements over those of others.

1. You shall not believe that you are somebody.
2. You shall not believe that you are as worthy as us.
3. You shall not believe that you are wiser than us.
4. You shall not imagine that you are better than us.
5. You shall not believe that you know anything more than us.
6. You shall not believe that you are more than us.
7. You shall not believe that you are good at anything.
8. You shall not laugh at us.
9. You shall not believe that anybody cares about you.
10. You shall not believe that you can teach us anything.

1   2   3   4

1   *The bow and Foc'sle head with crew quarters below. Not a very comfortable place to be in bad weather, or when letting go the Anchors.*

2   *The wheel house, chart room, bridge wings painted white. The pilot room below used by the Captain while at sea. The Mates quarters, and Officers mess hall on the main deck.*

3   *The engineer's quarters and entrance to the engine room were at the after end of the house. My room was below the aft lifeboat. The white canvas shoot aft of the name was used when the firemen dumped the ashes over board.*

4   *The poop deck, with the Captain and the Steward Quarters and dry stores room below with the saloon. The white box on deck was the meat box.*

You never forget your first ship SS Knud 1,940 gross tonnage built in England in 1900 and a coal-burning steamship making 8 knots, operated by United Steamship Co. (DFDS)

She had sailed under British flag during WWII and participated in the Allied invasion of Normandy in 1944. When the War ended, she returned to Denmark and DFDS and entered service between Denmark-Antwerp, Belgium, carrying steel and general cargo.

When I joined the ship she was in dry dock in Helsingor. I realized she was an old ship and that everything was a total mess with shipyard repair equipment all over the decks and very dirty. I learned later that is the way every ship is when in dry dock undergoing repairs.

I cannot say I was shocked when I saw my room because I had never seen anything else to compare it with. The room was very small, shared with 2 other kids, a deck, a mess boy and me, the cabin boy. There were four wooden bunks, one little table, one chair, and a few drawers and hooks to hang our clothes on. The one empty bunk was used for storage. There was no way we could get up and put our clothes on at the same time. On the Starboard side was a small wash room but no running water, only a hand pump and a bucket. When you wanted to take a bath you had to spend a lot of time pumping cold water into a bucket and placing it under a steam pipe to heat. So it took some time to take a shower.

Out at sea the electric lights were on all the time. In port the lights were turned off at 10 p.m., and kerosene lamps were used at night.

I started as a cabin boy. Most of the time I only worked a half day, 12 hours. My job was to clean the officers' rooms, help the steward and the cook.

If the captain wanted to eat on the bridge, it was my job to get the food from the cook and carry the tray up to the bridge. I was also a gofer for the steward, helping the cook peel potatoes and clean the galley daily.

Out at sea I was called out at 0320 to make and serve coffee and toasted bread to the chief mate on the bridge at 0400, and to the second engineer in the engine room.

Carrying coffee and toast up to the bridge in the dark on a windy night and down to the engine room in bad weather was not always easy. The ladder down to the engine room was always slippery from oil and grease. Then I would go back to bed for a few more hours before bringing the trays back to the pantry at 0600, and start my regular day's work.

Each officer had a small sink in his room with running cold water coming from a small holding tank way above the main deck. It was my job to pump the water up from the main tank to the holding tank daily, using a hand pump which took an hour.

The galley was amidships, and the steward's store rooms were all the way aft. Meat was kept in an old wooden ice box using block ice which was purchased from a ship chandler in each port as needed. It was my job to help the cook move the ice around to get the best use from it.

The captain's cabin was also located on the stern starboard side. To get to his cabin you had to walk through the saloon (the dining area for the captain, chief mate, and chief engineer.) Out at sea, the captain slept in the Pilot's cabin mid ship below the wheel house.

The captain had a large bathroom with an old fashioned iron bathtub, but no running water. When he decided to take a bath, it was my job to fill the bath tub with cold water, using an old slow hand pump on the poop deck next to the stairs leading down to the quarters.

I had to pump the water into a bucket and carry it over to the starboard side right above his cabin and pour the water through a funnel and pipe leading down to his bathtub.

Every four or five buckets of water, I would run down to check my progress, then back and pump some more. When the bathtub was full, he had to use the steam pipe inside to heat the water.

I was the youngest in the crew. The mess and deck boys were both a few years older. They were City slickers a lot more street smart and always trying to take advance of me.

Antwerp was our bunkering port; the coal would come alongside on railroad cars and then was lifted onboard in a big steel bucket by a crane dumping it through a narrow hatch on the port side. Since there was so much obstruction around the hatch, it was impossible for the crane driver to come anywhere near it. He was forced to dump it several meters up in the air, making a total mess all around the midshap's section.

The galley was right next to the bunking hatch, and even with the skylight and doors into the galley closed tight, coal dust still came inside. Some would end up in the food, crunch and crunch each time you chewed something. We never got the amidships area clean until we were out at sea. In addition to bunkers, we also took on fresh water in most ports. This was done by the deck department, using a fire hose connecting it to the hook-up on the dock.

In 1948, three years after the war, most items available in Denmark were still rationed. Antwerp was the shopping capital of Europe. For years after the war, cigarettes were common currency for most transactions. Tax free cigarettes were sold for around $ 2 a cartoon, and their demand was unbelievable in many countries around the world

Crew members who had the right connections and money to purchase cigarettes, cigarette papers, coffee, nylon stockings, and rugs in Antwerp, sold them in Denmark and made a lot of money on the black market. Customs in Denmark was watching the ship in every port, shaking us down without notice, posting people on the dock and by the gangway, but for the most they were outsmarted.

When I first came onboard, I spent my money buying clothes for myself, cigars for dad and chocolate, raisins and prunes to send home to mom.

Knowing how much money there was to be made on the black market, I knew I had to get in on it. My first investment didn't pan out too well. I purchased a carton of cigarette papers and found a good place to hide it.

A well-dressed man came onboard in Copenhagen, asking if I had anything to sell because he had some buyers willing to pay big money for cigarette papers. After we agreed on the price, he told me where to meet him. He also told me to be careful walking off the ship with it. When I met him outside the port area, he called for a taxi to bring me to the buyer. We arrived outside a large apartment building. He told me to hand over the carton of cigarette papers and he would do the transaction while I waited in the Taxi. After waiting for what seemed forever, I went inside to check, and realized what had happened.

He had walked right through the building, out the back door and disappeared, knowing I would not dare call the police. Not only was I cheated out of my investment, I was also stuck with the taxi fare.

While discharging steel plate in Copenhagen using ship cargo gear at # 4 Hatch, the load became too heavy for the old mast and the entire mast started to bend slowly, at first making a lot of noise before the mast and steel plate hit the deck. People were running in all directions. By bad luck, the cook happened to be back on the poop deck getting meat out of the ice box and was hit by the top of the mast. He wound up in the hospital with a broken leg and arm. When the captain found out, he responded "Well, that's the end of my good omelets."

I was working the officer's mess while the mess boy was off for the day in the Port of Odense. I was standing in the pantry washing dishes when the Second Mate and his wife came in to eat after everyone had left. He asked me to bring some hot food from the galley.

When he saw me drying my clean hands on the dish towel before heading for the galley, he got very upset and stormed into the pantry, slapped me several times, screaming, "Don't you ever dry your hands on the dish towel again." I am still looking for that SOB.

After four months as cabin boy, a great opportunity came along when the deck boy quit. The captain told me the job was mine. What a break. As deck boy, I would be able to join the sailor's union.

My job as a deck boy was a lot more exciting, and I was now part of the deck department. My salary was $ 42 a month. The unlicensed deck and engine crew quarters was up forward in the fo-c-sle head, the most dangerous place on the ship in case of a collision or in a storm when taking heavy seas over the bow. It also had very primitive sanitary conditions, using a bucket for showering or washing clothes. I kept the room amidships as before.

Now my day started at 0600, cleaning the sailors' mess hall, serving breakfast, cleaning the inside hallways. Then I worked on deck for two hours, washing down and chipping rust or paint, learning how to steer the ship, and serving a hot meal at 11.30 for the sailors going on watch and again at 12:00 for the ones getting off watch.

The hot meals had to be carried in special containers from the galley up forward. I would also serve coffee at 10:00 a.m. and again at 3 p.m. I had a break in the afternoon before serving dinner at 5:00 p.m. The evening meal was a cold table with a hot dish.

The cold cuts were served on a large tray prepared by the steward back aft. I would pick it up before 5:00 p.m. and stop by the galley to pick up the hot dish. It was always a challenge walking from aft forward with food in both hands. Out at sea I would walk on the lee side hoping for the best. In the beginning, I forgot to cover the tray and the cold cuts would blow off when turning the corners. I would clean it and place it back on the tray hoping nobody would notice. Beer was served with the evening meal.

I don't know what was worse, dodging the bad weather out at sea, or in port walking on top of hatch board, steel beams dumped all over the main deck by the longshoremen

At 14 years old, you don't like to be around dead people or even talk about it. One trip we brought back a dead seaman from another DFDS ship. The casket was stowed in the #4 hatches. The hatch cover was open for ventilation, and I could see the casket each time I walked by, and it made me feel sad.

Entering or leaving each port, my job was on the bow helping with the mooring lines and getting the spring wire on/off the real. Going through the locks in and out of Antwerp, I was lowered down onto the walkway, together with a cork fender. It was my job to run alongside the ship and be ready to lower down the cork fender between the ship and the cement wall as per the captain's instruction from the bridge. A cork fender is round made of rope and knots filled with cork. I don't know how much good it did because after a while the cork fender looked like a flat pancake.

I am in the middle

After I completed the first trip as deck boy, I went to join the Sailors' Union located in Herluf Trollegade 5 in Copenhagen. After showing my discharge book and a letter from the captain, the union official told me I was welcome to join the union but that I would not be able to vote or collect unemployment until I turned 17. That was OK with me.

After paying my dues and other small fees, I was presented with my union book. The union official said I was the youngest member he had ever issued a union book to, and he wished me good luck. I stayed on the ship a few more months before getting off and going home for Christmas.

A few days after Christmas 1948 I packed my sea bag and returned to Copenhagen hoping to get on another ship, assuming there would not be very many guys looking for a job between the holidays. If I didn't get a job, I would return home to spend New Year's Eve and Dad's birthday December 31st.

I checked in at the Bethel Seaman Home across from Nyhavn, the red light district. I had my list and addresses of shipping companies, and since I was all dressed up in my confirmation suit, I decided to go to them all right away and make out application.

Most of the companies said they already had a long waiting list and they would call. When the day was over, I knew my best chance would be at the United Steamship Company (DFDS) who I worked for before. I was sure Captain Søskov had given me a good recommendation from the SS Knud.

The hiring office at DFDS was just a small hole in the wall in the cellar below their main office on Larsen Place. When I stepped down into the dungeon I was surprised to see only one kid there. After making small talk, he asked me if I had sailed before. When I told him yes, he said I was lucky and that I would get out before him.

The last day of the year I decided to look for a job in the morning and go back home in the afternoon. I was just about ready to leave when the door to the office opened and the dispatcher came out asking if anybody here had sailed for them before. I jumped and told him I had been on the SS Knud for six months. He took me into the Office, told me he had a pier head jump as a cabin boy on the "M/S Florida" sailing to New York that same evening. He asked if I could make it. I said, "Yes I am ready to leave right away." I called home telling them the good news, picked up my belongings at the Bethel' and took a taxi directly to the ship.

The M/S Florida was a 3,538 gross tonnage dry cargo ship. She was built in 1944 and completed after the War, sailing between Copenhagen and North America and the Mediterranean.

I Right away I reported to the steward who instructed me on my duties and told me I would be working with the stewardess cleaning the officers' and 12 passengers' rooms

Since we had very little cargo aboard, the Captain sent word down to the Steward to secure everything well and prepare for a rough ride across the Atlantic. Sand ballast was loaded on deck to ease the rolling. To everybody's relief it turned out to be a very smooth crossing.

The last day before arrival, the sailors got busy shoveling the sand overboard. It was fascinating to see the New York skyline and the Statue of Liberty when we pulled in on January 12-1949.

I was told Denmark had a shortage of foreign currency so I could only draw $10 against my salary in New York and another $ 10 when we got to New Orleans a week later, which was still only 50% of my salary.

At the time, most major ports had stores selling clothing to seamen from all over the world. They would meet the ship on arrival, set up a time to pick us up and drive us to their shop for free. Since I didn't speak two words of English, it was important for me to go ashore with someone who did, and getting a free ride to town sounded very good to me. The store owners knew we only had $10 to spend, and the higher ranking seamen had a little more. There were many nice items in the shop, but I settled for a very nice good looking jacket, but to my disappointment it cost $ 10 which completed my shopping.

We decided to walk back to the ship and do a little sightseeing. We stopped and looked in a window, and to my disappointment, there was a jacket like the one I had just bought, selling for $8. I was very impressed with everything I saw in New York and New Orleans and was looking forward to getting back some day when I had more money in my pocket.

We were out at sea on my birthday, January 23. It so happened that there was an engine maintenance man who turned 50 that same day and had a party.

I stopped by to see what the party was all about. One guy looked at me, then at the guy turning 50 asking if he was jealous of me and wished he was turning 15 instead of 50. He became very quiet and said, "No I would not want to go through all that crap again"

I was sharing a room with a mess boy named Ole who was a few years older than me and very quiet. He had been on a school ship for six months but didn't talk about it. One day I asked him what he had learned on the school ship. He took his time before he responded that he learned to take a dump without eating. Guess the food must have been lousy.

My next two trips were to Mediterranean countries, Portugal, Spain, North Africa, Italy, Greece, Cyprus, Lebanon and Egypt. Alexandria, Egypt was a place where everybody you met had something to sell you.

Part of the deck cargo included a large truck to be discharged in Beirut, Lebanon. By the time we got there, the engine was missing. The chief mate suspected that the longshoremen in Alexandria had carried the whole engine off piece by piece.

On the way home we stopped in Spain to load oranges for Copenhagen. I bought two cases to bring home to Mom and Dad. My mother came to visit me in Copenhagen and to make sure the oranges got home. It was probably the best and most welcome gift I ever gave them. The whole town was jealous because none were available in the stores in Denmark at that time.

With my one year at sea on the book, I was ready to move up in rank. I sat down and analyzed my job as cabin boy, working 10-12 hours a day, walking around in a white jacket being a gofer for everybody. Not my idea of going to sea, and I decided to get off when the ship got back to Copenhagen.

My brother, Karl, came to Copenhagen to pick me up. I had a few big old fashioned five gallon bottles of wine. Karl placed them on the back seat of the car. We were almost home when Karl stepped on the breaks to avoid running over a rabbit and, by a bad luck, one of the bottles fell on the floor and broke.

Later, to my big disappointment, I found out that law required I had to be sixteen before I was able to ship out as an ordinary seaman, and I was only fifteen and half. My Father recommended I come home, work with them during the fishing season, and ship out again when I turned sixteen.

HOME FISHING

My timing was right. When I got home most of the hard work was done, and the nets were ready to set out when the season started in August.

The kind of fishing my family was doing is called Bundgarnd, a type of trap net. In addition to the eels, we also fished for herring, cod, and horn fish, but the bulk of the profit came from the eels. It was very labour intensive and also required a huge investment which could be wiped out in a few days of bad weather.

The eels originated in The Sargasso Sea in the North Atlantic and travelled with the Gulf Stream across the Atlantic Ocean. It took between two and three years before they reached Danish waters and turned around to go back to their breeding grounds in the Sargasso Sea which is over 5000 meters deep. Grey eels have quite a history behind them before they get into Danish water where some are caught. Smoked eels are considered a delicacy in Europe and Japan.

We had around 20 bundgarnd and 4 boats. In addition my father had a partnership with a man on the Island of Møen who had started working for my father as a young man. The partnership worked well for many years

In January the preparation started with repairing the old nets used the year before, and making new ones where necessary. The nets were made from cotton and had to be dipped in black tar before used.

The net was tied onto wooden piles hammered into the ocean floor. If we had a severe winter the ice would break them below the water line, which meant the old stumps had to be pulled out and replaced with new ones, which was a huge job and very costly.

When a net was set and the tar smell had gone away, the net had to be checked and emptied daily. Normally we would leave the harbour at around 0600 in two boats. The part of the nets where the eels would end up during the night would be emptied first.

If there were a lot of eels we would return to the harbour and unload them into wooden boxes full of holes, floating on the surface.

Each live-box held up to 10,000 lbs. of live eels. My father sold his directly to Holland where they would be smoked and sold at a high premium.

When the season ended in November with all the nets brought ashore it was very good with top prices for the eels. I can still see my father sitting behind the old adding machine totalling everything up, over and over.

Christmas was always a happy time in our home and lasted three days, a lot of work for my mother, followed by my father's birthday New Year's Eve. I will always have good memories of the holiday season. As it turned out, Christmas 1949 was my very last Christmas at home, ever.

BACK IN COPENHAGEN LOOKING FOR A SHIP

In Rødvig we didn't have any stop signs or signal lights, and every time I left home for Copenhagen my mother would remind me never to walk across the street when the light was red. This time in Copenhagen was a big step in my career when I was finally allowed to register for shipping with the sailor's union, and getting my jobs there instead of walking around with my hat in my hand or sitting in a small dark cellar waiting for a job. When I entered the union hall, I noticed a lot of old timers sitting around playing cards, but only a few youngsters which I took as a good sign.

The dispatcher checked my union book and discharge book to assure that I had one year of sea time, and that I was 16 years old.

When he gave me a shipping card, he explained it would take between 30-90, days to get a job. He kind of felt sorry for me that I was not able to collect unemployment before I was seventeen, which didn't matter to me because I had money in my pocket. As a matter of fact, I can't remember a time in my life when I didn't have money in my pocket. He also told me to make sure I had my shipping card stamped at the end of each week.

The job call was every hour on the hour from 0900-1700. I stayed around to watch and learn the system. There was a big blackboard hanging on the wall with permanent lines and symbols like B for Bosun and down the chain. When a job came on the board, each man interested would throw in his shipping card. The one with the oldest date on and most stamps on his card would get the job.

I checked into the Seaman home Bethel and paid for two weeks in advance. I made all the job calls daily, and noticed the crowd changed from day to day. At the end of the week guys would come into the union hall to have their shipping card stamped, collect unemployment and disappear.

Nyhavn, the red light district was right across the narrow channel from Bethel, full of Bars covering two blocks along the channel. When you entered a Bar you where met with loud live music, smoke and the smell of beer.

Quite often there was standing room only with people from all walks of life from all over Scandinavia. The waiters all had big beer bellies and often sat or stood around drinking beer by themselves and were not always in a hurry to take care of the customers. The prostitutes were drinking with the customers, speaking a language nobody in my home town had ever heard.

I would find a place in a corner hoping to sit and watch all the activity without being thrown out. One evening I saw something that made an impression on me. At one of the tables three young women sat drinking beer. Two of them were good looking and nicely dressed. The third one was not. One guy came in, sat down at their table and purchased a drink for himself and the two good looking ones but nothing for the not-so good looking one. I remember saying to myself, I hope I never grow up and become a jerk like that guy.

The bars were also full of black market racketeers dealing in stolen gods. Old time police officers walked the area constantly, carrying sticks and not afraid to use them if somebody stepped completely out of line. The Swedes seemed to be rolled for their money more than everybody else, but they kept coming back.

On March 8, 1950 several jobs came up on the shipping board. The jobs were on the M/S Korea East Asiatic Company back from a six month trip to Asia. Among them was a Jungman (Ordinary Seaman) job. I threw in my shipping card and was surprised when my name came up and the job was mine. I was told to report to the ship at 0700 the following day.

The following day when I walked up the gangway, I was impressed with the size of the ship and how clean and well maintained it was. The crew consisted of 48, and carried 12 passengers. At the time, the East Asiatic Company was one of the most prestigious companies in Denmark, and I was looking forward to making a trip to the Far East.

M/S Korea

The mid ship house was in two sections, the forward one being four decks high and including the wheel house, captain, deck officers and passengers' quarters, and the main dining room. The Engineers and Stewards lived in the mid-ship house above the engine room. The officers and crew mess halls were located close to the galley.

The unlicensed Deck and Engine crew lived back on the poop deck, two men to a cabin except for the Bosun and carpenter who had single berth cabins. The wash area was an open space, and you had to use a bucket when taking a shower.

Before getting ready to shower I had to fill two buckets with water and heat it up under a steam pipe controlled by a valve just like on the SS Knud. There was no washing machine.

My cabin was a small hole-in-the-wall on top of the poop shared with the deck boy named Jens. There was only one porthole and one fan. We each had a small locker and a drawer.

The Boson was a big man in his fifties who had a lot of sea time behind him and had sailed under the American Flag during WWII. Besides the Bosun, we had one carpenter, six able bodied seamen, four ordinary seamen, and one deck boy, a total of 13.

The Bosun told me I would be on the 4:00-8:00 Sea watch together with an able-bodied Seaman name Anton. I asked him why I didn't have a mattress on my bunk.

He explain that each man had to bring his own a mattress, sheets and towels and that we were paid extra to do so. When I went ashore to buy a mattress, the picking was slim, and I had to accept a thin itchy and very uncomfortable mattress made of burlap and straw and only 2inches thick. The day of sailing from your home port is always very hectic, making sure all the stores and spare parts are aboard. In this case I noticed several Carlsberg and Tuborg trucks on the dock bringing beer for the trip, all brought aboard by the company shore-gang. I was told the company believed in parties aboard ship for their customers.

Securing the ship for sea was done one hatch at the time. First the steel beams had to be placed across the hatch opening. Next wooden hatch boards had to be placed one by one between the steel beams covering the entire hatch, then covering them with canvas tarpaulins properly tucked in against the sides of the hatch. I worked with the

Carpenter, helping him secure the hatches; using wooden wedges to keep the canvas cover in place.

Our first port of call was Gøteborg, Sweden only a few hours away. The cargo booms didn't have to be lowered. When the last cargo was onboard and the ship was secured for sea, gangway up, the Bosun told us to split up, go fore and aft to undock, and make the tug boats fast. The captain, 3rd mate and one sailor were ready on the bridge to steer the ship with the harbour pilot to guide the ship out of the harbour.

When it was time to go on watch, the ship was well clear of Copenhagen, and Anton told me to take the first wheel at 1600. It was very exciting for me to get behind the wheel and steer a large ship like this, and I made sure I was on the bridge early to relieve the wheel man already there. When I entered the wheel house ready to take over, the Captain took one look at me and told the Chief Mate to get somebody else. He didn't ask if I was able to steer or not.

Anton took the wheel and another man was assigned to the watch, and I became a day worker for a few weeks, a big disappointment to me.

The next morning when the Swedish longshoremen opened # 5 lower hatch to discharge the copra loaded two months earlier in the Philippines they were shocked to find the entire lower hold full of rats, and they refused to go down there.

An exterminator was called in, and twenty-four hours later the hatches were open again. Dead rats were everywhere. The Bosun told me and a few others to go down and pick them up and put them in sacks, which we did. Copra is the dried meat of a coconut used to extract coconut oil, and it was not condemned.

A few days after we left Rotterdam the Chief Mate told me to come up on his watch to steer. After one hour behind the wheel he told me I was doing okay and that I would be standing the 4 - 8 watch in the future.

The Captain was a snoop, never talked to anybody or even looked in your direction, but the Chief Mate was about the nicest man I'd ever met, and very professional, and so was everybody else. It was a good ship all around.

I also felt for the first time that I was part of the adult world, standing Sea Watches, eating in the crew Mess hall, going ashore with the older crew members, heading to the bars checking out the night life in various ports.

My watch partner, Anton Bak Sorensen, was a strange kind of character and didn't get along with the mate in the beginning, always trying to be difficult. When on lookout on the bow from sunset to sunrise, the ship's bell was used to notify when a light was spotted. If a light was spotted on the starboard bow the lookout was to give one ring on the ships bell. If the light was on the port bow, he was to give two rings. If the light was dead ahead he was to give three or more rings. Anton was playing a game with the Mate and each time he spotted a light he would give five or six rings on the bell. The Mate would tell him the system over and over.

Anton acted like he didn't understand it, but the Mate was the one who outsmarted Anton, and after a while he came around.

Anton was building a house outside Copenhagen which was round like a light house. He liked to paint on canvas, didn't drink or smoke. Twelve years later I read in a Danish Maritime paper how he had invented a new type of life raft which would right itself when it hit the water. That was the beginning of a new type of life boat used today. Hope he made some money on his invention.

The galley food came out of three different pots. The best pot was for the Captain, chief engineer, chief mate, and the passengers. The second pot was for the officers, bosun and carpenter, and the third pot came down to the rest of us. The Steward was in charge of duty free items. Beer was available all day for 10 cents a bottle, Gin and whisky $2-3 a bottle. A carton of American cigarettes was $2. At the end of each month your purchases were subtracted from your salary.

As per union contract, the day worker was able to work 8 hours between 0600 and 1800. On this ship they started at 0700 washing down the wooden deck around the mid ships house.

Out bound we worked on overhauling cargo gear, replaced wires and ropes where needed, took steel cargo blocks apart, renewing parts as needed and keeping them well-greased. The bosun made sure we youngsters took part in that work to learn from the experienced sailors.

In the Mediterranean, we stopped in Marseille and Genoa to load. Genoa was a real seamen town with good night life. We all hung out at a bar named Black Cat a few packs cigarettes sold on the black market was enough Lira for the night. Someone was always coming onboard trying to sell us something. Sometimes there were unbelievably good deals and some were fake. I learned quickly not to ask any questions where an item came from. I bought a very nice looking gold casing Swiss made navigator wrist watch for one carton of American cigarettes. I gave it to my dad, who passed it back down to me, and I still have it.

By the time we left Genoa we had a full load of general cargo for Asia. Before transiting the Suez Canal, the Chief Mate explained that I had to watch the steering very carefully.

He recommended bringing a wooden box to stand on to get a better view of the ship's bow and what was ahead. By the time we picked up the pilot in Port Said, it was too late to make the convoy for the day, and we spent the night moored between two buoys across from the city of Port Said.

When we lowered the Gangway, boats full of salesmen were waiting to come onboard to sell us souvenirs, shirts, shoes, suitcases lots of items made out of leather, always started out with ridiculously high prices.

Each ship awaiting Canal transit got a number. A few hours before it was our turn to precede, a crew of canal workers came along side with two wooden boats. The boats were hoisted up along the ship's hull close to the rail and tightly secured, ready to be lowered down to the water in a hurry in case of a sand storm, or if the north bound convoy was late and not able to meet the south bound convoy in the Lake, or in case of engine problems. The boatmen would then lower the boat to the water and row our mooring lines ashore to keep the ship moored.

The Egyptians had a reputation for being able to steal the cream out of your coffee. I never liked to deal with people from the Middle East, never trusted them and always felt I had absolutely nothing in common with them. Even today I feel very uncomfortable around them, and I am sure they feel the same way about me.

Since the Suez Canal was under English Control, most of the Pilots guiding the ship through the canal were European and former ship Masters.

When it was my turn to go on watch to steer, I walked up to the bridge 15 minutes early carrying my wooden box with me and placed it on the stand. I remember the Pilot watching me carefully, but he didn't say anything. The Chief Mate was watching me and translated the Pilot's commands from English to Danish, and I never had a problem and was told I did a good job.

It was late afternoon when we dropped the pilot off in Port Suez and entered the Red Sea, and it got real hot and stayed hot all the way through. Our rooms became like a sauna, and to get any sleep at all we had to sleep on deck.

Each day after dinner the day workers had a party, sitting around drinking cold beer and telling stories. By the time I got off watch, the party would be well under way. This was the first time I ever enjoyed the taste of a beer.

In Penang, Malaysia we anchored on the stream to work cargo. After Dinner I decided to take a swim off the gangway amidships not realising how strong the current was, and before I knew it I was way back at the stern hanging on to the rudder. I managed to climb up and sit on top of the rudder, hoping some boat would come by. After a while it seemed the current got weaker, and I managed to swim back to the gangway.

Singapore was a busy port with ships from all over the world. It was fascinating watching the small Chinese coaster lying at anchor, or moving to or from the docks loading and discharging freight from all over Asia. I was told the entire crew was Chinese except for the Captain and Chief Engineer who were Europeans.

Business men came aboard selling different items, tailors taking measurement for suits and shirts. One man was selling fresh pineapples, cleaning and cutting them up, selling them for very little money. The carpenter took me up to see Boogie Street, the red light district, checking out the activity.

Reading the history of the company was fascinating. It started in Siam now Thailand by a young Danish sailor named Hans Niels Andersen who came to Bangkok on a sailing ship and stayed. He started his own trading company in 1887 under the name Andersen & Co. which later became the East Asiatic Company of Copenhagen. Shipping and trading were the core of the business, and the company did well for Denmark.

In 1912 the company built the world's first ocean going diesel ship, "M/V Selandia." EAC became the first shipowner in the world to use motor ships on inter-continental liner service. Perhaps even more significant is the fact that EAC within a few years had replaced its entire fleet of steamers with motor ships.

There were rumours among the crew that Andersen actually started the company with money from operating Bordellos in Bangkok Maybe they came to that conclusion because the EAC was the only Danish company that paid the doctor bills for venereal diseases.

Another interesting story and history is that the Oriental Hotel in Bangkok was started by two Danish Sea Captains back in 1865. The hotel catered to seafarers and business men visiting Bangkok and became a big hotel chain throughout Asia.

During happy hours there were a lot of stories about Bangkok and Siam/Thailand, and I was looking forward to seeing it for myself.

Unfortunately we were too deep in the water to cross the sand bar to transit the Menam River up to Bangkok, and had to anchor in Koh-si-chang, an island located at the end of the gulf of Siam and close to the entrance to the river up to Bangkok.

As soon as we anchored in Koh-si-chang, a large old fashioned steam powered tugboat with three huge barges in tow came alongside, ready to pick up our cargo and tow it up to Bangkok.

Each longshoreman brought his own straw mat to sleep on. Several men were assigned as cooks, always busy chopping vegetables, cooking rice and fish, or making tea for the workers. The ship carpenter made two wooden toilets hanging over the railing forward for the workers to use.

Just before dark, a boat load of girls came onboard climbing up on the ship ladder made of rope and wooden steps called a Jacob's ladder. The girls were from 16 to 30, the older ones keeping an eye on the younger, all available for your pleasure, staying with you until sailing time, for a fee.

It was only a 20 minute boat ride from the ship to the small village of Koh-si-chang. The company had regular boat service between the ship and shore. I was very much looking forward to seeing what it was all about, and decided to go ashore the second night to have look.

As soon as the boat landed I was met by another bunch of girls asking if I was interested in going with them to see their homes, or trying their local food. I decided to stop at the local bar and restaurant for a few beers.

The bar and restaurant was built on wooden pilings over the water. It had a good view and fresh sea breeze. It all looked like paradise to me. I never felt and appreciated the difference in people like I did here, always smiling, happy and friendly.

When the town turned off the lights and the bar closed, I realized I'd better start thinking about getting back to the ship. When I came down to the boat landing, I was told the last boat had left long ago, and I would not be able to get back to the ship until daylight.

As I was standing on the pier ready to stay ashore overnight, a fisherman came by in a small narrow boat with an outboard engine. Since there were no white people living in the village and only one ship at anchor out on the stream, he must have realized I had missed the boat, and he offered to take me back to the ship.

I was grateful and enjoyed the ride out toward the ship. Then half way between the beach and the ship, the engine died and he was unable to get it started again.

The boat was very light in the water and drifted fast further and further from the ship and the island. The guy didn't have a flashlight or any other kind of light on the boat, and I was thinking what an idiot going fishing without an emergency light. I noticed he was getting very nervous, and I realized I should not depend on him for my safety.

As we drifted further and further out into the Bay, we found ourselves surrounded by a fleet of fishermen all lit up. I called for help and, by good luck, one heard me and came over. I don't know if he was ready to head back or if he just felt sorry for us, but he to tow us back to the village, Then he took me back to the ship just in time to go to work at 0700.

I realized I was lucky getting back to the ship when I did and decided to stay onboard for the rest of our stay in Koh-si-chang, watching the cargo operation and joining in on parties back on the poop deck, which were a lot of fun.

Our next port of call was Saigon, French Indochina/Vietnam. When the river pilot came onboard he also brought along several French Foreign Legion Soldiers armed and ready to protect us during the river transit up to Saigon. At the time there were four battalions of French Foreign Legion soldiers stationed and fighting in Indochina/Vietnam. Many of them were Germens SS who survived the war.

We were advised not to go ashore at night because it was dangerous. Snipers were shooting at all white people. But since we docked close to down town, some of us went ashore in the day time, and I found Saigon to be very beautiful, like southern Europe with Oriental atmosphere, and it looked very peaceful to me.

The other side of the river was where the natives lived in small shacks. However, it looked like there had been a huge fire with many shacks burned down. We were told a French Soldier had been killed there, and the French retaliated by burning down their houses.

On the way between Saigon and Manila we discovered a stowaway. He was a German who had enlisted in the French Foreign Legion but was very unhappy and wanted to go back to Germany. I don't know the outcome, but he did get off the ship in Manila.

Manila was another busy Port with ships from all over the world. The Longshoremen at the time was a rough bunch to look at. In addition to the large hook Longshoremen use in most Ports some also carried a gun in their belts. I don't know how many watchmen we had onboard keeping an eye on things, but I was told lots of the cargo was stolen before it got to its destination.

There were lots of small bars outside the gate, full of sailors, the juke boxes playing various American songs. To us, everything was cheap, a bottle of Manila rum cost only a few pesos or a pack of cigarettes. San Miguel was the only beer available and was very good.

There were always a lot of homeless boys shining shoes, keeping themselves clean by jumping in the water now and then and washing their clothes down by the beach. Since we were good to them they were good to us. If someone got drunk and fell asleep they would sit next to him keeping an eye out for him to assure nobody came along and steal our money, or watch. One guy named Jacob was around all the time, and I guess I can say I saw him grow up and become a young man and very street smart.

HONG KONG

A city that never sleeps, it made a big impression on me, with the harbor full of ships, large and small sampans, moving cargo between Hong Kong and the mainland or from the docks out to the ships moored at the buoys.

Watching the large sampans and junks coming alongside our ship to deliver or pick up cargo was interesting, and I never got tired of it. It was not uncommon to have three generations living on a sampan.

The wife or grandma would often be at the rudder steering the sampan alongside, and the men would be busy making the sampan fast to the ship. The women would do the cooking on deck, using a small stove with scrap wood and taking care of the children, dog, and feeding the chicken. In the morning the older children would be dressed up in uniforms and taken ashore by boat to attend school. It was team work at its best.

I noticed a Danish Cable ship tied up to the buoys close to the Hong Kong side and learned that it was owned by the Danish "Great Northern Telegraph Company" which was a pioneer in laying telegraph cable across Russia to China and Japan in 1870.

The Great Northern had embarked on a venture that connected the European trade powerhouses in the Far East by telegraph with the rest of the world. The ship was on Standby and ready to leave port if repairs on the underwater cable became necessary.

It was very interesting to walk around the dock area in Kowloon where people lived in small apartments, most without running water, often used as factories in the day time and places to sleep at night.

There was a busy stream of rickshaw men pulling people around in all directions, and the Bian Dan, known as the pole men, a large bamboo pole over their shoulders carrying boxes, packages, cages with live chickens, birds, live fish in glass tanks, transported from one end of town to another.

The streets were full of small shops and restaurants, everybody trying to sell something, the whole family working together as a team. Late evening you would see children sitting under a street light doing their homework.

The original Red Lion Bar located on a corner across from the old Kowloon hotel, was the hangout for seamen from all over the world. It was a large old fashioned bar with swinging doors, Bataan furniture, large fans hanging from the ceiling black and white tile floors. It was an atmosphere no one has never been able to copy.

Construction was going on everywhere using bamboo scaffolds tied together with rope. The women seemed to do most of the hard work on the construction jobs, walking up and down on narrow bamboo ladders with a heavy load of bricks, all with bare feet.

While walking the streets looking at the shops and activity I recalled a Dentist working on a patient with an old fashioned drill powered by a boy sitting peddling with his feet supplying the power, talking about torture:

Our next port of call was Keelung, Taiwan where Danes were not allowed to go ashore because Denmark did not recognize Taiwan as part of China. Keelung was not very interesting to me anyhow, and what I saw from the ship did not empress me. The People on the dock and the longshoremen working on the ship were not very smart and very poorly dressed, working with old obsolete equipment. That was the first time I ever saw people eating out of the ship's garbage can.

Japan, our turnaround country, was still down-and-out after losing the War. However, the people working on the ship were hard working and well-organized both in Kobe and Yokohama.

Sailing from Yokohama heading back toward Europe, we stopped in Hong Kong and Singapore again.

The East Asiatic Company owned Copra, hemp and lumber plantations in the Philippines; so we stopped in several smaller Ports to load Copra to bring back to Europe. Copra is dried coconut albumen a hazardous cargo to handle. It came in bulk, and sacks had to be kept dry and well ventilated. The copra in sacks would be full of Copra bugs and they would be everywhere, in our beds and cabins and would sting us all the time.

Cebu, on the Philippine island of Cebu was a Port often talked about on this ship, and I was looking forward to seeing it for myself. We docked very close to town. It looked like a little paradise, nice and green with palm trees and very clean at that time.

Across the dock were small bars with loud jukeboxes playing American music, lots of girls smiling and waving us down. After work I went down there and had a great time.

We had real bad weather crossing the Indian Ocean. Since we had a big load of cargo and were deep in the water, we took some heavy seas over the decks. In situations like that flying fish would be caught in the heavy seas and thrown up on the ship often knocking them unconscious when they hit the deck and not able to get back out in the ocean

A flying fish can be up to 15 inches long and looks like a herring with wings capable of jumping out of the water and gliding through the air for up to 100 meters, usually to escape predators. Flying fish are very good eating. In stormy weather I would always check the decks in the morning.

Guess my roommate Jens, decided to get up in the middle of the night to search the deck for Flying Fish a flashlight. However, we never saw him again. Most likely he got taken by surprise and forced overboard by a big sea near the number 4 hatch. I felt sad for the rest of the trip.

Before we arrived in Copenhagen, I was told we would all be paid on arrival and relieved by a standby crew for about two weeks while the ship stayed in Copenhagen and then called at Poland and Finland. That was a company policy giving everybody a vacation. You were asked if you planned to make the next trip.

I took the train home, looking forward to seeing everybody again. The Fishing season had already started, my father and brothers were happy now that all the hard work and expenses for the preparation was behind them. All the nets were in the water and money started coming in.

I never talked much about my experiences on the ship or about the Far East because there was no way they could understand or believe my experiences, and most were not interested. After I had been home for a week, I started getting bored and looking forward to being back on the ship.

When I got back to Copenhagen and rejoined the ship, I met a lot of new faces in the deck department, but the Bosun and Carpenter came back, and I was happy about that.

All the officers where new. The Captain was a man in his late 50s completely different from the first one. Whenever he came up on the bridge, he made sure he greeted and talked to everyone.

He had sailed all his life, starting as cabin boy working his way up the ranks, and he liked to talk about it, telling good stories about his experiences

When we got out at sea in warm weather, he would come up on the Bridge with just a T shirt and a Thai Sarong showing his tattoos.

My new watch partner, able bodied Seaman Svend was a man in his mid-thirties, nice to work with.

Everybody had a good time in Hamburg again. This time I went to the biggest night Club I'd ever seen called "Lillie Put." It had a circus ring with full entertainment and girls galore. There was another night club where each table had a phone and a large number. If you wished to talk to any of the girls at the other tables you just picked up the phone.

We loaded a large dog in Marseille, France. Can't remember how long he was onboard. He was in a big cage placed inside the door on the twain deck, number one hatch. The owner had requested that one crew member would feed and walk him twice a day.

Since I was on his watch, the Chief Mate asked me if I would take the job and make a little extra money. I agreed. The first day out at sea, I went up to feed and walk him and got scared when I saw how big he was. I didn't dare let him out the cage. I gave him food and water and left. The Chief Mate called me up asking why I didn't walk him around the deck. I had to tell him I was afraid of him. Since he could not leave the navigation bridge, he told me to meet him up there later.

When he let the dog out of the cage it turned out him was more afraid of me than I was of him and we made friends. I missed him when he got off.

The ports of call were very much like the trip before except for two additional ports in China. Also Otaru on the Island of Hokkaido, Japan was added. After a few days ashore, three of us were heading back to the ship. As we got closer we, realized the ship was ready to sail, and the crew was standing by fore and aft. We were told that the Captain had waited over an hour for us. What luck?

We spent Christmas around the Philippines, and New Year's Eve in Davao on the Island of Mindanao. We anchored a couple of miles away from town. The cargo copra and hemp came out on a barge towed back and forth by a little old tugboat that often broke down. It was a very slow cargo operation. The company had a launch service between the ship and town every four hours. Since it was the New Year's holidays most of us were off duty and looking forward to spending a few days ashore

We checked with the Chief Mate regarding sailing time. He told us it was almost impossible to say, but since we had two days off, he told us to check back on the ship and he would try to get the word ashore to us with the man who operated the Launch service.

Davao was just like any other small town in Philippines, dirt roads, small shacks, children running around everywhere, several small outside bars and restaurants. We all stopped at the first bar by the boat landing, having a few cold beers to get the feel of things and to relax. After a while we all split up and went our own way with a girl. By good luck there were a lot of them my own age. The following day was the day we had been told to keep track of the sailing time. I went to the boat landing mid-day for information, but there was nobody to ask or talk to. I was able to see the ship out on the stream, cargo booms over the side which indicated they were still working cargo.

I still had money in my pocket, and I went back up to the village, stopping at the bars looking for my shipmates, but nobody was there.

At the end of the day, I went back down to the pier to get information about sailing time. Before I made it down there I was shocked to hear the ship whistle give three long blasts which is the signal for the crew to return to the ship. By now, it was getting dark. I could see the ship laying out there all secured for sea. The next shock was when I found out the Launch service had stopped, and there were no boats in sight.

My hope was that some tug boat or fisherman would come by, but no luck. The ship would blow the whistle every half an hour. I wondered how many guys were still ashore.

As I was walking back and forth on the pier, I noticed a small boat up in the corner. It had a lot of water in it, but no oars. I found a piece a wood I hoped to use as a paddle The boat was made fast with a chain around a bollard.

I climbed down into the boat, hanging onto the chain hoping I would be able to swing the chain off the bollard. No luck. I had to get back up on the pier to lift the chain off the bollard, jump in the water and climb into the boat and start paddling. It started out okay but after I cleared the end of the pier the current took me in the wrong direction fast with no way of getting back in again

The boat kept drifting faster and faster in the wrong direction, and it was getting real dark and I soon realized I was in big trouble. The ship was getting further and further away.

Soon I realized I was drifting down on a large steel barge at anchor, and to my surprise the barge was loaded with black pigs. Among the pigs, I noticed a watchman sound asleep, and in the middle of the barge was a large oar. However, I was not able reach it. I made the boat fast to the barge and climbed up. By good luck, the watchman didn't wake up, but the pigs did. I managed to get the oar carefully and put it in the boat.

Since I only had one oar I had to scroll, something I had done in my own boat at home a lot, so I was good at it. I started making headway determined to make it as I worked up a sweat.

I don't know how long it took me to get to the ship, but it seemed like forever. When I finally made it alongside, I called for somebody on deck to throw a Jacob's ladder over the stern.

When I stepped on the ladder, I let the boat loose to drift away. My hands were full of blisters from the oar and hurt badly all the way up the ladder, but I made it.

I was told to come up to the Captain's office right away. He took one look at me standing there dirty and wet with a big hangover after two days of partying. He asked how I got back to the ship, and when I told him my story, he said he hoped nobody would find out about the boat before sailing. Otherwise they would charge me for a Yacht. Next question was if I had seen Svend Pedersen, my watch partner, if I had any idea where he was and when I last saw him.

He also told me he had waited six hours for us and had to get underway at midnight to make his ETA in Singapore. As we were talking, the Mate on duty came and told the Captain that a small boat was approaching swinging a flash light it might be Pedersen and the ladder was already rigged for him to climb onboard.

When the boat finally made it alongside we could see Svend standing in the boat wearing a new straw hat and a guitar hanging over his shoulder. It took him a long time to climb on board. When he got up to the rail he just rolled across and landed on deck, smashing his guitar. He stayed there until I helped him back to his cabin. I heard the Captain telling the Chief Mate to start heaving up the anchor and get to hell out of here.

When on watch the next morning, sailing toward Singapore the Captain came up on the Bridge and started asking me about my time ashore in Davao and the Orient as a whole. He also told me stories about himself when he was my age and I think he kind of saw himself in me.

When we left heading back toward Europe, I looked back at Asia and found it all very exciting. I knew I would be back

The ship had two steering Engines Port/Starboard, only one in use at a time. The officer on duty swapped Engines at noon each day. The second steering Engine would be on standby in case the one in use failed. On top of the Steering stand were two buttons with a safety latch around the one not in use. If the steering Engine in use failed all you had to do was remove the latch around the button and press and the idle Engine would start up right away.

There was a rudder indicator showing the position of the rudder. Whenever you turned the wheel the arrow on the indicator would follow.

On the way home to Europe, I was at the wheel steering into Rotterdam. The Captain was out on the Starboard wing of the Bridge with the Dutch Harbour Pilot, the Third Mate at the Engine Telegraph giving command to the Engine room, as instructed by the Harbour Pilot.

The Engine Telegraph is placed close to the steering stand. When the Harbour Pilot gives an order right or left rudder or a new course to steer always in English, it's then repeated by the sailor behind the wheel. Since my English was not very good, the Third Mate would repeat the Pilot's order to the Harbour Pilot in English and then translate to me in Danish, and I would then repeat it back to him, and carry out the order.

The channel was narrow, traffic heavy with large and small ships all around. I was given an order to change the course easy to Starboard. When I turned the wheel to the right nothing happened. The arrow was stuck. I told the Third Mate that I had lost the steering. He panicked and ran out on the wing of the Bridge to tell the Captain and the Harbour Pilot we had lost the steering.

All three came running in at the same time. However, by then I had started up the standby Steering Engine and the ship started to turn to the right.

The Captain looked at the situation, gave me thumbs up, and turned to the Third Mate asking. "Why didn't you think of starting up the other steering engine instead of panicking?"

One reason I like to mention this is because when I first came onboard I was told I was not big enough to steer, but now a year later that my quick reaction saved us from a grounding.

The year I spent on the M/S "Korea" was unforgettable and a turning point in my life at sea. At the age of 16 I had been accepted into an adult world. With two years sea time behind me, short only one year, I would be sailing as an able bodied seaman. Life was good and exciting, my future looked bright, and I made sure I enjoyed it to the fullest.

After being home for only a few weeks, I was completely bored and realized I had nothing in common with anybody there and didn't want to listen to the same old stuff. I decided to go back to Copenhagen and look for another ship, making all the job calls and be ready to go on short notice, which was always my system.

SS "Marit Maersk," my first of five ships under the Maersk line, black funnel with a blue band and a white seven point star on each side of the funnel which had been their logo since 1886. When the company first started, their ship hull was painted black and ship's structure white. In my time the ship hull was grey with a buff mid ships structure. Now they are blue.

The ship was in the shipyard in Rotterdam.

The company issued me a train ticket and I was told I would be on the same train as a deck boy named Willy who happened to be in the office and invited me home for dinner to meet his mother and two sisters. I think his Dad worked for the rail road and was not home. At the dinner table the conversation quickly came around to the ship and the long train ride. Willy's mother must have felt that she'd better give us a little advice about the upper side sex before we left. She started out by saying that in countries hardest hit by the war, like Germany, Belgium and Italy, the girls around the bars would all have some kind of venereal decease, and we should stay away from them.

Willy looked at her and said, "Don't worry, mom, we are not going to screw around until we get out to Asia." The two sisters busted out laughing, his mother looked at us realizing nothing or very little had sunk in.

I called home to let them know about my new ship, and that I had to sign an 18 month contract. Little did I know it would be eight years before I would see them again.

Sitting on the train looking out the windows riding through Germany in ruins was depressing; Belgium and Holland were a little better. Stepping off the train in Rotterdam, we took a Taxi to the hotel where the crew was staying for the shipyard period. We met a couple of crew members at the Hotel who told us we would be notified by the Chief Mate when to turn to.

We went to the ship the day before sailing. We were only six men on deck, and a deck boy, no bosun. The Chief Mate would stop by and tell us what to do. We drew matches for the sea watches. I drew the 4 x 8 watch.

Marit Maersk

The ship was oil burning Steamship built in Norway in 1938. The amidships house was large for the size of the ship. The boilers were located above the main engine which allowed you to enter the fire room from the main deck, a short distance down to the main engine room.

She had five cargo hatches with double booms at each hatch and steam winches 3,300 DWT. She was in the tramp trade which is very competitive, but the company had a lot of experience in worldwide tramp trade and was good at estimating the cost of a voyage, and always on look-out for another load at or close to the discharging port. Keep in mind you can't make money sailing around with an empty ship.

After a short trial run, we sailed for Hamburg, Germany to load what became very interesting loads, a complete whale factory, owned by a Norwegian company. The factory was to be assembled on the Island of Sao Tome, a small Island in West Africa on top of the equator, in the Gulf of Guinea. Modern whaling was carried out from land stations. The catcher vessel would go out and kill the whales with a harpoon and tow them into the factory for processing.

Karl, the Chief Mate, was a man in his 60s, deep voice and a happy laugh, tattoos on his arms stomach. In addition to sailing all his life, he had been in the Spanish war, lived in Argentina, and Canada. He didn't miss anything. His nick name was Karl six shooters I enjoyed being on his watch together with A.B. Smith, lots of good sea stories

The ship was still very much like the day it was built. Hand steering using an old fashioned magnetic compass. The galley was on the main deck starboard side, with an old fashioned coal burning stove. The cook made us an offer we could not refuse. If we would keep the fire and stove hot at night, he would leave eggs and bacon out for us to cook ourselves.

One day at the dinner table one of the sailors mentioned that between the captain and the three Mates were close to 200 years of sea time. Someone else made a comment that it appeared that this ship must be some kind of punishment for them or the last chance before they got fired. I learned a lot from these men.

At that time it seemed like you couldn't even look at a girl, or use a strange toilet without getting the crabs. We had a special white powder onboard, also used by the military to kill crabs. But the ones I got in Hamburg were very difficult to get rid of regardless of how much powder I used.

One of the ship's fire and water tender pulled a fast one on me when he told me to use kerosene, and I was stupid enough to give it a try one morning before going on watch. It burned my skin around my manhood and hurt like hell for a long time.

When I entered the wheel house to take the wheel, I smelled of Kerosene from a mile away. The Chief Mate said those darn engineers were sending those smelly fumes all the way up to the bridge.

Besides standing the 12 x 4 watch, the 2nd mate was also the Radio operator, sending and receiving all messages and getting the weather reports, and often talking to other ships in between. One day he came out from the Radio shacks all shucked up and said, "Wow, I just talked to a Norwegian ship where the Radio operator was a woman. Guess in the future I will have to be a little more careful what I say."

We arrived in Sao Tome at daylight on the 4 x 8 watch; I was at the wheel. The Island is of volcanic origin and rises to 6,640 feet with a tropical rain forest climate and a thick vegetation cover.

The official language is Portuguese. It looked like a scene from a south pacific movie. The captain dropped anchor very close to the beach to make it easy to get the cargo off. I had never seen such clean, clear blue water with so many colorful fish all around us.

When the longshoremen came onboard, we found out they came from the main land, had never seen a ship before and were wondering how a ship like this could stay afloat. Not a very good beginning and only a few spoke English.

The Chief Mate wasted no time taking charge, told us we would have to set the cargo booms and make the cargo sling fast, operate the winches, basically discharge the cargo ourselves, hoping the longshoremen would learn quickly.

The first cargo to be discharged was the heavy steel boiler on deck which would float and be towed ashore. The longshoremen were standing around looking with very little interest at all. This was like teaching a child how to tie his shoes for the first time.

The man who was foreman didn't show any more interest in the operation than the rest of the gang. The Chief Mate started to build him up, hoping to get some fire under him. Instead of eating with the laborers out on deck he was invited to dine in the officer's mess hall. They gave him an officer cap, a pair of new gloves and cigarettes and allowed him to sleep in a spare room. After that the foreman was all over the workers and things turned for the better.

I was driving cargo winches by No 4 hatch for the first time in my seagoing career, standing between two steam winches in 100 degree heat. But I did okay. When using a single boom, the Chief Mate would line up the workers in a row to pull the rope to swing the boom out over the side, and he would yell real loud, "Pull the rope, pull the rope." A few days later the workers started to call him Mr. Pull the Rope.

A normal day's work was from 0600 to 1800. We spent our spare time fishing. I'd never seen so many good eating fish anywhere. As soon as the hook hit the water you had a bite. The fish were very colorful with sharp teeth.

The longshoremen ate fresh fish with every meal. Sometimes they would bring live chickens and kill them just before cooking. In addition they also ate beef, rice and vegetables.

A few of us went ashore one evening, walking through the beautiful jungle with birds and animals everywhere. We found a small grocery store owned by the only white man we met on the Island. Among other things, he also sold warm beer. It was a very exciting feeling sitting in the middle of the jungle, sharing a warm beer with the mosquitos and listing to all the strange sounds from the animals and birds.

It was fun to fish for barracudas and watch the longshoremen prepare their meal at the end of the day and play games for relaxation before going to sleep.

One young man seemed to have more ambition than the rest. He would come around looking for extra work, washing clothes or repairing shoes. He told us he would stay on the Island for six months to build the factory before going back to the mainland with enough money to buy another wife. He already had two.

When the cargo was all discharged we left for Casablanca, a city with a real North Africa atmosphere like we see in the movies, people sitting out on the street drinking tea, smoking water pipes, old cars, and horse buggies used as taxi. The French Foreign Legion had a big influence on the town, with soldiers everywhere.

My friend Erik and I walked around town in the evening and found ourselves outside a huge gate with two French Foreign Legion Soldiers standing guard.

Erik asked in German what was inside, and to our surprise we were told it was a whorehouse, and we were welcome to go in. The French Foreign Legion always operated large Brothels wherever they went. We no sooner stepped inside when a young girl came running up to me and grabbed my cap. I ran after her, and before I knew it I was inside her small room. She was my age. She told me she had been sold to the compound by her parents for a two year period.

By the time I was ready to leave it was around 2 a.m. I was in for a big surprise when I found the main gate closed and no way to get out. After searching for a while, I found a place where I was able to climb over the gate and out to the street. To my disappointment, there was no taxi or anybody around at all, and I started to walk hoping to find my way back to the harbor and ship. I notice a lighthouse shining up in the ski at a distance. I assumed that was the direction back to the harbor. I kept walking. When I finally stood in front of the lighthouse on the beach, the harbor was nowhere in sight and by then it was 0400, three hours before sailing on a long journey to Archangel, Russia. I started getting a sickening feeling. No money and no passport? As I stood there looking up and down the sandy beaches, I noticed at a distance to the right there were quite a few ships at anchor. Putting two, and two together I realized does must be the ships at the Quarantine anchorage waiting to clear to enter the harbor at daylight.

I started to run, and as I got closer I realized I was heading in the right direction and soon I was able to see the outlay of the city and the harbor. When I stepped on to the gangway, I counted my blessings. Casablanca was not a place to be left behind unless you were trying to run away from something.

We had a long trip ahead of us sailing to Archangel. The Captain decided to take the inside passage up the Norwegian archipelago, and we stopped in Bergen to pick up the local pilot who stayed with us for the next two days to Lofoten where he got off, and we were on our own sailing through the Barents Sea, passing Norkap, and Murmansk, before entering the White Sea, to Archangel where we were to pick up a full load of pit props for Liverpool used to shore up British coal mines.

When we first arrived and dropped anchor outside the harbor, various government bureaucrats starting coming onboard. First the normal health department, immigration and customs, then the military, and many unknown government agents and special police

We all had to stand in line in the cold rain on the main deck while our cabins were searched. They were some of the most suspicious and unpleasant people I ever met anywhere. Several personal items like cameras, film and radios were confiscated and never returned. And that's what they called the workers' paradise

Looking at the equipment they had to work with brought you back to the Stone Age. They all seemed to wear old military left over clothing. I was surprised to see the diversity in the people, white and Asian mixed. The sad part to watch was nobody ever smiled and they seemed afraid to talk to us.

It was in the charter that the crew had to drive the winches when loading. I volunteered to drive the cargo winches by number (4) four hatch again just like in San Tome. Since the only export they had was lumber they had a very good system. The first thing on the agenda was to hoist a large wooden ramp from the dock to the ship side. The ramp was about 10 feet higher than the ship, the lumber would come on a truck, all ready with a wire sling around it.

The truck would park in the middle of the ramp. Getting the signal from the person on the truck, I would lower the hook and he/she would then make it fast to the lumber. Then I would hoist it up the ramp slowly, at first, and when it cleared the top of the ramp, it would swing quickly, and I had to be quick to lower it down into the middle of the hatch.

One day I saw a young Asian looking girl working on the dock by # 4. Each day I tried to catch her attention or give her finger kisses. She not as much as gave me a look. One day when no one was watching she returned my finger kisses. That was the extent of our romance.

There was an armed soldier at the gangway at all the times. One cold night I went down and gave him a package of cigarettes, which he accepted and put it in his pocket.

Next day a Russian bearcat in full uniform came onboard to see the captain. He threw the same package of cigarettes on the captain's table, told him that one of the crew members had tried to bribe the security guard, and to let him know they don't smoke American cigarettes.

The weather turned quickly, and by the time we left the ice had started to set in. We had bad weather all the way to Liverpool.

The captain stopped close to the Norwegian fishing fleet to buy fresh fish in exchange for cigarettes and Snaps.

It was nice to go ashore in Liverpool and be back in the western world again where I was able to go ashore when I felt like it and be around people not afraid of smiling or talking to you.

Our next port of call was Hamburg for repairs. As per union contract, each member of the deck department was entitled to two days off a month. If you didn't take your days off, you would be compensated when you got off the ship. The Chief Mate told us we would be in Hamburg for at least a week and that would be a good place for us to take some time off. We were all very excited and looking forward to vacation in Hamburg, the town known for the best night life in Europe. Another plus for me was that I had a lot cigarettes hidden away which was better than gold. With just a few packs in your pocket you were a king for the night.

When we arrived in Hamburg, we tied up at a repair pier next to the ship yard where we were met by a company ship's inspector from Copenhagen who told the Chief Mate to have the crew paint the ship's hull while in port.

That put a big damper on our vacation break. The Chief Mate came and told us to rig a stage by the gangway for the inspector to see when he went ashore, making it look like we had started painting the hull. We left it hanging there until sailing time.

After a week of partying I was behind the wheel sailing but had a hard time concentrating on the steering. I kept hearing the German beer drinking song *"whim skall thas betale"* in the back of my head which was played on every jukebox, but it had been a fun week.

We sailed empty out of Hamburg through the Kieler-canal to Rostock East Germany to load a full load of onions to Haifa, Israel. The canal pilot brought his own quartermaster to steer the ship, giving us time to enjoy the nice and colorful scenery with farms and small villages all around us. Rostock was very much in ruin, and it looked like nobody was in a hurry to rebuild.

Various types of uniformed police were running around with high pressure hats everywhere; some looked like the SS and Gestapo I had to put up with during the German occupation in Denmark. The way they looked and talked to us showed that they didn't like us, and there were a lot of restrictions put on us.

Each man was issued a special shore pass to show at the gate when walking ashore and returning; worst of all there was a midnight curfew, and if you were not back onboard you would lose your shore privileges for the rest of the stay.

The buildings still standing were very much in need of repair and paint; the apartments were small some without heat. There seemed to be a shortage of everything.

To get away from it all, the younger crowd would flock to the bars, five women for every man. The young women were clean and fairly well dressed. That's more than I could say for the men.

I met a very nice girl. She invited me home to her small, and cold apartment. She had a 3 year old son name Peter who was asleep when we got there.

It was early morning and long past the midnight curfew when I walked back to the ship. By luck, there was only one man on guard duty at the gate, an older man who gladly accepted my one pack of cigarettes as a bribe. He also told me he would be on duty the following day and asked if I could bring him some coffee.

For the next few days I loaded up with cigarettes and coffee before going ashore, and I had a great time. The third morning my luck ran out when I returned to gate and found three young Gestapo looking officers on duty. They confiscated my shore pass, searched me, took my one pack of cigarettes and small bag of coffee for the guard who was no longer there. I was now banned from going ashore again.

During lunch hour I walked the dock in different directions away from the gate shack and noticed several holes in the fence; some places it would even be easy to jump the fence out to the street. I asked the Chief Mate for the following day off. I loaded up with cigarettes, coffee and soap, waited until dark and off I went and found Ingrid waiting for me.

The following morning I heard a lot of noise on the street and in the apartment below us. Ingrid told me the police were there not necessarily looking for me, but perhaps just a routine harassment. She told me to hide in the closet and told Peter to be quiet, and she would try to talk them away.

The Police were standing close to the closet, and I wished I could understand what it was all about. To make things worse, Peter started to kick the closet door, and I was sure it would give me away, but it didn't. We stayed indoors for the rest of the day and talked about the possibility of me coming back to Rostock soon.

When I returned to the ship the next morning before sailing, the Gestapo looking guards at the gate gave me a lot of crap, but since the ship was sailing that morning they decided to escort me down to the ship.

Looking back, 5,500,000 German soldiers died doing WWII, mostly young men leaving an overflow of women. Dating the available girls helped reproduce the population. I felt I did my share of rebuilding Germany.

It was fairly smooth sailing through the English Chanel out into the Atlantic, passing Gibraltar sailing through the Mediterranean to Haifa, Israel.

Israel was a new country with Jews coming from all over the world to help build it up. Propaganda posters stated that someday their currency would be the strongest in the world. Looking around, I found it hard to believe. However the people seemed very friendly and they had a dream for the future.

After discharging the onions, we loaded a full load of general cargo for Cape Town South Africa. It turned out to be second hand clothing and house wares in wooden boxes, most likely items donated from Europe, and they either sold it or donated it to somebody in South Africa.

The freight rate must have been good because it was a 30 day voyage at sea. The first day out I was standing back aft washing my clothes when someone tapped me on my shoulder asking if I spoke German. It turned out to be a German stowaway, and he asked me our destination. When I told him we were bound for South Africa he was very disappointed because he wanted to go back to Germany.

I brought him up to the Chief Mate on the bridge told how I found him on deck. The chief mate who spoke German, started asking questions, and why he decided to stow away on our ship. He told him he had come to Israel as a volunteer to help build up the country but decided he didn't fit in and wanted to go back to Germany, and that he was under the impression that we were heading for Germany.

It is very difficult and costly to get rid of a stowaway anywhere. The Captain made a quick decision to pull into Algiers, North Africa for fuel and water. When we arrived, not a word was mentioned about the stowaway. At the noon break when a lot of people were walking out of the gate the Chief Mate had the stowaway dressed respectably, walked him out through the gate, gave him some money in small bills, and wished him good luck getting back to Germany and to never mention the ship's name. A simple solution to a big problem.

The sea voyage from Algiers to Cape Town was very smooth, nice weather down the west coast of Africa. We took advantage of all the sea time and nice weather, cleaning and painting the ship.

Cape Town was a very segregated city. The Danish consul sent a letter to the ship explaining that it was against the law for white people to mingle with black people, and if seen walking the street with a black girl, we would go to jail, and there was nothing he could do to get us out. The city was very nice and clean, the white population seemed to be Dutch or British. We back loaded General cargo for Antwerp, Belgium, another long trip at sea, stopping in Dakar, West Africa for fuel.

We ran into a big storm when entering the Bay of Biscay, with heavy seas day after day, unable to make much headway. The 2nd Mate picked up a distress message from a ship in trouble ahead of us, that the crew and passengers had already abandoned ship, only the Captain remained on board. The following day we learned from listening to the Danish radio that it was an American freighter S/S

Flying Enterprise, owned and operated by Isbrandtsen Steamship Company, New York. We also learned that the owner, Mr. Hans Isbrandtsen, was a Danish American, and so was the captain, Kurt Carlsen, who became very famous for staying with the ship alone for 16 days. Just before the ship sank it was listing so much that he was able to walk on the smokestack to jump into the cold north Atlantic water where he was picked up by a British tug boat. Little did I know that 12 years later I would sail with him on the Flying Enterprise II

When we finally arrived in Antwerp, the Captain and most of the other Officers went home on vacation, and a new bunch came onboard before sailing for Cardiff, England to load clay for Portland, Maine.

By now it was late January and getting cold, lots of rain and always windy, not a very nice time. Customs came onboard to shake the ship down and found two cartons of cigarettes not declared on the Customs declaration.

They took the cigarettes and gave me a big fine. The way it works on a ship is customs Collects the money from the captain, then he deducts the amount from my salary.

The Pubs had some strange hours, only open for a few hours at a time but always full of people, everybody smoking, some talking, some singing, very happy people, but loud. Everybody was making fun of the English cooking, which had a bad reputation, and rightly so at that time.

Two days out at sea, the Captain told me Customs had presented him with an addition fine before sailing and he had paid it. That made me upset because I was told that when I paid my fine I would not hear any more about it, but I had no choice but to pay it.

The weather across the Atlantic was not the greatest, gray, cold and windy all the way. I started dreaming about sunshine, getting back out to the Far East. I was upset about the second fine from the customs in Cardiff, and I made up my mind I would try to get off the ship in Portland, Maine if the Captain would let me go before my 18 month contract was up.

There was an Able Bodied Seaman who had been on the ship for two years and decided to get off in Portland, Maine and go to New York to get onboard a ship heading for Asia.

He told me the Danish Sailors Union had a hiring hall in New York, and that U.S. Immigration would allow you to stay in America for up to 60 days as long as you were registered and looking for another ship. At the Danish union hall, he had done that before.

He also told me how the system in America worked. When a foreign ship comes into a U.S. Port from overseas the U.S. Public Health officials came onboard checking the ship and crew's health for deceases. Next came U.S. Immigration checking passports, asking if you ever belonged to the communist party, or if you had ever been deported from the U.S. If not they would ask if you wished to get of the ship. They would give you a special pass. U.S. immigration is very lenient toward Scandinavian seamen because so many of them sailed on American ships during the war.

I went to give the captain my 7 days' notice and told him I wished to get off in Portland, Maine. He told me he would not let me break the 18 months contract, case closed.

There was a snow storm when we arrived. The pilot came out on what looked like an old fashioned sail boat. A small boat was used to bring the pilot from the pilot boat over to the ship. The pilot brought out the mail. I received a letter from my mother which had been lost or following me around for 8 months. It had even been in Australia even though the ship had never been there. After docking, we were told to present ourselves in the officer's mess hall with our passports. First we were checked for venereal diseases by the public health Doctor.

Next, immigration checked my passport and my name against a large blacklist of seamen not allowed to enter the U.S. When all clear he asked me what was music to my ears. "Do you want to get off the ship?"

The chief mate sitting at the table next to the immigration officer tried to answer for me. "He said. "He can't" He is on 18 months contract with 8 more months to go." The immigration officer looked at me and repeated the question, "Do you want to get off the ship," My answer again was yes. He told the Chief Mate to go get the captain. The Captain came running down looking seven feet tall and started running off his big mouth about my 18 months contract and that I was not allowed to get off. The immigration officer turned to him and said "Captain, pay this young man off today." The captain was shocked, turned red in face from anger.

The immigration officer turned to me and told me I couldn't stay in Portland. I would have to go to New York directly, register for shipping at the Danish Sailor's Union when I got there. He issued me a 30 days pass with optional extension for another 30 days.

The chief mate asked me to stay until my replacement came up from New York in two days. I agreed. I had approximately 300 dollars coming. Since my English was very poor, A.B. Smith went with me to the railroad station to check the schedule and help me buy a ticket for the following morning.

The next morning I was standing on the dock with my suitcase and sea bag, waiting for a taxi, all dressed up in my new suit, freezing. Standing in two or three feet of snow, I started kicking my feet in the snow to keep warm when I noticed something green in the snow. When I bent down to picked it up, to my surprise it was a roll of dollar bills, mostly small bills. What a welcome to America: Sitting in the train heading for the Big Apple I was kind of nervous, afraid I would not get off at the right station. One friendly passenger told me not to worry, New York was the end of the line and I would recognizing the Big Apple.

When I got off the train in Manhattan and collected my suitcase and sea bag, I walked out to get a taxi. Showing the taxi driver the address of the Danish Sailors' Union in Brooklyn, he tried to tell me it would be much cheaper and faster to take the subway. Since I didn't have a clue what the subway was or how to use it, he decided to drive me to Brooklyn. I was grateful when we arrived in front of the Scandinavian sailor's union hall.

After I registered for shipping, Mr. Clausen, the man in charge of the Danish sailor's union, gave me various addresses of ladies who rented rooms close by the union hall. I took the first room I saw. The rent was $8 a week and very nice, and I was happy to have my own room, and happy to be in New York. I paid for weeks rent in advance to make sure I would have a place to stay in case my money ran out.

NEW YORK

New York was a fascinating city in the 1950s for an 18 year old like me. The movies were open day and night, good restaurants, bars open until 4 a.m. and closed for two hours and opened up again at 6 a.m. The drinking age was 18. I met a few young Danes at the union hall the following day. They told me where to go for entertainment, where to eat, and where to have fun.

They hung out at bars named Kronborg, Montero's, Casablanca, and International, all within walking distance from the union hall. A glass of beer cost 10 cents. If you purchased three glasses the fourth glass was on the house. In addition they served boiled eggs, ham and other things to eat for free with your beer or drinks.

There were lots of small Greek and Puerto Rican restaurants, a good meal for a dollar, soup and a large piece of French bread or a large sandwich for 50 cents. The Puerto Rican restaurant had loud Spanish music blasting out of the juke box. Movies were less than a dollar for three and if you wished to see them twice you stayed. By the time I was settled I still had around 250 dollars left, not bad. The way the shipping situation was, I expected to get on another ship within a month or so. In the meantime I would enjoy the Big Apple to the fullest.

I followed some of the others over to Manhattan and quickly learned the subway system, the best way to travel in the Big Apple, but most of the time I stayed in Brooklyn hanging around Montague

Street and Atlantic Avenue and had a ball. Some of the Danes hanging around had left Denmark before the War and never went back. Some sailed on American ships and were U.S. citizens.

The younger crowd was waiting for a Danish ship. Some were waiting for Maersk Line ships for the Far East, some for J. Lauritsen for South America, and some for Torm lines for the Mediterranean. Some didn't care. A ship was a ship. I was hoping to get on Maersk Line for the Far East.

The fellows who were on ships and on the pay roll seemed to set up the bar most of the time. Even if we were 20 people in the bar it was still only $2 to buy a round for everybody. The bars and glasses were always full, the juke box always playing How Much Is That Doggie in the Window. Or drink rum and Coca-Cola, five songs for a quarter.

Shipping was slow and a month later, still no job. I had to go to the Immigration to get another 30 days extension. That was not a problem, but I was almost out of money and realized I'd better start to take it a little easy and watch my money and start hanging around the union hall hoping for the best.

One evening, walking home after spending most of the day between the Casablanca and Montero's bar, I got hungry and stopped at a little Puerto Rican Restaurant where they served soup and a large piece of French bread for only 50 cents.

The girl behind the counter was about 20 years old, very dark. She served me the soup, told me if I would wait she would get some bread. She asked the owner if she could go next door to get some more bread. The owner told her not to bother because it was almost closing time and to give me the soup and forget about me, and start cleaning up and prepare for closing. I was hungry and asked her to give me some more soup in place of the bread. She was upset with the owner and told me to wait for her outside, and she would take me to another restaurant to get a real meal.

I guess I was naive enough to believe it but still surprised when she showed up and off we went to another restaurant close by. She told me she had seen me several times with my friends.

We talked. Her name was Maria. She was from a small town in Puerto Rico, related to the owner of the restaurant where she worked, didn't like him much but she needed a job, and that was it until she found something better. I told her my situation, that I was looking for a ship and in the meantime I was not allowed to work or make any money while in the U.S.

She told me she had her own place in lower Manhattan and invited me home, like a dream come true. Her place was typical for New York at that time. It was a family's apartment, who again turned around and rented out a small room, all sharing the kitchen and bathroom. The family was Puerto Rican and very loud. Okay with me.

Maria was very nice and a happy person. To me it was like living in paradise. To play it safe I kept my room in Brooklyn, stopped by every now and then to change clothes, and the union hall to check on the shipping and listen to rumors on jobs coming up in the near future.

When I met some of my friends there, they were wondering what had happen to me, or where I was hanging out. When I told them where I had been and what had happened to me, they were all jealous, and wished they were in my shoes. Life was good.

I dreamed that someday I might be able to live in New York and sail on America ships, not an impossible dream, but a long road ahead.

After two months on the beach my visa expired for the second time. I was a little nervous when I went back to the U.S. Immigration for an extension but they gave me another two weeks.

Shortly thereafter I got a job on the "Olga Maersk" as an ordinary seaman.

Olga Maersk

It was a new ship built in 1949, one of the Cadillacs of the fleet. For the first time I had my own cabin. The average age of the deck department was 24.

We worked hard and played hard. At the time, everything was made from scratch by the crew, and this is where I learned to splice both rope and wires used for the cargo operation. On the second trip I had enough sea time to sail as an able-bodied seaman and was promoted accordingly, quite an accomplishment since I was only 18 years old.

Our schedule was the U.S. East Coast through the Panama Canal to Los Angeles, San Francisco, then cross the Pacific to Manila the Philippines, Hong Kong, Saigon, Bangkok, returning through the Philippines, Hong Kong and four ports in Japan before crossing the Pacific back to San Francisco. It was a good run with a lot of sea and port time. A round trip New York -New York was four months. I made five trips in 20 months

After making the loop on the East Coast we left New York with a full load of cargo for the Far East via Panama and stopped in Cristobal for bunkers, (fuel oil) and water and groceries shipped over from Denmark. Cristobal was a wide open town with good night life, and everyone had a great evening ashore.

Next morning the Panama Canal Pilot (who were all American at the time) came aboard with the Canal Authority native line handlers who stayed aboard for the transit to heave the heavy wires from the four electric mules used to pull us through the locks. It was a great experience standing behind the wheel steering through the canal and locks, watching the beautiful tropic scenery.

We had nice weather sailing up along the West Coast, and I did a lot of painting on deck. After two days in the sun, I got the worst sunburn I ever had in my life. I had to stand under the shower for a long time to ease the pain on my back and neck.

We stopped in a small port in Nicaragua, very primitive, but that didn't stop us from having a good time. The small village looked like a tropical paradise with outdoor bars and restaurants with plenty of available girls to keep us company. We spent the night in a small cozy hotel. Outside the hotel was a well with an old fashioned hand pump where the girls gave us a bath in cold water in the morning.

We found a small lost puppy, took her back to the ship and named her Peggy. She became good company for all of us and also for our dog, Tommy who had been on the ship for a year. As on all Danish ships, the unlicensed crew lived back aft and both Tommy and Peggy spent most of their days back with us. Out at sea when the cargo hatches were closed and covered over with tarpaulins they both liked to run around and play on the hatches. Once or twice a day they would wander amidships stopping by the galley, checking out the menu by jumping up on # 4 cargo hatch to look through the port hole into the galley. One day when in port the cargo hatch was left open. Tommy jumped up to see what was cooking in the galley not aware that the hatch was open, and he fell all the way down into the lower hull and broke a leg. The Bosun made a wooden cast and tied it around the bad leg which made him walk with a limb. Walking around slowly, he must have realized he was getting a lot of extra attention by being injured and was in no hurry to get better. The crew members sent out from Denmark were on 18 month contracts. Everyone else was able to get off anywhere but had to give 7 days' notice. On one trip in New York, a new ordinary seaman came on board who was 17 but looked like he was 12. When he presented himself to the Captain he took one looked at him and asked if he had ever sailed before. The kid looked at the Captain and said "What a stupid question. Do you think I walked over here from Denmark?"

Baltimore was known for its famous crab cakes, men's clothing, Polish jokes, and East Baltimore Street was loaded which strip clubs, prostitution and adult entertainment. Close to the piers were some well-known local bars, and some not so well-known. Once I happened to walk into a bar where I had never been before and didn't know it was off limits for white people. Before I had a chance to sit down or turn around, I was lifted off the floor by two big guys and thrown out on to the street hearing words and language I'd never heard before.

Another time in Baltimore I was sitting in a bar right outside the gate down to the piers when a man in his late twenties came storming through the door, ran up and down looking at everyone sitting at the bar. He grabbed me and took a couple of swings at me, and before I knew it I was on the floor. Guess I should have stayed there because when I started to get back up he grabbed me again and pushed me out through the door which was still closed. Guess that's why it hurt so badly. It took me a long time to get over that.

A few years later when sailing 3rd Mate on the Export Ambassador, a well-dressed man carrying a brief case came on board saying he was from the U.S. Weather Bureau and here to pick up our weather log and weather reports sent in during our last voyage. Since he looked very legit to me, I told him to wait in my room while I went to the bridge to get the weather information he requested.

Shortly after he left, I noticed my Gold Omega watch and some cash were missing.

The following day I contacted the Weather Bureau in New York who informed me they didn't have anybody representing them in Baltimore. The only nice thing I can say about Baltimore is I still like their crab cakes.

On the third trip, the schedule was changed eliminating the west coast port and sailing direct from Panama to Manila, a 17 day voyage at sea. Before arriving in Cristobal the Chief Mate instructed the carpenter to fill the after fresh water tank completely. As soon we were tied up to dock the carpenter connected the hose to the water hook up on the dock, pulled the hose onboard, secured it and turned the water on. Everything worked perfectly with just a few small drops leaking from the hook-up which was normal. He figured it would take eight hours to fill the tank, and instead of sitting around waiting for the tank to run over, he decided to go ashore and have a few rum and cokes.

Eight hours later and a lot of rum and coke, he returned to the ship and found the water turned off, the hose hanging slack between the ship and the dock. He assumed someone must have seen the tank running over and turned the water off, and he went to bed.

The next day out at sea as he was taking routine sounding of all cargo holds and water tanks, he was in for a big shock when he found the after water tank was almost empty.

I don't know how many times he measured before he realized the tank was empty and he knew he was in serious trouble.

When he found out, the Captain was furious. For the next seventeen days we showered and washed clothes in salt water. We never knew what went wrong, but most likely someone on the dock turned off the water for some unknown reason.

Three weeks later a few of us, including the carpenter, were sitting in a bar in Cebu across from the ship having a great time, when one of the girls came running in telling us our ship was sailing.

At first we didn't believe her, but when I looked down toward the ship I noticed the headlines were already gone, and the ship was ready to move away from the dock. We ran real fast and yelled to throw a rope down for us to climb up, and we made it.

The following day, the Captain told me he was not trying to leave me or my friend, Arne, behind, but he wanted to get rid of the carpenter. He had instructed the agent to send Arne and me to the next port, but leave the carpenter there.

Bangkok was a paradise and our turnaround port, staying 6-7 days discharging and loading cargo. The company took advantage of the cheap labor and hired lots of workers to clean and paint, giving the crew time off. Regardless what time of the day we arrived at the Klong Toey pier, a boat load of girls came along side and crawled up a Jacobs's ladder back on the stern where we lived. Most of the girls were young except for a few who were keeping an eye on the young ones. Some had a boyfriend from the trip before others were available for whoever needed a warm friendly Thai girl to sleep with, and keep your room clean, wash your clothes and be your escort ashore.

The Mosquito Bar located close to the piers was known by seafarers from around the world. It was on the second floor in a building looking very much like an, old warehouse. When you walked up the stairs to the bar you were hit by the smell of booze, beer, cigarettes and a lot of noise from the ceiling fans. The tables and chairs were metal, suitable for throwing at people when a fight started which happened quite often.

Many of the girls had their own little shacks built on stilts over wetlands in an area we called for swappen. The best way to get there was by boat. After a night at the Mosquito bar, my girlfriend decided to spend the night at her house, and go there by taxi. The Taxi driver tried to get as close as possible to her house before he stopped. As I started to open the door I heard my girlfriend screaming, "No, No." but it was too late, and before I knew it I was standing in mud up to my waist. After getting into the house she took my muddy clothes to some old lady who washed and ironed them and brought them back the following day looking like new.

All the shacks looked alike, without electric lights or running water. The toilet was just a hole in the floor. She had a large bucket full of rain water. During the dry season she had to buy water from venders coming around by boat. The area was a breeding ground for mosquitos, and you had to have mosquito nets around you when you slept. Years later the shacks looked the same except they all had TV antennas on top of the roofs.

Manila was another swinging town with ships and seamen from around the world. The bars and nightclubs were full to the brim and tables were full of San Miguel beer and Manila rum and smiling Filipino girls.

Stepping into an adult world at an early age, I had a lot to learn. The girls in Asia taught me a lot and what they had to do to survive. We shared our life stories and dreams. My friend, Judy, in Manila was a few years older than me and a real entrepreneur, buying and selling American cigarettes, exchanging U.S. dollars into Pesos. Her dream was move to the United States, and she was willing to do whatever it took to get there. 16 years later I was on the Bucyrus Victory operated by American President Line docked in San Francisco.

Walking off the ship through the parking lot, I was in for a big surprise when I heard my name being called by lady sitting in a yellow Volkswagen. It was Judy and her daughter. She told me she was married to one of the Cooks on my ship, but please don't ever mention to him that I knew her because he was very jealous of her past. After a short conversation, we parted knowing we both had our dreams come true. I was happily married and had two nice children, she had a life she had always dreamed about.

Back to Manila. The party had started and was well underway at the Legaspi Garden. The place was full of people, mostly Norwegian. To get to the restroom I had to walk through the dance floor which was crowded. A Norwegian couple was dancing and blocked me from walking through; each time I stepped to the left or right he did the same on purpose.

I finally had enough, tapped him on the shoulder and asked if he would please step aside, there is a Dane coming through.

He turned around and took a swing at me. My friends and his friends got into the act, and before you knew it, the whole bar was turned upside down with chairs flying in all directions.

When the police came and things calmed down, the question was who started the fight. The fingers were pointed at me and the Norwegian. By good luck for me, one of the police officers investigating was the same guy I had sold cigarettes to that day. The bar owner was willing to forget about the damage. The Police officer took me aside and asked what had happened. After telling him my side of the story, he asked me if I was willing to pay $ 20 to bribe the other police officers, which I did. He then asked the Norwegian if he was willing to pay $ 20 which he refused, to pay, and instead of being quiet he started running off his big mouth. The police officer asked me if I was willing to pay $20 for him, which I refused. He asked me "What do you want me to do with the guy?" I told him to lock him up, and off to jail he went. I am sure he is still looking for me.

On the ships we didn't have a toilet facility for the longshoremen which meant they had to walk off the ship and down on the dock each time they had to go to the toilet, which of course you can't do when out at anchor.

To eliminate them from using the ship as a toilet, the carpenter built a wooden toilet to hang over the ship's side attached to the railing. They were usually placed out of sight forward or back on the stern of the vessel.

One evening sailing from Manila after several days in port working and partying ashore, we were all tired and happy to get out to sea and get a good night's sleep. Next morning we discovered that the carpenter was missing and had not been seen since we sailed.

We searched the ship without any sign of him. When we arrived in Cebu with the flag on half-mast, we noticed a man standing on the dock watching us approach, and to our big surprise it turned out to be the carpenter. We were all happy to see him and to find out what had happened to him. He told us that sailing from Manila, he decided to try out the portable toilet he had made hanging over the port side forward of the propeller. When he jumped up and turned around inside the wooden frame he lost his footing grabbed onto the ship's rail and fell in the water. By good luck he cleared the propeller and came up quickly, seeing the ship sailing away. He was able to stay afloat and swim around until some fishing boat came around and rescued him. The fisherman brought him to Manila where he borrowed some money from one of the bar owners to buy an airline ticket to Cebu and was happy to be alive.

I didn't spend much money on work shorts. Mostly I would take a pair of old work pants and cut the legs off, as short as possible. One time out at sea I was laying on the wooden deck taking a nap during the meal hour. I was wearing shorts and my private parts must have been showing. When I woke up I felt something very strange in my groin. When I checked I found one side of my testicles had been painted green and the other red. Since it was oil paint I had to use paint thinner to get it off, and that hurt: Never did find out who did it.

One trip in Hong Kong tied up to buoys working cargo from the Sampans, the sailing time was set for midnight. We were called out one hour before sailing to secure for sea and bring home our anchor chain which was secured to the buoy with a slip wire. When we turned to on deck, the Bosun was not there and his door was locked, but we were able to look through the Porthole and saw him lying in his bunk all passed out. We decided to let him sleep in and went ahead and did the work without him.

Next morning out at sea, steaming down the South China Sea toward Saigon the Bosun finally woke up and so did his girlfriend who was supposed to have been off the ship before sailing from Hong Kong. The problem was, she did not have a passport or any kind of ID. We all got together agreeing not to tell anyone midships that she was here. If the Captain found out he would be required to report it to Port authority in Saigon and have her sent back to Hong Kong. She visited Saigon, Bangkok and the Philippines without any problems with the Immigration or the ship's officers finding out.

It was still a very difficult time for the people of Japan getting over their defeat from the War, but working hard to rebuild their nation. So many men had been killed, and the unemployment was high. Oil and raw materials had to be imported and paid for in hard currency. Meat was hard to come by; their diet was mostly fish and rice. Many small farmers found themselves unable to feed their families. Some brought their daughters into the port cities to become bar hostesses, hoping they would be able to take care of themselves and send money home to help the family, or perhaps get a ticket out of the country to start a new life by marrying a foreigner. Many did and became good wives and mothers.

I knew one girl whose father collected two hundred dollars from a bar owner in Kobe, with the understanding she would work there for two years. The girls lived three or four in a small room above the bar, without heat or water, using public Bathhouses located throughout the city. Any young male who didn't like the Japanese girls had a problem.

The small hotels were very primitive, with small charcoal stoves which sometimes would give out dangerous gas fumes. However, they had some of the most comfortable heavy comforters I had ever seen anywhere, the kind where you didn't feel like getting out of bed.

Like one cold windy night in Shimizu the end of November, 1953. We had been there for three days loading mandarins for Vancouver BC. We were to sail around midnight and to be back a few hours before sailing to secure the ship for sea. Laying under the warm comforter with my girlfriend, thinking about going back to work in the cold windy night, secure the ship and then sail across the Pacific, was not what I had on my mind, and I must admit that was the only time in my seagoing career that I ever considered jumping ship. I heard the three long blasts of the ship's whistle calling everybody back before sailing, but I didn't get out of bed.

My girlfriend showed me her bank roll and assured she would take care of me. Since there were only a few bars and hotels in town, the Bosun had no problem finding me and knocked on the door and told me to get my butt back to the ship, and I did. A month later, I got off in New York after 20 months without a break, and not very much money to show for it, but I had a lot of fun.

NEW YEAR EVE
IN NEW YORK

t was winter and cold in New York, and after a week of partying I
was ready to ship and get away from the cold weather. I managed
to get a job on the Laura Maersk, built in Denmark in 1939, and
in good shape even though she had been through the war as a U.S.
troop ship under the name Day Star.

Laura Maersk

Our schedule was a little different than on the M/S Olga Maersk.
U.S. East Coast through the Panama Canal, Los Angeles, San
Francisco, Japan and Hong Kong twice, Saigon, Bangkok.

The captain and chief mate were two old timers with many years
in the company, and thanks to them it was a very relaxed and happy

ship all around. We did have a gyro compass but no Iron Mike and it was hand steering only.

The Bosun was Jens A, a man in his late 40's. That was old to most of us. He was a good bosun and seaman from Vendsyssel in the northern part of Denmark, and sometimes he was very hard to understand. He was very emotional, especially after a few drinks. If you told him a sad story he would start crying.

We stopped in Boston where I met my uncle Hans and aunt Magda. Together with my cousin Harold and his wife, Doris, they all became very important people in my life later on.

We stayed overnight in Cristobal before transiting the canal and I went ashore for the evening and learned a good lesson that night. After a few rum and cokes, I went to the red light district where I picked a girl. She had a nice clean good sized room. There was a gap between the walls and ceiling and you could hear what went on in the other rooms.

I hung my pants on a chair up against the wall. As I was getting comfortable in bed I noticed a hand reaching over the wall from another room digging into the pocket of my pants and stealing $ 20 dollars. I got mad at the girl and everybody around there, put my clothes back on and walked out of there.

Since there was a police station close by, I went to file a complaint. The Police said it was a false complaint because nobody in Panama steals. They gave me two choices. Pay a $ 25 fine or go to jail for making such an accusation. Since I had money in my socks, I paid the fine.

In Hong Kong I went to the American Embassy to find out if it would be possible to apply for a visa and immigrate to the U.S. without going back to Denmark to apply.

The lady at the embassy told me it could be done, but it would take 18-24 months. She also told me I had to have a sponsor in the U.S.

She gave me a complete package with the application and requirements for me to fill out and return. I left the embassy with a good feeling and was very impressed at how nice and helpful they had been to me. I wrote to my uncle Hans in Boston who agreed to sponsor me.

In Bangkok, we loaded a baby pink elephant and about 30 monkeys. The elephant was to stay on board to Los Angeles and would be part of a private estate. The monkeys were for a zoo in San Diego, California.

The monkeys were kept in a special room forward port side called the tally room. The pink elephant was kept in a wooden stall and allowed to walk around in a small space on the main deck aft, a lot of freedom compared to the monkeys.

On a Sunday afternoon in the South China Sea, a day of rest, it was the kind of weather people pay big money to experience on cruise ships. We had a party going with plenty of cold beer, gin, rum & coke. Jens A was right in the middle of the party. One guy mentioned that here we were sitting in a nice cold breeze, drinking cold beer, and those poor monkeys were sitting in that hot little room drinking nothing but water. Jens was listening to the conversation and started to cry. To make things worse someone said to Jens," You have the keys and can do something about it, which we can't." He was still crying when he left.

Shortly after the phone rang in the after mooring station. It was the Mate on watch on the bridge telling us the door to the Checkers room was wide open and the monkeys were out and running all over the deck. When we got up there not only were they all over the deck, but also climbing up the mast and guy lines. The first thing we had to do was get Jens off the deck and put him to bed before anybody realized what had happened. I can't remember how long it took us to gather up the monkeys using special treats. It was a miracle we didn't lose any over the side.

The second trip, the schedule was changed to the around the world service through the Panama Canal west bound and the Suez Canal east bound, Japan and Hong Kong only once every four months. Montreal and Havana Cuba were added to the schedule. Sailing up through the gulf and straight up the Saint Lawrence River to Montreal was a new experience.

Havana, Cuba was one of the few ports in my time where you could go ashore with $ 5 and stay all night. A bottle of rum and five cokes was one dollar. A night in the biggest and most up to date Brothel was only $3. That left you one dollar for a breakfast and a taxi back to the ship in the morning.

I had someone help me complete my application for the U.S. Visa and turned it all in to the U.S. Embassy in Hong Kong.

I decided I would try to get off, or swap ships with someone from the Maersk Line ships shuttling in Asia, nicknamed China Coasters, or the Monkey fleet

Before getting into Singapore, the captain knew the Mathilde Maersk would be there also. He had been notified there was a sailor out of the hospital looking for a job on our ship, which gave me a double chance to swap ships or get off in Singapore.

Mathilde Maersk

When I walked onboard the Mathilde Maersk in Singapore, I knew I was onboard one of the most desirable ships and runs for the seamen who liked Asia.

I went to see the Bosun asking if anybody was interested in swapping ship. He didn't think so. However, the Engine department was short a motorman (engine maintenance man). If I took the job I would be able to move up to the deck department later.

When I went to see the chief engineer, asking for the job, I told him I was an AB and had never sailed in the engine department before. He asked if I was a good painter because my job as a motorman would be, cleaning, painting and handling tools to the engineers when working on repairs. Next he told me his system. We work like hell out at sea, and go dancing in the good ports.

He asked if I drank. I do, good, because everybody here does. Since we just came back to civilisation from the Persian Gulf we all took time off in Singapore.

The Captains on both ships agreed on me swapping ships. It didn't take long to pack and bring my personal belongings over to my new home. Since I was told not to turn to before we got out to sea, I felt like celebrating. First I met some of my old and new friends at the brightest seaman club.

There after we went to my old time favourite, Car Park Restaurant It was a parking lot for Robinson department store in the day time, and after 5 p.m. it was turned into an outdoor Restaurant, a family operation, mom and pop doing the cooking, the kids serving and taking care of the tables. It was a place with an atmosphere that will never be repeated.

Later I met a few of my new ship's mates at the Straight Caprea. I remember the crew from a Polish ship started a big fight, and we moved on up to Boogie Street. The party went on for another twenty-four hours.

When I worke up I had the biggest scare of my life when I found myself laying on a wooden poop deck on a ship out at sea. Hearing the propeller going blom, blom, blom I didn't have a clue what ship I was on or how I got there I was looking up in the sky seeing stars and a few low clouds. I noticed several crew members sleeping on army cots all around me. I went over to see who they were and found they were all Chinese.

The first thing that came to my mind was I was on a British ship with a Chinese crew. My head was pounding, and I felt sick to my stomach and disgusted with myself and swore I would never drink again.

A few minutes later the moon came out from behind the clouds, and as I looked ahead I noticed the moon shining on the ship's funnel and realized I was looking at the Maersk Line black funnel and blue band with the white seven pointed star. I went to check the name on the life ring "Mathilde Maersk." What a relief. I started feeling better right away. One thing I didn't know was that over half of the unlicensed crew was Chinese. When I went down below I found my suitcase and sea bag placed outside an empty room which became mine. I was told later that one of my new ship-mates had found me uptown and brought me back before sailing and dumped me on the poop deck to sleep it off, and I am forever grateful.

We were three unlicensed crew members in the Engine department. The 1st Engineer was in charge of all maintenance and gave us an option to work our eight hours between 0600-1800. He also gave a lot of piece work.

I was happy working in the Engine room and didn't miss the deck department as much as I thought I would. However, two months later I went back on deck as able bodied seaman since I knew my future would always be in the deck department.

Japan was our home base. The schedule called for a six week trip from Japan, Hong Kong, Bangkok, Singapore, Indonesia and occasionally stop in the Philippines or Taiwan, with two weeks on the coast of Japan.

Second schedule was a 10 weeks trip from Japan, Hong Kong, Singapore, Colombo, Saudi Arabia, Iraq, Iran, Bombay, Cochin India, back to Singapore, Hong Kong and Japan

The Persian Gulf countries were never very exciting, neither were the people. The heat was unbearable in ports like Al Basrah, Abadan, and Koramshar, Iran.

Sometimes we stayed days out at anchor before a berth would be available to discharge our cargo from Japan. The cargo operation was very slow, mainly because everything was done by hand. Mechanical machinery like fork lifts were not used.

It was difficult to watch the cargo operation in Basra, Iraq where I saw large heavy wooden boxes being discharged and lowered down on men's back's, moving them away from the dock area step by step. I was told the average male life span was 36 years in Iraq at that time.

The star of the ship was our female dog name Tory after the Japanese Sun Tory whisky.
She was from Osaka and had followed us back to the ship.

Tory loved ice cubes when it was real hot, and when I had a chance I would steal a few pies and give them to her. If I gave her two pieces she would hide one underneath the mooring line to save for later. When she came back to get her ice cube and was unable to find it she would get very upset. She never learned that they melted. When nature called she had a spot up forward by # 1 hatch where she did her business.

One trip out of Bangkok with a load of teak wood logs on deck, I happened to watch her jumping up on the logs to get forward. The ship was rolling and shipping water over decks and logs. I watched her stand looking at the sea and the roll of the vessel waiting for the right opportunity before she ran. She was a real sea dog. I had many good walks ashore with her in various ports, looking at the ships from around the world and watching the activity around the port areas. She would have a bath before we came back to Japan, and dressed up wearing her best. Sometimes I would take her with me to the bars in Kobe.

The Bosun Gunner (nick named Gunner gold tooth) was a man I will never forget. He was in his mid-50s. Every tooth in his mouth was plated with gold, a huge tiger head tattoo was on his chest, and a pair of fighting gloves tattoo on his private parts.

Gunner had been stuck and forgotten in Shanghai during WWII when Japanese invaded China. He spent two years dogging the Japanese living with the prostitutes without any help from anybody else.

Since this was before air conditioning it was often too hot to sleep in my room when we were around the Persian Gulf and India. I built a free swinging bed frame and hung it underneath the life raft. It turned out to be a great idea, giving me a nice breeze up there. Tory would sleep on deck below me.

Coming back from the Persian Gulf, we stopped in Bombay, Cochin and other small ports in India. Bombay was a busy port and very congested with many ships lying at anchor awaiting berth. When entering port and transiting the locks, we were always assisted by two old coal burning tug boats huffing and puffing like, an old steam train blowing off smoke and fireballs which made it necessary for us to water down the canvas hatch covers to eliminate fires or ruin the canvas hatch covers. While in Bombay I took many walks around the docks with Tory on a leash, looking at the ships and watching the homeless children hanging around the water front.

On one trip in Cochin, I had another unforgettable experience which could have changed my life for ever. During my lunch break I was standing back on the poop deck with our rooms below, watching the longshoremen eating their lunch down on the dock. A Fisherman in a small boat came along side trying to sell his catch of shrimp. He told me he had enough for a big bucket full, and they could be mine for six packs of cigarettes. I went down to get a large bucket and a heaving line, and six packs of cigarettes. I lowered my empty bucket which the man quickly filled up whit beautiful shrimps, and I quickly pulled up on deck. As I started lowering the six packs of cigarettes a man wearing a long white sheet came running toward me yelling. "Hold it, hold it."

He told me he was a Custom's officer, and I was not allowed to sell cigarettes. I told him I was not selling cigarettes but exchanging them for food. The fisherman asked for 30 rubies instead of cigarettes, and he was happy and left. As I started picking up my shrimp and cigarettes the guy dressed in the white sheet told me to hold everything, that he was calling the chief Customs officers. Since my bucket of fresh shrimp was sitting in the hot sun, I told him I was taking my bucket of shrimp away from the sun.

When I picked up the bucket and started walking away he put his hand on the bucket. I told him to take his hand off my bucket. Next thing I know was he lay out on deck screaming like a pig calling for help. The longshoremen now back onboard gathered around him. Shortly thereafter the ambulance came, and he was carried off the ship on a stretcher.

An hour later the police came, and I was called up to the Captain's office where the police and another customs officer were waiting. The Captain asked for my side of the story. The company agent who was called down to assist us deal with the Police.

The Police officer claimed the man who had been attacked by me was very weak and unable to walk or talk.

The Police officer told the Captain it had to be settled in court someday down the line when the man was well enough to get out of the hospital, and that in the meantime, I would be under arrest.

The Captain refused to let them take me off the ship without having the Danish consul here who would have to come down from Bombay. The agent started getting nervous because now we were talking about delaying the ship which was scheduled to sail at 8 p.m.

that same day. He talked to the Captain in private. Later they both agreed I was not at fault and that they were trying to make some easy money on my situation, and admitted we had no choice but to play along with the game.

The Captain and the agent guarantied me they would make sure I would be taken care of while in jail and that the company would hire lawyers to represent me in court and send me back to the ship. The Captain told the Steward to make up a box full of various types of canned food, hard boiled eggs and bread to take along.

The Police station and jail were inside the port area, with only one small cell with a cement floor and one small window with steel bars across it. I was given a straw mat to sleep on, and the duty officer would let me out to use the toilet which was very primitive.

Before the ship sailed, one of the Chinese crew members came and told me through the window and bars that he had a friend in town who would look out for me.

Each morning for the next several days I was told that the report from the hospital was that the man was still very weak and unable to leave or to appear in court. I was given soap and towel and a bucket of water to keep myself clean and often allowed to sit in the office looking down over the harbour. One thing that went through my mind and scared me was What if the man in the white sheet was sick with some kind of disease and died I would be a murderer, and in serious trouble.

Finally, one morning I was told today was the day I would be in court. I was able to take a shower using cold water from a bucket. I was given a nice clean white shirt, and at around 10:30

I was brought down on a small ferry and sailed across the Bay to the court house. When we entered house I was met by the company agent and three attorneys, one British and two Indians. They told me they would do all the talking, and if I was asked if I spoke English to just say no. That was not very far from the truth anyhow.

The court house was a large low building without windows but it had a mosquito net all around to take advantage of the breeze. There was a large heavy desk for the judge and chairs and wooden benches for the public to sit on.

In the middle of the room was a round stand where I was placed. I stood there for what seemed forever. Shortly after 12 noon a ferry arrived loaded with people from all walks of life. I found out later that some of them were longshoremen.

As they got off the Ferry and entered the courtroom they had to walk by me on the stand. Some of them came over, pointed at me and said, "You bad man. You hit one of our people, bad man," and they spit at me.

Soon the court room was full of people all mad at me. Around 1230 an ambulance came. Two men in white carried the man in the white sheet into the courtroom and sat him down in a large chair close to Judge. He appeared to be very weak. The two Ambulance drivers had to hold him up straight in the chair.

The judge came in, listened to the Custom's officer complaints. He pretended he was really hurting and unable to speak or stay in focus. My Attorney went into action, presented the case the way it happened. The Judge asked me if I understood English and per instruction I said, no.

I believe as time went on the custom officer was losing ground with his story. He became more alert and louder. At the end he was standing up yelling with his fist up in the air. Witnesses were brought in. I had none, all were in his favour.

Around three o'clock most of the people had left. On the way out they would look at me like I was the worst criminal they had ever seen, pointing fingers and spitting at me again.

The Attorneys on both sides were now putting their heads together for what seemed forever. Finally the three who represented me came over and took me off the stand and gave me the news. The custom officer had four witnesses, all testified they had seen me hit him six (6) times in his chest. I was told I had two choices.

(a) Declare I was guilty of hitting him six times in his chest and pay a fine of 250 US Dollar

(b) If I declared not guilty I would get three or more months in jail.

I chose (a) and walked out a free man, thanks to Captain R. Mogensen for standing up for me and hiring the Attorney, making sure the company paid the bill except for the fine which came out of my own pocket. The agent told me the ship was still in India loading cargo for Singapore and he issued a train ticket. I was on my way. The train was an open car without windows, black smoke and soot blowing in my face, but I didn't mind. When I finally made it to my destination, the ship was laying at anchor outside the harbour waiting for me.

Sitting in the boat approaching "Mathilde Maersk" I saw her as the flag ship of the fleet, and I was home. I went up to see the Captain right away and thanked him for his support and for sticking up for me. After that experience, India was never my favourite place to visit, however I still like shrimp. Later I was reading in a "NY TID," the Danish Sailors union paper an article about harassment seamen had to put up with out in the world. The more I read the more I realized it was a situation in Cochin identical to mine and what I had been up against. After reading it the second time, I noticed the name of the writer was our Bosun. He wrote a very nice article and told my story without telling me first.

Three months later we were back in Cochin. During the noon hour the Chief Mate happened to be by the gangway when a man looking familiar came up asking for Mr. Pedersen. He asked if he was the man who was here last trip and got a free ride to the hospital.

The man said, "Yes, and I am here to say hello to my friend Mr Pedersen." The Chief Mate quickly realised that if he went back to see me the trouble might start all over again, and told him since he was not on duty on this ship he better get off the ship and down the gangway before he hit him six times in his chest. He took off.

Several months later I was notified by the American Embassy in Hong Kong that my visa had been granted and was ready to be issued after my final medical examination at the Embassy.

It was the end of October, 1955 when I went for my final interview and complete physical. The Doctor checked for tattoos or marks for identification. Having none, he noticed my two little fingers on both hands are bent. I have to admit I had never noticed that myself. Later I found out that my father and brothers had the same. The Staff at the Embassy was gracious and went out of the way to help me, and I'm forever grateful.

I gave my seven days' notice and got off the ship in Tokyo Nov. 2, 1955. I took a Taxi to my apartment in Yokohama looking forward to a nice vacation

My girlfriend had decorated the apartment, but it was still not very comfortable except for the warm comforter. We had no running water or heat. There was a motorcycle style toilet where you had to bend your knees and squat, the honey bucket was emptied once a week. We used a public bath house close by. The apartment was on top of a beauty shop, in the middle of a vegetable market in China Town located in Yamashita-cho, Naka-ku a place where many Chinese and Koreans live and form a community that is a mixture of businesses and residences.

*Chinatown around 1955 (b). From the collection of the Yokohama
Archives of History, photographed by Haruchika Hirose.*

At the time there were over sixty bars in China town. The Danes
were partying at the Copenhagen, Scandia and Viking Bar, the
Americans at the Pilot House which also had a shipping board, if jobs
where available.

After a nice vacation in Yokohama. I decided it was time to move
on with my new life, and I took a job as Motorman on the "Jeppesen
Maersk," destination New York via San Francisco, and Panama.

When I arrived in San Francisco and presented my sealed yellow
envelope to the immigration officer, he looked at me and asked me if
anybody had told me that when you enter the USA as an immigrant
you are supposed to enter as a passenger, not as a seaman. If anybody
ever asks you, tell them you came from Hong Kong as a passenger on
the "Jeppesen Maersk".

I got off the ship in New York and took the train to Boston to
meet my family who opened their doors for me. Uncle Hans was
father's older brother who had shipped out as a young man, and

jumped ship in Boston in 1908 with four dollars in his pocket. He was the most positive person I ever met, only talked about the good things in life, and never mentioned the hardships he had as a longshoreman in Boston during the depression, raising four children.

He was a member of the longshoremen's union for over forty years when he retired. He found it very difficult to stay away from the waterfront and was given a job taking care of the longshoremen's card room on the Commonwealth pier. It was his job to keep it clean and go for coffee and sandwiches when they were playing cards.

The Boston waterfront was dominated by the Irish. The walking boss who hired the gangs would get up on a large stand to pick his men by pointing and calling out there names," Kelly, Murphy." With a name like Pedersen you knew you would only get the left overs, yet Hans never complained or bore a grudge. The union was a closed organisation with union books passed down from father to son only.

My Aunt Magda was Norwegian and came to the USA as a third class passenger on the SS Hellig Olav in November, 1914. She was sixteen years old and on her own. Instead of getting off the ship in Boston, she got off in New York, where she was told that she would be better off in Boston because of the large Scandinavian speaking population there.

She was given a train ticket and a contact in Boston. Years later she met my uncle Hans at a Norwegian club, got married and raised four children. Thelma, Norma, Edna, and Harold.

I received my green card and Social security number right away. I went to the US Coast Guard to apply for my seamen papers. They accepted my seven years sea time on the Danish ships and issued me an Able Bodied Seaman ticket, but first I had to get a lifeboat ticket. I was given a book to study, and told to come back the following week for the test.

It was snowing and cold when I showed up for the test which was to be conducted on one of their cutters just back from the North Atlantic ice patrol. The bosun mate who walked me down to the cutter to watch and grade me, explained that I would be in charge of four sailors who would follow my orders. Everything started out well, but when the boat was hanging free in the davits, and I gave the order to lower away, nothing happened. Everything seemed to be frozen, not just because of the ice but also due to lack of lubricant. They started hitting the brake ban with a hammer, but nothing happened. When we returned to the office, the Coast Guard inspector asked how I did. The Bosun mate didn't know how to bring the news to him, and when he told him what had happened the inspector got very upset and said. Here we are inspecting the merchant ships, and the equipment on our own ship doesn't work. He then looked at my application and sea time and told the inspector to pass me, another good luck.

My next step was to register with the draft board. The lady in charge was very helpful. She gave me a date to appear for a complete physical. She explained that if I was on a ship when receiving my notification for military duty not to get off the ship but let them know what ship I was on.

My uncle Hans and aunt Magda lived in an apartment building on Centre Street in Jamaica Plain. The whole family made me welcome, for which I was grateful. I worked as longshoremen for a while, taking the jobs nobody else wanted, usually down in the hulls on the lumber ships coming in from the West Coast. I also walked the docks trying to get out fishing on the large trawlers. I was told by the skippers that they could not hire me unless I belonged to the Fisherman Union. When I went to join the union, I was told I could not join unless I had a job, one of the many confusing problems I ran into in years to come. Ten years later I read an article in the Boston

Globe wondering why the fishing industry was not able to attract young people. Guess they didn't do their research?

My Aunt told me a story. During the depression she had one of her Norwegian friends over for coffee one day and her friend asked her if she was buying a new hat for Easter.

My Aunt answered that they could not afford a new hat this year. My uncle, who had listened to their conversation, said, "Of course you are going to get a new hat for Easter. Here is $10." After the friend had left, my uncle told her, "Give me back the $10.00, you know we can't afford to buy a hat."

CHOOSING A UNION

At the time, America was still a major seafaring nation with New York being one of the busiest ports in the world. Lower Manhattan was the home for many large and small shipping companies, and also the first Port of Call for ships returning from overseas and the Pay-off and crew replacement Port. The National Maritime Union and the Seafarers International unions both had their Headquarters there.

It was just a few years after the Korean War had ended, and the union had taken in many new members to crew the ships taken supplies to our military there. Many of them were now unemployed, and the union was not taking in any new members.

I knew it would take a lot of foot work to get started, but I was determined to do what it took to join in any of the three major unions.

> National Maritime Union of America (NMU)
> Seafarers International Union (SIU)
> The Sailors Union of the Pacific (SUP)

My first choice was the Sailors Union of the Pacific, headquartered in San Francisco, with a hiring hall in New York I spent the first evening visiting the sailor's hangout in Brooklyn where I met Willy Roy, an American Dane sailing in the SUP. I told him my situation, and he told me he would try to help me getting started. We agreed to meet outside the union hall the following day around 10 a.m. He told me I would not be able to enter the union hall without him because the doorman checked everybody and only members were allowed inside.

Willy was one of the 6,500 Danish seamen sailing for the Allies during WWII. During the war, the SUP and the Danish Sailors Union shared a building on Broad Street in Manhattan. There was a shortage of American seamen and the SUP called on the Danes to help crew up the ships. When the war was over the U.S. Immigration offered the Danish seamen U.S. citizenship, and the SUP offered full membership to the ones who decided to stay.

The SUP shared a union hall with the SIU located at 675 4th Ave in Brooklyn.

After standing across the street in the cold rain watching guys entering and leaving the union hall, I decided to take a chance getting inside the hall by running up the stairs, waving my hand at the door as if I belonged there. It worked.

When Willy finally showed up, he was dressed up in a suit and tie. Morris Weisberger the SUP port agent had his office on the second floor. He was happy to see Willy, who introduced me as his friend from the old country, and told him I had just received my AB ticket and Green Card, and that I would make a good member. Mr Weisberger got up from behind his desk and told Willy he could not take in any more members until the shipping improved.

Willy appeared to be astonished. He walked over, looked directly at him and just stood there like he could not believe what he was hearing. After a while I started to feel uncomfortable and ready to walk out, but Willy did not budge and just stood there looking directly at him for what seemed to be forever. Finally, Mr Weisberger said, "Okay, I know I did promise that when the war was over I would not forget you guys." I was issued a Permit also known as a trip card. He told me I had to understand I would only be able to get the jobs the book members didn't want, and since I only had a green card I was not allowed to work or sail on government subsidized ships.

I was grateful for an opportunity to get started, and I knew if it had not been for Willy being so insisting it would not have happened. I sailed together with him several times later on.

I made all the job calls and talked to as many members as possible to learn the ins and outs. Most of the men I talked to lived in New England or Maryland and only came to New York when ready to ship out or to attend union meeting. Some guys were looking for a particular ship or run. Most didn't like tankers, which made me see an opportunity.

The SUP had contracts with all major shipping companies operating on the West Coast.

Shipping cards were issued for a 90 day period. The full book member's shipping cards were white, and the Permits had blue cards, the white card had priority over a blue card regardless of the dates. A full book member was allowed to stay on the ship for a year and a Permit member one trip or 60 days. It took three years of sea time to become a full book member; later changed to six years. As a Permit man you were supposed to be seen but not heard.

Me on "SS Big Bend"

After a few weeks hanging around the union hall a full crew came up on the SS Big Bend a T-2 tanker and I manage to get a job as an Ordinary Seaman. The Company hired a bus to take us from Brooklyn down to Wilmington, Delaware. The crew getting off was waiting and happy to see us. The bosun told us watch standers to draw cards for the sea watches. I drew the 8 to 12 watch. I was told that I had the sanitary job. I didn't have a clue what the sanitary job was all about. The Bosun told me it would be my job each morning from 8 to 12 to clean the unlicensed sailors quarters, showers and passageways, bring clean linen each Friday and take the dirty laundry back to the steward.

I shared a room with two AB on that watch.

The meals on Danish ships were served family style. On American ships we had a menu with three different entries to choose from. There were two mess halls, one for officers and one for the crew, all eating out of the same pot. Each mess hall had a large blackboard where the steward would write the menu using white chalk.

Lunch was my first meal. When I walked into the mess hall and looked at the menu on the black board, I was completely lost and didn't have a clue what I was looking at. After looking at it for a while I recognised entry # 3 EGG SALAD SANDWICH and that's what I had. Later I would watch what the others were eating, telling the mess man to bring me the same.

The first time I entered the Engine room I was in for a big shock. Instead of seeing a big Diesel engine as I was used to, I saw compact 6000 HP General Electrical Turbo-Electric propulsion making a loud whistling sound.

Our first port of call was Maracaibo, Venezuela to load lube oil for Los Angeles and San Francisco. It was a pleasant trip down the East Coast through the Caribbean. The loading went fast, and a few days later we transited the Panama Canal heading north. When the last oil was discharged in Richmond California, we went out into the Pacific to clean tanks. It was a special cleaning job and the next voyage depended on our success.

It took 10 days around the clock of tank cleaning, first by butter worthing using hot water through heavy rubber hoses with a double-opened brass nozzle that spun rapidly and blasted hot water onto the tank bulkheads and overhead.

The hose was lowered and raised ten feet at a time by hand. It took two to three men to handle the hose when pulling it up from the bottom. When the tank cleaning was complete we entered the tanks for mugging up the dry oil, using brass tools to avoid sparks. The tanks were dried by using wind sail, and later by hand using rags.

Grain was normally carried in dry bulk carriers or on regular freighters, which required wooden bulk heads to be built throughout the cargo holds to eliminate the shifting of cargo in bad weather. Someone figured out that if grain was carried on a tank vessel, those bulk heads would not be necessary since a tank vessel is already made up of many compartments. We became one of the first tankers to try it, and it worked well.

After we returned to San Francisco various inspectors and cargo surveyors came onboard to inspect the tanks. With minor corrections we passed and started loading grain for Brake, Germany, which turned out to be a 30 day voyage with nice weather most of the way down the West Coast, through the Panama Canal, and across the Atlantic.

We had two strange characters on the same watch in the engine department. The fireman believed he was Jesus Christ, and he looked like him with long red hair, always walking around in bare feet.

Frank, the oiler was even nuttier, wearing real thick glasses. One evening I saw them both back on the fantail watching the sunset and the ocean. Jesus was standing with a wooden stick painted all different colours with a cross on top. He was swinging the stick violently, yelling for the wind to blow and for the sea to rise.

Frank was standing next to him with a tray of left over hamburgers from dinner, pretending they were hand grenades. He'd take one small bite and spit it out like he was pulling the pin before throwing the grenade, then place both hands on his ears waiting for the explosion.

We changed sea watches every 60 days, and I was now on the 4 to 8 watch, working six hours overtime daily, chipping, sanding, priming and painting the after mast from top to bottom sitting in a Bosun chair day after day.

Brake was a small port between Bremerhaven and Bremen. The night life was not the greatest, but after 30 days at sea, it was better than nothing.

We bought a fresh supply of Beck's beer. The deck department shared a large refrigerator placed in the biggest foc's'le. After getting off watch the first night out at sea, I volunteered to go get three beers out of the refrigerator. Since everybody was a sleep, I didn't want to turn the light on when I entered the room, and I heard a strange sound like someone was crying.

When I turned my flash light on I saw Alf, a Norwegian A. B. sitting there drunk, crying louder and louder. When I asked him what was wrong, he explained that he felt so bad because the chief mate was such a nice man who had given him four days off to go back to Norway to see his mom and dad, but when he got to Hamburg he I started partying and forgot to home.

After sailing out of Germany we started another tank cleaning job in route to Aruba, a Dutch Island in the Caribbean where we loaded heating oil to Boston. This was my first time there, and I went ashore to see what it was all about. It was a fun place.

Our Bosun was a man in his early 60's with a lot of sea time behind him, and he had been in Aruba many times in the 30's. He asked me what the girls at the Bordellos charged for a short time, and he was shocked when I told him the price was $3. He told me he used to get it for an empty paint bucket.

I was very optimistic about the future, but there were a few who were pessimistic, like the 3rd Mate, a Texan in his late 50s, who told me I was wasting my time going to sea and that I would be better off becoming a longshoreman or a fisherman. He told me that during WWII he was sailing as a captain, then back to 3rd mate. During the Korean War he was back sailing as a Captain and now back down to 3rd mate on the Big Bend. He also told me that someday all the ships would be flying the Panamanian flag. Now 50 some years later he turned out to be right, but in the meantime I had a job I enjoyed and made a good living doing it. He also said that the U.S. State Department was our worst enemy, always putting the rest of the world first, and the unfavourable Tax structure was a nail in our coffins.

A young Norwegian by the name of Arnie Hindenes was on board sailing as a pump man. He became a lifelong friend. I told him what the 3rd mate had said. Forty years later I retired as Captain, Arnie as Chief engineer. Good thing we didn't listen to him.

We sailed coastwise carrying various types of heating oil from Texas to the North East. On one trip at dock in Brownsville, Texas, a man in a clean khaki uniform with a gun hanging on his belt came onboard. He looked like a police officer or security guard who came to see the captain. I asked if I could help him. He said, "No I am here to see the steward and pick up the dirty laundry." When I asked why the gun? he said, "I have to drive through the Mexican section to get here."

At the time there were several small oil docks on the Mississippi river with no houses or anything around, except when a Tanker came in. Then a mobile bordello came down from New Orleans with a few ladies of the night.

After eight and a half months we pulled into New York, and the Union told me I would have to get off.

After a trip to Boston to see my family, I was back in New York and had a job on another tanker, SS Cornell, owned and operated by Hilcone Shipping Company of San Francisco.

She was a T-3, a little bigger than a T-2 tanker in the coastwise trade carrying various types of fuel oil from Texas to the North East. We also made a trip with molasses from Venezuela to New York. I managed to get three months in before the Union pulled me off. That completed my first year in the S U P with eleven and a half months sea time and $ 5000 in the Bank, not a bad start.

I still had a language barrier, but everybody was very friendly and went out of their way trying to help steer me in the right direction.

When in New York I stayed at the Seaman Institute, 25 South Street in Manhattan. There was everything you needed, free Post office box for seamen, bank, great library, cafeteria, and movies.

The Marshall Plan started in 1947 when part of Europe was in ruins and had just survived one of the worst winters on record. Secretary of State George C. Marshall, stated that something had to be done, both for humanitarian reasons and also to stop the potential spread of communism.

The U.S. offered the Europeans up to $ 20 billion for relief, but only if all the nations could get together and draw up a national plan on how they would use the aid. A lot of the aid would be in food such as grain, soybeans, also coal and Iron. 50% of the aid had to be shipped on American ships.

That gave many small ship-owners an opportunity to cash in on carrying coal from the U.S. East Coast to Europe, or by just operating the ships for the Government, with a lot of jobs coming our way.

At the union hall the SIU had the job call on the hour, and the SUP in between on the half hour. One day the SIU were looking for a volunteer for an organizing job. I volunteered and was called in to see one of the officials who explained what it was all about.

It was a small company operating two Liberty ships under the Panamanian flag with Italian crew. 50% of the foreign aid like grain, coal had to be carried on American ship.

This company decided to change the flag to take advantage of the foreign aid cargo.

The NMU and the SIU were always fighting among themselves to get the contracts for the unlicensed crew. In this case the ship-owner didn't care who got the contract, and to make it fair they invited Seamen from both unions to apply without mentioning their union affiliation on the application.

They gave everybody three days to apply, and on the fourth day they would pick the crew and sign a contract with the union that had the most men on the ship.

When I went to make out my application for an Able Bodied Seamen job, in the column where they asked for the name of the last ship and how long you had been there, I realized it would be easy for the company to figure out what union you were affiliated with since most of the lower seniority men in the SIU were only allowed to stay one trip or 60 days on each ship, whereas the NMU guys had years on the same ship.

Since I had three and a half years sea time on my last two Danish ships alone I decided to write down those two ships only to make myself look completely different

A week later I received a message that I had been accepted as AB on one of their ships and to report at their office at 45 Broadway ASAP.

Before reporting to the company, I went to the SIU and showed them the message. They were happy and told me if I would stay on the ship for one year they would give me a full union book. Paul Hall the SIU President gave me 50 cents for the Subway.

The company instructed me to check with them daily, which I did. The day I was told to report to the ship to sign on, I was shocked to be met by two picket lines outside the gate, one from NMU and another from SIU both claiming unfair labor practice.

As the picket line and union dispute got nastier, the company changed their mind, and put both ships back under the Panamanian flag and called the Italian crew back. It was a big disappointment.

Since I had wasted two weeks on the above, the SIU told me that if I ever needed a job on one of their contracted ships to let them now. They also gave me a card stating that I didn't have to pay union dues in addition to my SUP dues. When the shipping was slow for the SUP, the SIU often passed jobs over to us.

Helen Hunt Jackson

In 1957-60 a total of 600 Liberty and Victory ships came out of lay-up to carry coal and grain to Europe and India, which created a shortage of sailors to crew them. I was at the union hall looking for a job. A full crew on the SS Helen Hunt Jackson came on the board, and I took one of the AB jobs. The ship was operated by Shepard Steamship Company named after a writer and activist of Native Americans. It took several days to get a crew.

The ship had been laid up in Norfolk, VA ever since the Korean War. She had been through a complete overhaul and was freshly painted before we joined her at the shipyard in Philadelphia. Shortly thereafter we sailed to Newport News to load 9,000 tons of coal for Dunkirk, France, part of the Marshall Plan.

The loading went fast. The coal came alongside in railroad cars and was dumped onboard. We sailed out of Newport News April 15, 1957 and the very first day, we ran into a storm, which stayed with us for most of the way.

She was number 673 out of 2,711 Liberty ships built by the US Maritime Commission during WWII, nicknamed the ugly ducklings by President Franklin Roosevelt. They were essential to our victory. Without them, the war would have dragged out much longer. They carried jeeps, tanks, rifle ammunition, bombs, troops, tanks, planes, torpedo landing crafts, first aid supplies, trucks, food, and U.S. Mail, across the Atlantic and the Pacific Oceans under unbelievable circumstances, battling winter storms, enemy submarines and air attacks.

She was 441 x 56 x 28 ft. with a crew of 40. Her three-cylinder reciprocating steam engine was fed by two oil-burning boilers producing 2,500 hp, speed 10 knots and built by Kaiser Steel in California in 1942. It was a great concern to a number of quality-control experts that Kaiser decided to venture into a new method of building ships in mass production. Once the keel was laid, ships sections were fabricated in various locations away from the yard, transported to the keel site and lifted into position by large cranes.

In lieu of the older method of riveting sections of the ships, they were now constructed by the use of welding techniques. All Liberty ships were constructed this way which was much faster but did not allow the hulls to flex in heavy weather. Several Liberty ships broke in half, not a very comfortable feeling when one is out in bad weather in the middle of the Atlantic.

She was not build for comfort. With three men to a room, only two were able to get dressed at the same time, shower and toilets were down the passage way. Later I sailed with some old timers who liked the living conditions with all the rooms amidships, running water in the sink, cold water fountains, and refrigerators in the mess halls, which was superior to ships built prior to World WarII.

Liberty Ship Crew of 37

Deck Department	Engine Department	Steward Department
Master		
Chief Mate	Chief Engineer	Chief Steward
Second Mate	First Engineer	Chief Cook
Third Mate	Second Engineer	Second Cook & Baker
Bosun	Third Engineer	5 Steward Assistant
1 Carpenter	1 Deck Engineer	
1 Deck Maintenance	3 Oiler	
6 Able Seaman	3 Fire/Water tender	1 Radio Operator
3 Ordinary Seaman	2 Wiper	

A few days out in the North Atlantic, I was awakened one morning by six short blasts on the ship's whistle (the danger signal). I jumped out of bed, looked out the porthole and saw the mast and side light of a ship very close heading directly at us It looked like she would hit us but nature help when a couple of long heavy swells came along and pushed the ship away from us and she missed us by a ship length.

Our captain was an old timer who came out of retirement and was happy to be back at sea again. His quarters was next to the wheel house. He liked to come in and talk to whoever was at the wheel. He chewed snuff and carried an empty coffee can to spit in. One day he came in and said, Pedersen, I see you are new in this country and making your home in Boston. I don't know if you plan to stay in Boston, but if you are I would like to give you a little advice. Either change your name to Kelly, Murphy, Mc-Nab, or get the hell out.

Most of the unlicensed deck department were not professional seamen. My watch partner, Chicken Sam, drove a taxi most of the time. Charlie Brown, an ordinary seaman, was a bookie and card player. Another made his living drawing cartoons for newspapers and magazines. There was a poker game every night with plenty of beer, scotch and bourbon on the table. Charlie Brown ran the games.

The Steward department were all members of the marine cooks and steward union.

The menu and meals were fantastic. Before dinner the Steward walked around singing today's menu, his favourite saying was come and ha-va some more.

The 8 to 12 watch has always been my favoured but not on this ship because when midnight came you never knew if you would be relieved on time. The 12 to 4 watch were all poker players and heavy drinkers.

One dark and stormy night, standing behind the wheel waiting to be relieved, I heard a loud noise which turned out to be a coffee cup flying over the deck in the wheel house. At the same time I felt something falling over my feet.

I turned on my flashlight and saw AB Mickey bleeding by my feet completely passed out Guess he was late getting away from the poker game and forgot his flashlight.

When he entered the wheel house the ship took a heavy roll and he lost his footing, and hit his head on the handle to the engine telegraph. We did manage to stop the bleeding and get him back on his feet.

A few days out of Dunkirk, the weather improved. The captain mentioned that he was running out of clean clothes and had to do some laundry. He asked Micky to get him a clean bucket and some soap powder. Micky told him we had a washing machine back aft next to the carpenter shop and that he would be happy to do the laundry for him. Since we didn't have a dryer, Micky strung a rope on the sunny side of the boat deck next to the smoke stack and hung the captain's clothes out to dry.

I guess nobody was watching the wind direction because at 4 p.m. the wiper blew tubes to clear them of soot which sometimes come out as small fire balls. By the time they were finished blowing tubes, not only were the captain's clothes black from soot but full of holes. He went shopping for new clothes in Dunkirk.

Entering the English Channel we ran into fog. The 2nd mate mentioned to the captain that it would be nice if we had radar. The captain looked at him and said. "Radar why would you want radar? All you see on radar is a little blip. It doesn't tell you if it is a ship or an empty beer case coming down the channel." I guess he had never sailed with radar.

After twenty-two days of rolling and pitching, we finally arrived in Dunkirk. The French harbor pilot was a man up in age and had a hard time climbing the pilot ladder and walking up the steps to the bridge. As we entered the harbour, the captain and pilot started a conversation about retirement. The pilot told him he had retired before the War, and every month he gets a pension check and every month he takes his wife out for lunch, and the money is gone.

After the ship was safely moored alongside the dock, the chief mate told the bosun we would stay 7-8 days to discharge the coal due to a shortage of rail road cars and working with old stationary cranes, which meant we would have to haul ship ahead or astern when a hatch was completed. He also told the bosun he would leave it up to him to give time off. One crew member decided to make a trip to England, another wanted to go to Paris, and the rest of us just went bar hopping in town.

American cigarettes were still king on the black market and we had plenty well hidden, easy to turn into cash. The carpenter took up a collection to purchase beer and booze for the return trip home. We also bought perfume to bring home.

After eight days of partying the sailing day came and the ship had to be secured for sea, one hatch at a time. First we placed the steel beams across the cargo hatch, then we put the wooden hatch board down covering the entire hatch, before covering them up with three canvas tarpaulins properly tucked in against the side of the hatch before securing them with wooden wedges. Last, the cargo booms had to be lowered and secured for sea.

During WWII, Liberty ships sailing empty were known for being stiff which caused them to roll excessively. The U.S. Maritime Administrations issued instructions that at least 1500 tons of ballast be divided between the lower holds and between-decks before crossing the Atlantic Ocean. Sand was used for ballast.

After the war, private companies didn't always believe in spending the money. Some companies left it up to the captain, and sand was often not available.

When we sailed we didn't have any ballast except for some salt water in the # 5 lower cargo hold to keep the propeller in the water which left the bow high, making the ship pound when heading into the seas.

Water was moving from side to side in the lower hull, increasing the ships rolling. Later we had a hard time pumping the water out before arrival in Hampton Road Again. We had bad weather all the way across the Atlantic and one day we went 95 miles the wrong way. In nice weather it should have taken 12-14 days to cross, but it took us 28 days. By the time we picked up the pilot for Newport News we were out of fuel.

We loaded another 9000 tons of coal for Dunkirk, and shifted from the loading dock to Norfolk to pay-off and sign on for another voyage.

Just a few of us showed up the next morning to carry the voyage stores onboard. Some of the crew had their wives or girlfriends staying in a motel, others were out partying.

The shipping commissioner and paymaster came onboard to pay off and sign off/on at 1300 as planned. Sailing Board was posted for 1700.

The bosun and the deck delegate came back drunk around noon, telling us to go ahead and sign off, but not to sign on again. The captain asked for a reason. The only thing the bosun came up with was a shortage of fans in the rooms. The captain told them he would get new fans before sailing, but nobody was listening. Sailing time was cancelled; and the company filed a complaint against the SUP for delaying the ship without cause.

The following morning, which was Saturday, a local union official from the Seafarers International Union (SIU) came onboard with instructions from Harry Lundeberg, the President of the Sailors Union of the Pacific. Replace everybody who refused to sign on, and to get the ship out ASAP. He also said that every SUP member refusing to sign on would be brought up on charges and lose their union status.

I signed on, and took a taxi up to the motel where the bosun was staying and told him the news. When Harry Lundeberg's name was mentioned, he started paying attention and decided to return to the ship and sign on. By late afternoon we had everybody back.

I was at the wheel steering out of Norfolk, and the captain and the pilot were talking when the door to the wheel house flew open and the carpenter, who could hardly stand up, yelled, "Turn this fucking ship around I didn't get my new mattress." Nobody paid attention, and he left. The pilot said to the captain, "I think you are in for an interesting trip"

A few days out, a carrier pigeon landed on the foredeck to rest and for water. One of the Abs told the captain that it looked like the pigeon had a message tagged onto his leg.

The captain responded, "Well, it is probably from Harry Lundeberg telling you guys to sober up, and get with it."

It seemed like this ship was cursed with radio officers. The one we had on the first trip was an alcoholic, drinking everything he could get a hold of. The captain told him to stop stealing the crews shaving lotion.

It sounds like something out of movie, but on the second trip, steaming up the English Channel a British Navy ship came alongside and signalled asking for the ship's name, and later told us to stop. The 2nd mate was very good with the signal blinker and was in charge of communication. He told us they were there to rescue the radio officer.

The guy had sent out a position and a SOS stating that he had locked himself in the radio shack, and someone was trying to kill him with a fire axe. The captain assured them that was not the case and he would take care of it.

When we arrived in Dunkirk, the radio officer was brought ashore for observation. The captain insisted to come along to see where they took him because with a crew like this he wanted to find out if they had room for more. Otherwise our stay in Dunkirk was very much a repeat from the trip before. On the way home we stopped in the Azores to pick up a spare engine part. The steward asked the captain to give him some money to go ashore to buy fresh vegetables. The captain told him. If I do that I am afraid I won't see you again? I will go myself. Later he returned with several baskets full of beans, and nothing else.

Packing my suitcase after two unforgettable trips, I came to the conclusion that I had never met so many different characters from all different walks of life on one ship. You had to be there and have a good sense of humour to appreciate the day to day circus. I never saw any of them again on other ships or ashore.

SS NORWALK VICTORY

After the Helen Hunt Jackson, I was looking forward to going back to Boston to see my family. That changed when I walked into the union hall to register for shipping. I noticed right away there was an open AB job hanging on the board on the SS Norwalk Victory.

The dispatcher, Bill Armstrong was standing behind the counter waving me to come on over right away. He asked me when was the last time I had been back in the old country which was seven years. Well here is your chance to go back. "We still need one more AB on the Norwalk Victory. She is not exactly going to Denmark but Reykjavik, Iceland.

"She is laying down in Norfolk loading military cargo and will probably stay in Reykjavik for a week or more. Pope & Talbot who are operating the ship are very good with time off in port, and I am sure it will be easy for you to get a few days off to fly down to Copenhagen."

It seemed like a good idea, and I decided to take the job. Before heading for the Airport I stopped to buy a new suit and a nice coat to wear going home.

A ticket had been issued to me to fly from New York to Norfolk with Delta Airline's my first flight and a whole new experience.

It was very pleasant. The service was great. I had an unforgettable Fillet Mignon wrapped with bacon. I also remember when I went to the bathroom I was afraid to press the big red bottom to flush in case something else would happen.

I took a Taxi from the airport to the ship. By the time I walked up the gangway it was 9.30 p.m. The shore side watchman asked me who I was and what business I had onboard. When I told him I was the new AB, he told me the Chief Mate had left word for me to check with him right away. I stepped into his office to fill out the routine paper work personal information sheet and I was to go to the shipping commissionaire to sign on early in the morning.

I asked him how long he expected us to stay in Reykjavik. He started to laugh and said, you have been Shanghaied. We are not going to Reykjavik. We are sailing tomorrow for Thule, Greenland with a load of asphalt and some special radar equipment. Still laughing he said, "Don't feel bad. There are seven Danes and a Swede on deck were told the same story."

SS Norwalk Victory, my first Victory ship, was 455 feet long; 62 feet beam, 8500 HP 18 knots built in 1944. She served in WWII, Korea and later Viet Nam

I was happy to learn I would be watch partner with Willy Roi and would meet all the other Danes onboard; most of them I knew from the bars in Brooklyn. Most of them had not been back to Denmark since before the War and some didn't care where the ship was going, like Willy who owed a $ 2,000 bar bill, hoping to pay some of it off after this trip.

We left Norfolk the following day steaming north toward Thule, a distance of approximately 3, 800 miles. The weather was very nice most of the way. A few days out we were told to stop in Sondre, Stromfjord to discharge some radar equipment, which didn't take long.

The next day out of Sondre Stromfjord was when our trouble started, first by running into fog and then ice. The fog became very heavy as did the ice, and after a while we were completely stuck in the ice and remained stuck for several days. When the fog lifted, there was ice as far as eyes could see. Since there was no wind to break up the ice it looked like we might be stuck for a while.

The Captain notified the company regarding our situation and that we might not be able to make Thule before it froze in.

Routine sea watches were maintained as before. The second day I noticed two large polar bears walking on the ice approaching the ship. They stopped, standing up on their two legs looking at us.

At that time all garbage from the galley was thrown over on the lee side of the stern.In this case it landed right below the ship on top of the ice.

It didn't take the bears long to check out the garbage and find the menu satisfactory because they both decided to make camp close to the ship.

When I looked down at them standing on the ice 10 feet below looking up at me, I decided I would never go on a ship again without a camera.

Guess the U.S. Air force needed the asphalt real bad to repair or extend their run way; a lot of Government pressure was applied on the U.S. Coast Guard who dispatched an Ice breaker out of Boston to assist us. However, a few days out she developed rudder damage and had to return to Boston

I don't know if the Polar Bears knew something we didn't because a few days later they walked around the ship for the last time and disappeared.

Shortly thereafter a strong cold wind came along; the ice started breaking up, leaving a small opening for us to navigate out toward the open water.

The Captain started out on slow ahead for several hours. When he finally was able to maneuver better he rang full ahead, but soon the ship started to vibrate heavily which indicated the propeller blade was bent and damaged by the ice. Since there was nothing wrong with the rudder we were able to proceed on half ahead. The Captain decided to take a chance on making Thule.

When we arrived in Thule, a special trained military gang came onboard to spot the booms and started discharging the asphalt, all in drums. Most of them were only 19-20 years old. I was impressed the way they spotted the cargo booms and how they handled the cargo winches.

They worked around the clock to get us out as fast as possible

The next day I went to the PX to shop for a camera, bought two, one 16 mm Bell &Howell movie camera and a small 35 mm Kodak, a $300 investment.

I also bought a book about Greenland and the Thule base built in 1953 and had a variety of both wartime and peace time missions. The support of research and exploration in the Arctic has always been one of the main functions of the base, or so they said. Greenland is the closest land mass to the North Pole, and it felt like it. Thule is at 76.32 N, Latitude 68.45 W.

Denmark claimed Greenland in 1605 and attempted to make it into a productive colony. Fishing was the main source income for the 55,000 people living there at that time; I never met any Danes or Eskimos on the base, only U.S. military.

We left Thule with orders to proceed to New York. Because of the bent propeller, we preceded on a slow bell, about 10 knots. I don't know what caused, it if it was the cold wind at night when standing lookout or how it happen but a few days out I got a bad ear ache. The whole left side of my head around the ear was swollen up and became very painful. I was still able to stand my watch every day, but didn't get much sleep.

We made two stops in Canada homebound, picking up damaged military equipment, wondering why it would even pay to bring them back. While at anchor outside Halifax I lowered an old crab pot, using meat as bait. A few hours later when I pulled the pot back up I was surprised when I saw the biggest lobster I'd ever seen hanging outside the pot, one claw stuck inside. The cook steamed it for me. It was a fantastic meal.

A few days out of New York the Captain received a message that we were to proceed to the Army base on Staten Island to discharge the cargo, and then shift into a shipyard in Hoboken for dry docking to repair the damaged propeller. The crew would be paid off after dry-docking, and the ship would go into permanent lay-up in the Government Ready Reserve fleet. (RRF)

By the time we got back to New York, the whole side of my head had swollen up, I had a lot of pain in my left ear, and I went to the Marine Hospital on Staten Island right away.

The Doctor declared me unfit for duty and the nurse gave me a shot of Penicillin. Guess she hit something because now 50 years later I can still feel it every time I get wet or cold.

Since I was unfit for duty, I had to get off the ship and check back with the doctor every other day. When I called my uncle in Boston I was told there was a letter from the draft board and that I had to report three weeks later. After two weeks the infection was gone and the USPH gave me fit for duty. I sat down to analyze my situation to come up with the best way to fill my military obligation. The U.S. Coast Guard was by far the best option, for me but they told me I had to be a U.S. Citizen and would not accept me on a green card. My only option was the U.S. Army and I accepted that and was looking forward to getting it over with.

THE DRAFT BOARD

I went back to Boston where the family had a going away party for me the night before I went down to the Boston Army base, where I was told to report. I also gave my clothes away to the Salvation Army.

When I arrived early in the morning, I was told to pick up my medical file from my prior physical, then strip and get in line. It looked to me like we were around a 100 guys from all around the Boston area. I noticed most were a lot younger than me.

There were several tables with a doctor sitting at each table, ready to check our paper work.

I was one of the first guys in line and presented my envelope to the doctor, which he jerked out of my hands and without looking, asked me if I had been sick since I had my last physical I responded telling him about my ear infection. Without looking at me or my medical records, he said, "Don't worry about it, we will take a fucking bullet and shoot it right through your head. That will clean them out". That was before the F word was used in every day conversation. Next to him was an older Doctor who didn't like the way he talked to me, and asked him, "What happen to you, did you get out on the wrong side of the bed?" The young doctor responded saying he was sick and tired of listing to everybody's phony excuses.

I tried to tell him my ear was okay now, but he didn't listen. The older doctor called me over and asked me to explain my ear problem, which I did. He then asked me if I had any medical records from the Marine Hospital in New York. I showed him all the information I had.

One thing I didn't know was that some of the doctors at the Marine Hospitals were expert in their fields and volunteered time each week. It so happened the doctor who had treated me was a well-known ear specialist. The older doctor checked my left ear and claimed that I still had an infection. He went back to doctor smart-ass, and told him that in the future he'd better check the medical records people bring. He also told him the name of the doctor who had treated me in New York, and that I still had an infection in my left ear. Before I knew it, doctor number three got into the act. Shortly thereafter I was told to put my clothing back on, and go up to the third floor and wait. By now it was around 10 a.m.

I was the only one in the waiting room, and I sat there for what seemed forever. Finally by 3 p.m. I heard over the loudspeaker, "Pedersen you can go home." That was in 1958, and I haven't heard a word since. However, I am still A-1 and may be called any time.

A few days later I was wondering what next? I decided to go back to New York to look for another ship, and buy new clothing. The union dispatcher told me there were a lot of guys on the beach looking for jobs and my best chance would be to get on a Navy Tanker which the book members stayed away from mainly because Navy Tankers sometimes went overseas and stayed out for a year.

A few weeks later, a Deck Maintenance job on the USNS Tallulah, a T-2 Navy Tanker operated by Joshua Hendy of Los Angeles, went open and the job was mine.

The Tallulah was built and commissioned in 1942. During WWII she was assigned to the Asiatic Pacific and took part in the invasion of Luzon, Iwo Jima, and Okinawa. She was awarded seven battle stars during WW II and one during the Korean War.

After the War she was turned over to the War Shipping Administration who transferred her to the Military Sea Transportation (MSTS) who turned around and had a private company operating her, using civilian union crews. Together with others she carried Jet fuel to any part of the world where it was needed by the military keeping the Navy and Air Force well supplied with jet fuel and oil for many years. I came aboard in Newport News when she was discharging Jet fuel. After a few more coastwise trips between Texas and the North East we went through the Panama Canal to Los Angeles where we signed one year foreign articles, and sailed for Yokuska, Japan with a load of Jet fuel.

In the beginning there was a big poker game going every night. I am happy that I never learned to play poker because I saw people losing their money fast. One AB lost over $4000 in a week and was not allowed to play anymore until he paid up. It could take him up to a year to earn that kind of money.

This was my first opportunity to get back to Japan which I was very much looking forward to. Yokosuka was only an hour by taxi from Yokohama and I went there daily, hoping to catch information about my old friends

After discharging our cargo, we proceeded to Ras Tanuara, Saudi Arabia, which became our future loading port bringing jet fuel from there to the U.S. military bases in Japan, Philippines, Guam, and Turkey.

The "Tallulah" was one of the 481 T-2 Work horses very much like the "Big Bend" who survived the German and Japanese U-Boats. She was capable of carrying 141,000 barrels or 6 million gallons of jet fuel. The tanks were dement-coated to which oil would not stick, which made them easy to clean.

There was a lot of sea time between ports. Ras Tanuara had a Seamen Club with air conditioning, serving tea and soft drinks only, showing movies each evening, a nice place to go and cool off.

Subic Bay in the Philippines was the largest naval support base outside the United States, capable of dry docking and repairing large vessels. The base had a U.S. post office, banks, barber shops, restaurants, and clubs serving drinks for only 10 cents during happy hour. It was a nice port to visit after a long sea voyage.

When you left the base and walked across the bridge you saw dirty water full of young Filipino boys swimming, hoping you will throw coins which they would then recover. Stepping off the bridge, and entering Olongapo City was like entering another world, the streets full of children some living on the street, shining shoes, or begging. The bars, night clubs, brothels and gambling casinos were open 24-7. Several thousand women were registered as entertainers.

I walked ashore on a Friday evening with the weekend off and money in my pocket, but little did I know I was in for an unforgettable weekend. After stopping in various bars drinking San Miguel beers and Manila rum and coke, I decided to go home with one of the girls sitting around waiting for a live one. We took a taxi to her place and we barely got into bed when there was a knock on the door. The girl panicked and told me I had to get out right away because it was her steady Navy boyfriend returning early. She knocked on the wall to the girl in the next room, telling her she was sending me over and for her to take care of me. I didn't have time to put my clothes back on before she scuffed me out the window onto a narrow ledge were I walked with my clothing in my hands toward the next window. When I finally reached the next window and stepped inside, I felt like I was in paradise or just dreaming before me stood a real Filipino beauty my own age wearing just a pair of white panties. I stayed with her for the next two days without ever leaving her room, and I remember when making love how the sweat ran out of both of us. Life was good.

The next load out of Ras Tanuara was for the U.S. Air Force in Turkey. I remember visiting a local restaurant and ordering roast duck. The owner showed up with three live ducks and asked me which one I would like. Since I don't like to kill anything, I asked someone else to pick one. It took several hours and many drinks before dinner was served.

The steward bought fresh vegetables and other fresh provisions. Two days later half the crew came down with severe diarrhea. We went through the Suez Canal south bound on January 23, 1959 my 25th Birthday.

I had bought a lot of beer and liquor planning for a great party, and the Bosun gave me a break that day. Crew members coming and going took part in the party all day, a good time was had by all, and an unforgettable birthday for me.

One day out in the Indian Ocean, the Captain called down and told us a Russian tanker was sailing next to us, the very first Russian tanker we ever saw sailing the seven seas. A few years later they were everywhere.

Nobody knew how long we would be out there before returning to the U.S. For me I was hoping for a full year to get as much sea time as possible towards my union book.

When laying in RasTanuara loading jet fuel for Japan, a Navy officer came on board with a huge German shepherd named Valdemar. He asked the captain to take care of the dog for him, and that he would have someone pick him up on arrival in Newport News. The captain told him we were heading for Japan, and not Newport News. The Navy officer responded. "Trust me; you are heading for New Port News," and we did. By the time we returned to New Port News we had been out about ten months.

After the pay-off and before taking an overnight bus to New York, I decided to go to Western Union to buy two thousand dollars' worth of money orders. The girl behind the counter told me it would take a while because the biggest money orders she had were 50's, and she had to sign and number each one.

When she handed me the money orders, I gave her my $2000. I walked away from the desk and sat down and counted them and it came to $3000. I counted them several times before calling her aside and telling her she had given me $1000 to much. At first, she didn't believe me but as she was counting, and came close to the $2000 mark she started turning red in her face. The Manager came out and thanked me. He told me she would be the one who would have to pay for the mistake. Just before I left, the girl told me that if she were not married, we would sure have gone out in town tonight.

SS John Weyerhaeuser

Weyerhaeuser was one of the largest lumber and paper companies in the U.S. It began operating its own shipping between the U.S. East Coast and the Pacific Northwest in 1923 and continued until 1968. After WWII they used Liberty ships carrying lumber from the Pacific North West to the East Coast and steel and canned food on the way back. I was on three of their ships, the SS W.H. Peabody F

F. Weyerhaeuser and the John Weyerhaeuser. A round trip from the East Coast through the Panama Canal was two months. Due to SUP shipping rules I was never able to make more than one trip on each ship. The SS W. H. Peabody was the first one. We left Baltimore with a load of heavy steel, canned food, and pleasure boats on deck. The officer on watch told me that if everything went right we should be in L.A. in 18 days, which made me feel like I was on slow boat to China. When transiting the Panama Canal, my job was to stand by the two large ventilators and turn them into the wind to get fresh air down to the engine room. That job gave me a great opportunity to enjoy the sightseeing.

Ten knots, the normal speed for a Liberty ship, was just right for fishing for tuna around Panama. I caught several nice sized tuna and gave them to the cook. We had several Hawaiians on board who ate them raw.

Later on the SS F. E. Weyerhaeuser we started loading lumber in various small lumber ports in Washington State, all hand stowed below and above deck. Our final loading port was New Port, Oregon. After several days of loading and securing the deck cargo with heavy chain six feet apart, a wooden catwalk with handrail was built on top and when you looked at the heavy chain you assumed that it would never move regardless how bad the weather was. When the ship was secured and ready to sail for Boston, the weather turned against us and for several days we were stuck alongside the dock waiting for a break in the weather for the sea and swell to die down to let us cross the bar outside the harbour.

It was still windy when the captain and pilot decided to give it a try. The pilot also owned the tug boat, which his son was operating, assisting us to get away from the dock and turn us heading out of the harbour. The pilot sent word down not to rig the pilot's ladder but just to have ready. He didn't trust anybody but himself to make it fast.

It took us a long time to get away from the dock and get the ship turned heading out of the harbor. Outside heading across the bar, it became a challenge for the tugboat to come alongside to take the pilot off. It took several attempts before they made it. It seemed like it took forever heading into the big long heavy swells to get across the bar and into the open Pacific.

When we finally made it out, the captain changed course heading south. The vessel took a couple of long heavy rolls which put such a strain on the chains around the lumber on deck that they snapped one after another, and we lost a lot of the deck load overboard on the foredeck. It all happened so fast. One minute it was there, the next minute it was gone.

Later when I shipped on S.S. John Weyerhaeuser, two things happened which changed my life and future for the better. My watch partner was a fellow named Gene Dorothy from Pennsylvania. He was the first man I ever met who was investing his money in the stock market. He would walk ashore in each port to buy a Wall Street Journal and bring it back to study it page by page. One day he said he noticing me reading various magazines.

He also mentioned that he knew I had a language barrier and that I was trying to improve my English by reading what came easy to me. "But you can do the same thing by reading something meaningful, like the Wall Street Journal and learn to invest and make money at the same time." We started picking stocks on paper and followed them. It was a whole new world for me and very interesting. Gene was the kind of guy who never paid more than $75 for a car.

I learned a lot from him when it came to handling my money. Shortly after we parted, I made my first investment on Wall Street, I purchasing 25 shares of Sperry Rand, 25 shares of Black & Decker, two companies I could relate to. Sperry Rand was making gyro compasses and radar used on board ships, and Black & Decker made tools.

I have been investing ever since, but to be honest I never made much money on Wall Street. I guess one reason was that I became a speculator instead of a conscientious and long term investor.

My belief was that every company started out small, and if I was able to pick one and stay with it I would be set for life, but it never came about. I did all my research at the stockbroker's office reading the ticker, or studying the research available to customers. I also spent a lot of time at the business library.

I was happy sailing as an Able Bodied Seaman, making good money and had no plans to go any further. Thanks to the Chief Mate Bill Lancaster, a man in his late 50's from San Francisco, my future took a turn for the better without me knowing it. Sailing intercostal, we had a lot of sea time and not much traffic, which gave us a lot of time to talk when on watch. He was very interested in hearing about my background from Denmark and my life on Danish ships.

One day he told me he had been an instructor at a maritime school in Alameda, California during WW II and that there had been several Danish seamen among his students.

Some of them were sailing as captains today, and that I could do the same. I told him it had never crossed my mind since I had no education and was not able to master the English language. He told me that since I had two more years before I could become a U.S. Citizen, which is required before you can become a Licensed Officer, I should sign up now with a navigation school of my choice, attend classes in between ships, and take the school material with me to study on board. That would prepare me to sit for my license at the same time I was to get my U.S. citizenship in 1961.

He also told me that the Danish sailors who attended his classes in Alameda were not any better in English than I was. He pointed out that it was not a language or spelling test, but a navigation and ships handling test with the U.S. Coast Guard. I must admit most of his suggestions fell on a deaf ear, and that I felt everything he said was way out of my reach. However, Mr. Lancaster didn't give up. He kept hammering it into my head day after day. He also pointed out that sailing as a Able Bodied Seaman was okay now when I was young, but when I got older it would be boring, and no fun sharing the foc'sle with two other guys day after day. He also said that as long as I kept sailing going from company to company it would be difficult for me to borrow money from a bank when it came time for me to invest in a house.

When I got off the ship in Baltimore, he told me he would be very disappointed if I didn't give it a good try to become a licensed officer, and if there was anything he could do to help me he would be very happy to do so. Even though due to union rule I was only on the SS JOHN WEYERHAEUSER for two months meeting Gene Dorothy and Bill Lancaster made a big change in my life

WATERMAN TO THE FAR-EAST & EUROPE

Waterman was an old family Steamship company out of Mobile Alabama. I sailed on two of their ships, SS Afoundria to the Far East, and the Wild Ranger to Northern Europe.

I joined the Afoundria in New York Sept. 10, 1959, together with John Cunningham, a native New Yorker. On the way down to the ship he asked me if I ever had sailed with Waterman or with crews from Mobile, Alabama before. Since my answer was no, he laughed and said it would be a whole new experience for me.

The SS Afoundria was a special-built Waterman C-2 Freighter and later converted to a Sea Land containership and renamed the SS Beaurgard. The crew quarters were back on the stern. John and I both shipped as Deck/ Maintenance (AB day worker). We were three men to share a small room on the main deck Starboard side.

There were three steel bunks, three lockers for clothing and personal belongings and a small table, a chair and a sink and one porthole facing forward. Since one of the lower bunks was already taken, John and I flipped a coin for the other lower bunk, and I won. Toilets and showers were down stairs, not much for comfort.

The third day worker was a fellow named Hans from the swamps of Mississippi, not the neatest fellow to look at, or to be around. Hans had been on the ship for several years sending all his money home to his wife and five kids. He proudly told me he made more money each month than anybody else in his home town, I soon learned he could not read or write.

After sailing from New York we made several stops down the East Coast and gulf ports

I don't know what happened, but just before sailing the Bosun was fired, and there was not enough time to get another before sailing for Panama and Los Angeles. The Chief Mate came to me and asked if I would take the Bosun's job until we got to Los Angeles. I told him to ask Hans since he had been here for a long time. He told me if he made Hans the Bosun the Captain would fire him.

We had a pleasant but uneventful trip between Texas and Los Angeles, except for the heat. Our little room had only one porthole which had to be kept closed most of the time because of soot coming from the smoke stack, particularly when they blew tubes in the morning and evening. One night I saw a rat running around out on deck. I asked Hans if he knew we had rats onboard. "Yes, we always had rats, and last trip we had bedbugs to."

Sitting around talking, the guys from the south were always making fun of John, he being a New Yorker and a darn Yankee. Strangely enough they had no problems with me being from Denmark. They considered me one of them.

We all had a great time out in Asia. The Captain was a party man. I saw him several place ashore in Yokohama and Kobe, always wearing dark sunglasses both day and night.

After turning around in Hong Kong we returned to Japan to load for the U.S. East Coast, stopping in Los Angeles for fuel and supplies and a few crew replacements.

We had a lot of bad weather coming across the North Pacific, and everybody was happy when we pulled into Los Angeles early in the morning. Everyone went ashore except John and I who both had to work all day. As it turns out, I ended up working most of the night also.

It seemed like everybody came back drunk and headed for the sack. The sailing board was set for 8 p.m. which meant everybody had to be back 7 p.m. Some did and some didn't.

Since there had been no cargo work, the ship was secured for sea ever since Japan, so it was just a matter of letting the mooring lines go, and sail. The Bosun told me that the two 8-12 ABs were unable to steer or to stand watch and asked me to step in and take the first wheel, and the watch.

When I walked into the wheel house a little before 8 p.m. I saw the Captain all dressed up wearing his dark sunglasses the harbor pilot was there but the third mate was not. After testing the steering engine I walk out to the wing of the bridge and noticed a taxi coming along side. It turned out to be the 8-12 3rd Mate all dressed up in a suit and necktie, and that was how he came up to stand his watch.

The undocking went very smoothly, and the harbor pilot got off after we cleared the breakwater. The Captain set the course out through the Santa Barbara Channel, instructed the 3rd mate and showed him the courses on the charts, and what to look out for, and where to set the course for Panama, before he went below.

I knew I would be in for a long night; the only break I would get from standing behind the wheel would be after we got out clear of the channel and the ship would be on auto pilot.

The new ordinary seaman standing lookout on the bow was making his first trip to sea and didn't know what to report and what not to report. Halfway through the channel, I noticed an inbound ship dead ahead at a distance. The lookout called the bridge several times to report the ship ahead.

Since the 3rd mate didn't answer the phone, I started wondering what had happened to him. I ran up to the flying bridge above the wheel house but didn't find him.

The radio officer happened to walk by. I asked him to steer and ran down stairs to look for the 3rd mate. When I opened the door to his room, I found him laying on his bunk sound a sleep. I tried everything I could think of to wake him up. No luck, he was completely passed out.

When I came back up on the bridge to take the wheel, I noticed the inbound ship was very close but that she would clear okay. I called the captain to come up to the bridge right away, which he did and stayed there until midnight when we were relieved by the 12 - 4 watch.

The next day the 3rd Mate came and thanked me for trying to wake him up. He felt bad and knew he would be fired. We arrived at New York the day before New Year's Eve. I was hoping I would be able to stay on for one more trip, but the union rules applied and I had to get off. The Captain overpaid me a hundred dollars, which I returned. The 3rd Mate was not fired.

A couple of years later I shipped out on the SS Wild Ranger as AB. I was assigned to the 8-12 watch. My watch partner had joined the ship a few days before. He never talked, just sat there staring out in the air or at me.

He kept his union book under his pillow and would sit and look at it, turning the pages like he was reading a book. At first I didn't know what to do? And since he didn't seem to know time and what was going on, I knew there would be problems. He was sent to a doctor and never came back. Later we were told he had just been released from a mental hospital and most likely returned there.

After sailing from New York we went down to Newport News and Norfolk, loading military cargo for Bremerhaven, thereafter Antwerp and Dunkirk. One morning in the English Chanel while on lookout for one hour and twenty minutes I counted 144 ships, many of them small coasters, It was a busy place.

Our first U.S. port of call was New Orleans where we stayed for a week alongside the old Orange dock awaiting cargo. My job with a few others was to hang in a bosun chair, chipping the old paint off the stack down to the bare metal, then prime and paint it.

Since we had full steam up, the stack itself was very hot, and so was the sun. It was a job I will always remember. There was a small bar and restaurant on the dock, can't remember the name of the beer they served, but it was served in large ice cold glasses, and only 19 cents per glass. Each time we had a break we would run down the gangway and gulp down 2-3 glasses of beer. Can't ever remember a beer tasting that good before or later.

SS Steel Worker 1960   SS Steel Artisan 1962,   SS Steel Director 1970

Isthmian Line was a subsidiary of U.S. Steel and operated over 25 ships mostly WWII C-3 dry Cargo ships on three different trade routes around the world, India and the Persian Gulf. The Company had a contract with the Master, Mates & Pilots (MM&P) for the licensed deck officers, MEBA district II for the licensed Engineers, and the Seafarers International Union (SIU) for the unlicensed crew.

My suitcase was always ready to go and when a pier head jump came up on the SS Steel Worker a C-3 freighter on the Persian Gulf trade, I had no competition for the job, and I made it down to the ship before sailing

Our outbound cargo was mostly supply for the 10,000 American oil workers and their family working in Saudi Arabia for ARAMCO which was Exxon, Mobil, Chevron, Gulf oil, and Texaco working and developing oil files, which was later turned over to the Saudis. I don't know why.

After crossing the Atlantic, we stopped in Genova and Beirut in the Mediterranean before transiting the Suez Canal, which went very smoothly except for the usual harassment. The Red sea was calm and hot and very uncomfortable.

We stopped in Djibouti for Bunkers and fresh water before proceeding for Ras Tanura/Damman where we arrived two days ahead of schedule, but that didn't do us much good because we spent the next two weeks at anchor awaiting berth due to port congestion.

While at Anchor we spent a lot of time fishing for sharks. We had boat service which brought us into the air conditioned seamen club where they showed movies, no beer or alcohol served.

Since there were hardly any roads anywhere, I was surprised to see so many new cars sitting on the sand next to the dock in Daman, covered with sand and no doubt the engines ruined. The first off shore oil rig had arrived from Mississippi and was operating well.

After complete discharging we sailed for Khorramshar, Iran to load cotton. We started cleaning the cargo hatches right away, hoisting all the 2 x 4 and wooden boards that had been used to shore the outbound cargo, and stacked it on deck. Since most of the wood was in very good condition, the Chief Mate decided to wait to throw it overboard until we came close to land, giving the local people a chance to pick it up and use it. After we anchored in Khorramshar close to land we started dumping the wood overboard, and before you know it people came out in small boats to pick it up. One boy came out sitting on a few bamboo reeds paddling his way to get a few 2 x 4 and tow them ashore. I have it on an old 16mm movie

It was another long delay at anchor awaiting berth, but at least here we had a very nice Seamen Club, each man was allowed two cold beers a day. The Manager of the club invited us to come to a special party the following Saturday. Each day everyone at the club kept reminding us about the special event, but did not want to give us any clue what it was all about. We started guessing and assumed by the excitement of the people at the club it had to be something big. We started taking bets on what it would be. First bet was Belly dancer.

Second bet Iranian folk dancing. Flyers were sent to all the ships in port reminding everybody not to miss the big event.

We were all very excited when Saturday evening finally came, and the club was full of people all waiting for the big event to start, which turned out to be a BINGO GAME-big disappointment to everyone aboard.

Bombay, India had not changed for the better doing the five years I had been away. There were just as many beggars and homeless children walking the streets, living in cardboard boxes on the docks, eating left overs from the ships, and always asking for small change. Young women walked the street wearing hand-me-down clothing carrying two small children in their arms. Quite often one of the children would have a missing hand or a foot which would make it easier for the mother to beg for money. Women would train children to beg.

The homeless children stuck together and helped one another. The ones with only one leg were helped by the others when they had to run away. One day I was watching a bunch of boys sneaking around a fire hydrant, and when nobody was watching, they stripped and open the water spigot for the water and took a bath using soap I had given them.

It was hard to watch people living in such abject misery and still find contentment with their lives, nothing to look forward to, but always big smile to share. One day walking ashore I was followed by a boy about 10 years old asking me for small change. He asked if I was of the Steel Worker and I told him no. He kept following me asking what nationality I was.

I don't know why, but I told him I was a Greek? I will never forget the way he looked at me and said oh no, an f...... Greek and he left. Guess the Greeks were not known for giving anything away. Later I gave him some money on my way back to ship later.

Someone in the royal families in South Arabia gave one of the Aramco executives two small Arabian horses as a gift to bring back home to Houston Texas. The horses were loaded on to our ship in special made wooden stalls. We also loaded a big supply of hay for the trip. After a week onboard the female horse went into heat and the male standing next to her got very excited and kept kicking the stall trying to get to the female.

On the way home we stopped in Port Sudan located in the Red Sea to load coffee to New York. The longshoremen came from the mountains walking around in rags, no shoes with cow dung in their hair. We were told not to take pictures.

Two years later I made an identical trip on the sister ship SS Steel Artisan. And like the Steel Worker the Steward department was Filipinos, the food was outstanding, like eating in a five star Restaurant every day.

CITIZEN PAPERS & NAVIGATION SCHOOL

After five years on a green card, I applied for U.S. citizenship in New York where I lived and attended navigation school in between ships. The immigration told me it would take several months to process my application, and I would be notified by mail. I was given a booklet of U.S. history and the constitution to study.

I took a job on a coastwise tanker, the" USNS Cache" carrying jet fuel from Texas to the military on the East Coast. When off duty I spent my spare time studying U.S. history to prepare for my test. One day I was sitting studying when my watch partner, Bill, asked what I was reading.

He looked at me and said, "Forget it, you will never make a good citizen." I got a little shocked and started to wonder what I had done to him to make such a statement. Then he told me. "You have two strikes against you."

(1) You don't like peanut butter, (2) and you don't know fuck all about baseball.

In 1959 when I signed off a Waterman ship, the Captain gave me a letter of recommendation.

He pointed out that since I was here on a green card, it would help when I applied for U.S. Citizenship so he took time out to write a personal one. He was right. By the time I applied for U.S. citizenship I had four letters of recommendation and the Immigration Officers took them all seriously

I was notified to appear for the final interview on April 17, 1961 and to bring two witnesses who had known me for five years or more. I called Arnie Hindenes who had just become a U.S. citizen himself, and a fellow name Andy whom I had sailed with several times.

The Immigration Office was huge with a lot of small booths each big enough for a desk and two chairs. While sitting in my assigned booth waiting for the Immigration officer I was able to hear the conversation next door between an immigration officer and a German or Eastern European sounding lady. She was crying. The immigration officer had told her to stop coming here because she would never become a U.S. citizen. "You have two children with two different men and you have never been married. We do not accept people like you to become US Citizen. Since you have a green card you can stay in the U.S. but will never become a citizen.

I was asked several questions about the U.S. history and the Constitution, all very simple, and I had to prove I could read and write. Everything seemed to be in order until he checked my draft card which was A-1

The Immigration officer called the superior officer and told him that everything was in order except that I was 27 years old and never served in the military and my draft card was A-1. The superior officer looked at my draft card and said to my interviewer, "That's none of our business. Our job is to make sure he has a draft card and that is where our responsibility stops. Pass him."

Many of my friends and shipmates tried to discourage me from getting a license. "The way shipping is going you may never get a Mate's job anyway." I knew I would be in for a hard time getting started and that nobody would come along giving me a job, but I would keep looking and find one.

I decided to go to school full time, and to sit for a 3rd Mate license. The Coast Guard approved my sea time and application to sit for 2nd or 3rd mate license. The Coast Guard office and license department was located at the U.S. Custom house in lower Manhattan just a few blocks away from the school. The Exam room was large with many desks spaced far enough apart to eliminate cheating or contact with one another.

You were not allowed to bring anything into the exam room, and scratch paper had to be turned in and checked by the inspectors before going in the trash can.

Since my spelling was poor, I asked if I would be allowed to bring in a dictionary which was denied, and the inspector told me it's not a spelling test, so don't worry as long as I can understand what you are trying to tell me.

The questions were typed on cards; you had to accept five cards at the time. It was up to the inspectors which five cards to give you from the file. You were not allowed to leave the exam room before you had completed and turned in all five cards. The good part was there was no time limit. I was not very good at passing tests and did only five cards in the morning, and five in the afternoon. Then I would go home and study more for the next day.

The Rules of the Road and Navigation both needed 90% passing, and I never had any problem with them because those were two subjects I enjoyed studying and learning.

The other subjects required a 70% passing grade. What made the test very unfair was if you failed the test at the end and were given a pink slip, you had to start all over 30 days later.

I was disappointed when I got the pink slip half way through the test. When I started again 30 days later I was less nervous and took my time making sure I understood the question correctly before I answered it.

It took me ten long days to complete the test, but I passed except for the signal blinker Morse code. That was a subject done early in the morning and you were allowed to come back until you passed.

OUT OF THE FOC'SLE

Looking back, on my fourteen years in the foc'sle from 1948-1962 on 23 different ships was by far the most exciting time of my life. It was the Golden Age after penicillin, and before the Exxon Valdez Oil spill which changed the shipping industry forever and cut out the happy hours and parties on merchant ships forever.

I am on record as being the youngest ever to qualify to join the Danish sailors' union, and never had to waste time on a school ship and learned my skills from older experienced sailors as I went along and become an expert in splicing rope and wires and moved quickly up the ladder sailing as an Able-Bodied Seaman at the age of 18. I saw ships change from coal to oil and from steam to diesel, from General cargo to containership. I saw Europe in ruins with high unemployment and food rationing. On the ships the food was good and plentiful. Cigarettes were plentiful and better than money. It was a time that can never be repeated, and Hollywood would not be able to recreate it, just as today's seafarers would not believe it. The Sailors Union of the Pacific (SUP) in 1956 was the most respected maritime union in the nation. There I met men who had survived the great Depression and WWII where 1500 U.S. merchant ships had been sunk by enemies when crossing the Atlantic, or the Pacific Oceans bringing supply to our troops and allies troops. 8000 U.S. merchant seamen lost their lives and 1200 wounded.

Some of my ship mates had taken part in the invasion of North Africa, Sicily, and Normandy. Some had been torpedoed several times and spent time on lifeboats for days and weeks before being picked up by ships passing by.

One thing they had in common was loyalty to the union and their union officials, creating a real union sprit which I have never experienced anywhere else.

One old timer told me, "We pay our union dues first and eat later." I read the history of the SUP and the struggle they went through,and listened to the old timers' experiences.

Andrew Furuseth, was a Norwegian immigrant who some call the Abraham Lincoln of the sea. A self-indicated conservative man, he concluded that everywhere in Europe workers were under the influence of the socialists, and he was convinced that the socialists were looking not for freedom, but for government control and the destruction of individualism.

He almost single handedly brought the sailors into the twentieth century by his patient lobbying in Washington DC.

A few of the old characters would tell some hair rising stories. Suitcase Larsen, an old Dane got the nick name from saying, "Never mind what the captain says I can take my suitcase and go my way."

He left Denmark as a kid to see the world and have fun. Now 40+years later he still wanted to see the world and have fun. He was proud of being known up and down the West Coast and the Orient.

One guy told me he met Suit case Larsen in New York during the War and asked him how he got there? Larsen told him he was on a Liberty ship out of Los Angeles heading for North Africa. Two days out of the Panama Canal, the ship was hit by a torpedo and started sinking, giving them just enough time to get into lifeboats and get away from the ship before she went down. As they were rowing away from the sinking ship, the German submarine came up real close to his lifeboat, and the German captain appeared in full uniform with his binoculars looking directly at everybody in the boats. He got all excited and yelled through the bull horn "My God, is that Suitcase Larsen over there? Come over here and I will bring you back to the old country." Suitcase Larsen stood up and yelled "f... you, I am going the other way, and kept on rowing."

Another old character was nick-named the Ambassador from Finland. He had checked in at the Fairmont Hotel in San Francisco as the Ambassador from Finland. He called some of his fellow ship mates to join him.

The Hotel staff started wondering about some of the men in black Frisco jeans and white SUP sailor caps coming to the front desk asking to see the Ambassador from Finland. As the party got louder they were quickly thrown out.

I had a watch partner by name of Ski from Brooklyn who had been a professional fighter and it showed. His nose was completely flat, and he had many scars all over his face.

One day he saw me using a Danish-English Dictionary and asked what I was looking up.

I told him "I'm looking up some of the big fancy words I don't understand". He said, "It's a waste of time. Look at me. I am sixty years old and never had to use any of those big f...... fancy words." I took a good look of him and went back to my studying.

THE MASTER MATES & PILOTS

The MM&P did me well over the years by giving me the job opportunity, good Benefits. I received my 50 year pin in 2012, and my dues are always paid in advance. Like so many others, I had a rough time getting started.

With the ink barely dry on my 3rd mate license, issued April 12-1962 by the U.S. Coast Guard in New York, I proudly went to join the International Organization Master, Mate & Pilot Union, local 88. The secretary treasurer gave me an application to fill out, took my $300 initiation fee, and issued me a shipping card. When I asked him how long it would take to get a job, I was shocked when he told me I would never get job. He went on telling me that shipping was very slow and I was starting in group C which meant I would only get the jobs that group A and B didn't want.

He also told me that it takes a group "A" member up to a year to get a permanent job. So your chances are not very good.

The only way for you to get started is to go out and look for non-union job. When you have accumulated one year sea time as 3rd Mate on any American ship, you can come back and register in group "A" and wait your turn.

I could not believe what I was hearing. I asked, "Do you mean to tell me here I come with a license just a few hours old to join the union, you take my money, and then tell me to go out and look for a non-union job? What kind of organization is this?" He refused to give me my money back. I asked to see the President of the local who agreed to return my money.

Since I did not want to go around looking for a non-union job with the oil companies I decided to go back to the SUP asking for advice, which turned out to be a good idea because Bill Armstrong, the port agent, told me he might be able to help because the man in charge of MM&P local 14 in Philadelphia owed him a favor.

After a short phone call I was on my way to Philadelphia a few days later. The captain in charge told me an unusual situation had come up on the SS Alcoa Pilgrim, shuttling out in the Orient for States Marine Line, where a relief 3rd Mate wanted to get off to go home to attend school and was willing to pay his own way home and a ticket for his replacement to fly out there. Since my passport and U.S Public Health card were up to date, the job was mine.

I received a $ 1000 check for the airfare to Taipei and I was given two assignment slips, one as permanent 3rd Mate and one for relief 3rd Mate, hoping for the best. I managed to get a ticket to Taipei via San Francisco for $700. Flying Pan American across the Pacific I sat between a Chinese lady who had lots of paper bags with her, not just on her seat but also all over mine as well. On the other side was a Japanese man sitting there sucking his teeth all the way.

When I arrived in Taipei, I was met by the runner for States Marine office who told me the bad news. The ship was five days late. Since I was traveling on my own my expense, it was up to me if I wished to stay in Taipei or go directly to Kaohsiung.

I decided to go to Kaohsiung. Sitting on the train looking at the countryside, and going from one end of the island to the other, I was impressed by how every little piece of land was used to grow vegetables and other farms products. The train was an old coal burner steam engine without windows, and it didn't take long before I was full of soot.

Five days later I was standing watching the ship approach the dock. A small boat went out to get the ship's head line to bring it ashore which is standard procedure. The boat was laying close to the ship, waiting for the ship's crew to lower the mooring line. Next thing I saw was the anchor coming out the hawse pipe sending the two men flying into the water just before the anchor went right through the boat sinking it. Luckily they were both able to swim.

Watching the event, I started to wonder what kind of ship is this? But it turned out to be OK. She was a WW II built C-1 B five hatch cargo ship, 418' long, 60' beam, 6,750 gross tons, 4000 HP steam Engine, speed 14 knots. She had left the States with a lot of military cargo, and then started carrying cement from Taiwan to Vietnam to build up the US Air Bases.

The 2nd mate showed me the ship, and prepared me for my 1600-2400 port watch, and good luck for me, he explained how the CO_2 fire system worked. On my second night watch the Longshoremen stopped for meal hour at 1900 and left the cargo hatches open. Shortly thereafter a fire broke out in #3 hatch with a lot of black smoke pouring out.

Unfortunately everyone was ashore except the second engineer, and fireman on watch in the engine room a sailor at the gangway and the chief cook.

I rang the ship general alarm, to get everybody to give me a hand. I sent the cook down on the dock to get somebody to call the local fire department, who showed up very quickly.

The fire department wanted to fight the fire with water, and I wanted to use the CO_2 system, because the water would damage all the cement already in the lower cargo hull and also make it impossible to get the cement out later. There was a big language barrier and they kept insisting on fighting the fire using water, and I kept saying no.

I made sure there was nobody inside the hatch before I covered it up tight, told the sailor and the cook that I was going down to the CO-2 room to start the system and for them to stay by the hatch to make sure the local fire department didn't open up the hatch and start spraying water inside.

In the CO-2 room, I took my time to read the instructions, what to do step by step. It didn't take long to extinguish the fire, which turned out to have started on the lower twain deck in a bundle of straw mats used for separation. Guess it started by a cigarette butt earlier when the longshoremen were working.

The local fire department was still there when the Captain and everybody else came back, requesting a statement on how the fire may have started and why I didn't want to fight the fire with water. It was a good experience which worked out OK.

Unfortunately, we only made one more trip to Vietnam, then stopped in Yokohama to load before proceeding for San Francisco, where I had to get off as the permanent man assigned to the ship decided to come back. I collected transportation to New York and went home.

Spent two months at home in New York enjoying married life, and our small apartment at 633-171 St on the West side close to George Washington Bridge. It was a nice feeling to have the experience from the first ship on my license behind me, and I felt I did OK

I checked out all my options getting another ship out of New York but found nothing promising. I volunteered to stand picket duty for the MM&P who had just walked off two harbor dredges, the "San Captain" and the "Zanzibar" while the MM&P was negotiating a new contract with the company, the SIU and MEBA district 2 now the American Maritime Officers (AMO) walked through our picket line and sailed the dredges for less than what the MM&P had walked off with. So much for the Brotherhood of the Sea.

Sometimes when everything looks bleak a window of opportunity opens up. Isbrandtsen Steamship Company merged with American Export line, the name becoming American Export-Isbrandtsen Lines (AEL). Isbrandtsen had a contract with the MM&P, and American Export Line had a contract with The Brotherhood of Marine Officers, (BMO) a small company union affiliated with the National Maritime Union (NMU). The court ruled that the MM&P had to get off the Isbrandtsen ships and be replaced with members of the BMO. The company agreed that the MM&P could stay but had to join the BMO, and all new officers would be members of the BMO only.

I went to apply for a job with the BMO, where I was told the same old story that they had a long waiting list and they would call me when something came up.

Instead of them calling me, I kept calling them. After a while the secretary recognized my voice or accent right away, and her answer was always the same, nothing yet, Georg.

I decided to double my chances of getting a job by heading back to the MM&P Local 14 union hall in Philadelphia during the week then come home for the weekend and keep calling the BMO twice a week from there. There were only a few guys like myself hanging around the hiring hall. The Captain in charge didn't spend much time there either; his assistant was a man named Frank, who spent most of his time on the phone. You never really knew how many jobs were dispatched since there was no record, and I never saw any jobs heading the shipping board. If you asked, the answer was always the same, shipping is very slow. Port Relief Officers were all dispatched by phone. Frank would walk through the hall to get to the water cooler which had a small space built into the back big enough for a few bottles. I don't know what he had in the bottles, but I know it was not juice or coke, because as the day went on he would head for the water cooler more often, and became more talkative and friendly.

One morning Frank came out and asked if any of us had a car? One fellow jumped up and said yes. Frank told him to come into the office. After several phone conversations, the guy came running out of the office smiling and waving to us. We all assumed he was doing Frank a favor and would soon be back.

Around 3 PM Frank told us we might as well go home for the day, but it looked like the kid made it.

I asked. "What are you talking about?"

Remember this morning when I came out and asked if any of you had a car?

"Yes, I do," he said he told me there had been a 3rd Mate job on a Grace Line ship lying in Baltimore and they were not able to fill the job so they called here.

I was still in shock when I asked him" Do you mean to tell me you gave him that job because he had a car?

"Frank looked at me and said how else would you get there."

I could not believe what I was hearing. After I calmed down, I told him for a job with Grace Line I would have hired a taxi to take me to Baltimore instead of wasting my time in this place. I wanted to raise a complaint, but I soon came to the conclusion that there was nobody to complain to. I decided not to spend any more time there, and I have never been in Philadelphia since.

Shortly thereafter the secretary from the BMO called me and told me they had decided to hire me and start me as a Port Relief Officer (Night Mate). She told me to stop by their office the following day for more information and instruction which turned out to be a good deal for me. If I played my cards right I would have a permanent job with American Export Isbrantdsen Line. She told me she would be the one calling me for Port Relief Officer (PRO) but when an offshore came up I would be dealing with the company personnel manager.

American Export Line was a leading US-flag shipping company with service from the U.S. to the Mediterranean, Pakistan, India, Bangladesh, and Burma. In addition they operated a fleet of passenger ships in the Mediterranean service. The best known were SS Independence and the SS Constitution. Isbrandtsen Steamship Company operated 12 freighters on the around the world and Northern Europe service.

Export Adventure   Export Ambassador   Export Agent   Export Aide

My first job with AEL was on the SS Export Adventure, a nice new ship built by New York Ship Building Corp Camden NJ in 1960. 17, 498 tons six hatch cargo vessel with modern cargo gear and Macgregor hydraulic hatch covers. Before we left for India, the company instructed the Chief Mate that only the license deck officers were to open and close hatches in all Indian ports.

We sailed out of New York December 21, 1962 with a full load of cargo of heavy machinery, tractors, trucks, Coca Cola syrup, and flours for India. The reason I remember the Coca Cola syrup is that a barrel became damaged during the voyage and the syrup spilled on the twin deck and became very hard and the only way we were able to clean it up was by using power thistle to get it off the steel deck.

We made several stops in the Mediterranean, Barcelona, Genova, Alexandria and Port Said, Egypt before transiting the Suez Canal. At the time we had to prove that ship had not been in Israel or had any Israeli cargo onboard, before we were allowed to transit the canal.

We stopped in Djibouti, French Somalia for fuel and to discharge mail and supplies to the American Embassy before entering the Gulf of Aden, sailing through the Arabian Sea to Karachi, Pakistan, Bombay, and Madras, India. All the ports had long delays at anchor awaiting berth and long slow cargo operations when alongside the docks.

After several days at anchor outside Bombay awaiting berth and several days alongside the docks working cargo with two mates on duty at all times checking out special cargo, we didn't get much sleep for several days. By the time we finally got out of there I had been on my feet for 18 hours straight and had just enough time to take a shower and go on sea-watch from 20-2400.

I always make sure I relieve 20 minutes early to check the position on the chart, stepping off where I can expect to be each hour on my watch. In addition, I write down the names of the lighthouses which in many cases are long and difficult to pronounce. Therefore I always wrote down the characteristics of the lights as well in my note book, and kept it in my shirt pocket.

Half way through my watch the Captain came on the bridge and stood there to adjust for the darkness before asking me, "What is the name of the light forward of the port beam?"

Since it was one of the names I had a hard time pronouncing I took my note book out of my shirt pocket and used my flash light to read the name. Right away he blew his stack and started screaming at me that I didn't even know the name of the light house. I tried to explain to him that not only did I know the name and characteristics of the light, but I had been using it to take bearings and plotting them on the chart every 20 minutes as he had already seen before coming in here, and furthermore we were right on course as we were supposed to be, but he didn't let up. After a while I had enough of his BS and told him to step out on the wing of the bridge away from the quarter master steering the ship before I told him, "If you are unhappy with my work, I will get off the ship tomorrow in Cochin and pay my own way home and you can sail the f..... ship yourself." And I went back inside the wheelhouse to attend to my duty. He remained out on the wing of the bridge for some time before coming inside to go below and for the first time ever he said "Goodnight Pedersen" before he went below. After that incident he let up on me and became a little more human when talking to me. However, the 12 x 4 3rd mate making his first trip after graduating from Massachusetts Maritime Academy was not as lucky because the Captain drove him to a nervous wreck, and he lost 20 pounds during the voyage and was declared to be in a run-down condition and unfit for duty by the U.S. Public Health Department on Staten Island Marine Hospital when we returned to New York

The trip up the Hugely River to Calcutta took all day. The scenery was unforgettable with hundreds of people taking baths, bare breasted women washing clothes swinging them above their heads. Some were washing dishes, others taking a dump and some were cooking, creating a smell and smog you could never forget. The local pilots conning the ship up or down the river were dressed to kill, wearing white uniforms and gloves.

The schedule called for two weeks in Calcutta, but we always stayed longer, discharging, and back loading very expensive carpets and carpet backing which came in long rolls, also various textile items, cashew nuts, burlap, pepper and other spices, all high quality cargo.

The labor was cheap and the longshoremen worked around the clock in three shifts. The gangs from midnight to 0800 never accomplished much. It seemed like both the workers on the dock and aboard the ship either sat around resting or slept on deck with newspapers over their heads.

One morning, walking on the main deck, stepping in between the sleeping longshoremen, one man sat up and asked me if I was the duty officer and what time it was. When I told him it was 0700, he said," Thank you. One more hour and my duty is finished," and he went back to sleep.

Rangoon, Burma, our-turn around port, was a short stop, discharging supplies for the U.S. embassy, back loading teak wood and teak wood products. Homebound, we stopped in Colombo loading tea and coffee beans in Port Sudan for New York.

When we arrived in New York, I took two weeks off when she made the loop and had a great time at home, before returning for another voyage to India. When I returned, I found the ship all dressed up with signal flags from mast to mast, red carpet leading up the gangway, and I knew it was not because I had returned.

As it turned out, James Cagney, everyone's favorite movie actor and entertainer at that time, was coming onboard as a passenger with his two brothers, all newly retired. They had decided to take a vacation together on a freighter, and I was happy they chose our ship.

I had many interesting conversations with them when they came up on the bridge on my watch in the morning socializing. I missed them when they got off in Genova to take another ship back.

What a difference a few new faces can make on a ship. When arriving in port on the 8x12 watch, it was my job to handle the engine telegraphs as per Captain or pilot instruction, and to keep the bell book, logging all changes in speed and to keep the deck log up to date. After I finished with Engine (FEW) and pilot and tugs were away, it was also my job to make up the arrival slip which included the arrival draft, miles and average speed from the last port or from noon the day before and deliver the slip to the Captain and Chief Engineer.

When I stopped by with a copy to the first old grumpy Captain he used to pull it out of my hand, and without looking at it, he would ask me, "Are you sure its correct?"

Now one trip later with the new Captain I didn't know what to expect when I knocked on his door to deliver the arrival slip and to my surprise he asked me if I was finished on the bridge. If so, sit down and have a beer, or drink. I don't have to tell anybody that the second trip went twice as fast as the first one and without any problems.

Boston was the first U.S. port of call before proceeding to New York through the Cape Cod Canal. Sailing through the Cape Cod Canal was always very interesting, watching people standing outside their houses waving at us as we went by. A few hours out of the Canal getting off watch, I was sitting in the dining room waiting for my lunch when the waiter let out a scream and pointed aft. When I looked out the windows I saw a large submarine surfacing from underneath our ship. It looked like she came out from # 4 cargo hatch.

By good luck, she didn't touch our ship. We stopped the ship and set up communication with the sub. The Commander from the sub came onboard to give his apology.

He asked our Captain to sign a statement that there was no damage to our ship which he refused to do. A diver was ordered to check our bottom for damage on arrival in New York which turned out okay.

My next ship was the Export Ambassador, a sister ship to the Export Adventure but sailing on the Mediterranean run. In addition to the scheduled ports of call, we also stopped in various ports in both Greece and Turkey to load tobacco for Newport News. Tobacco demanded a lot of attention, keeping it dry and well ventilated. It t was a nice and enjoyable ship.

AROUND THE WORLD IN 120 DAYS

SS Flying Endeavor, SS Flying Enterprise II.   *Pictures from Isbrandtsen calendar*

The Flying Endeavor a former Robin Line special built C-2. The Flying Enterprise II, a Standard C-2 built doing WWII, crew of 40 with accommodations for 12 passengers

A fter making the loop on the East Coast ports with New York being the last U.S. Port, the schedule called for Barcelona, Spain, Genova Italy, Beirut Lebanon, through the Suez canal to East Africa, before crossing the Indian Ocean to Karachi, Pakistan, Bombay, India, Colombo, Ceylon, Singapore, Saigon, Indochina, Hong Kong BC, Pusan, Korea, Moji, Kobe, Nagoya Yokohama Japan, before crossing the North Pacific to San Francisco, Stockton, Los Angeles through the Panama canal to San Juan Puerto Rico and New York, our final port, covering approximately 25,000 nautical in four months.

The Around the World service was an interesting run with a lot of sea and port time, and it must have been very profitable for the company because we actually carried 4 loads in 120 days. The first outbound cargo from the U.S. was mostly for the Mediterranean ports and Karachi, Pakistan and Bombay, India, where we would back load for Singapore, Hong Kong and Japan, and then back loaded for San Francisco and Los Angeles and back loaded rice, canned fruit and Tuna fish in cans for Puerto Rico.

The Chief Engineer on the Endeavor was an old Export line chief who was used to having a reefer engineer to maintain the reefer cargo boxes. Isbrandtsen ships did not carry a reefer engineer and the chief engineer was supposed to be in charge of maintaining the reefer cargo boxes, and the oiler on watch was checking the temperature on each watch. Each day at noon when out at sea, a noon report was made and recorded in the deck log, giving the 1200 position, miles and speed made good from noon to noon, sea/air temp, fuel oil on hand, and the temperature in the reefer boxes. A few days out at sea the Captain noticed that the temp had been rising daily since we left New York, and he started wondering what was going on.

As it turned out the reefer cargo was for the U.S. military in Pakistan who had an inspector come on board in Karachi and condemn all the meat, a very costly mistake and the Chief Engineer was fired on the spot.

In Saigon we moored between two buoys, loading rubber in bales for Japan, and water buffalos for Hong Kong. The advantage of carrying livestock was that regardless what time of the day or night you arrived in Hong Kong you went directly to the dock or buoys and were able to start working cargo right away.

The buffalos were brought out to the ship on a barge just before sailing and hoisted onboard with a rope and canvas sling around their belly. The buffalos were huge and heavy and when the sling was in place the buffalo would be lifted slowly up a foot or two and stopped until the barge was moved away in case the sling would part which it did once when hanging half way up in the air. The rope parted and the buffalo fell into the water. It took what seemed forever before he surfaced and swam across the river and walked up on the beach and was brought back again. We sailed from Saigon in the morning on my watch, and after getting underway, the 2nd mate came up on the bridge laughing, telling me that walking from aft toward the amidships he saw a Vietnamese man running out from the amidships house with a large transistor radio, and he jumped in the water and swam ashore with the stolen radio. The 2nd mate thought it was funny until he found out it was his own radio the guy had stolen by reaching in through the open port hole. At the time and still in some parts of the world longshoreman will hide just before sailing and enter a room and steal whatever he can find in a hurry then jump over the side and swim ashore with his catch.

SS Flying Enterprise II was known around the world because of Captain Kurt Carlsen, the permanent Master. Captain Carlsen had been the Master on the original Flying Enterprise back in 1951 when in route from Hamburg, Germany to New York they got hit by a ferocious storm and the vessel suffered hull damage and took on water making the ship list heavily to port. After getting all the passengers and crew safely off the ship, he remained onboard for 13 days before he was forced to abandon ship when the list increased to a fatal degree and water came through the smoke stack on January 10, 1952 when in tow to Ireland.

When he returned to the U.S. he was honored with a ticker tape parade in New York City which drew 750,000 people. He was offered lots of money for book and movie rights, but turned it down saying he never wanted a Captain's honest attempt to save his ship to be commercialized. Life Magazine made him the man of the year in 1952. In Cork's Ireland is a very glamorous bar and restaurant named "The Flying Enterprise" with a special Captain's table. He was also known as a ham radio operator, call sign W2ZXM, talking to people around the world.

I don't know the reasons, but we had 3 different Captains when I was there. When I first came onboard in New York, the NMU had a union beef over a sailor who had been fired after getting caught in San Juan with some kind of narcotics customs found in his room. The NMU claimed it was not enough reason to fire the man. The new Captain had just come onboard and just like me didn't know anything about the firing.

When he returned to the ship at around 5 p.m. after spending the afternoon at the Custom house clearing the ship for sailing, the NMU patrolman was waiting for him on the ship to settle the firing dispute. I happened to be on the bridge writing up the deck log when I heard a lot of yelling coming from the next deck down.

When I went down to see what was going on, I saw the Captain staying outside his room with his brief case trying to open the door to his office and the NMU patrolman who must have lost his cool was choking him rapping his necktie around his neck. I managed to get a good grab on the guy pulling him away from the Captain and knocking his head against the bulkhead which seemed to calm him down. Shortly thereafter the chief mate came and walked the guy down the gangway. The Captain, a man in his upper 50's was the kind of man who could not get mad even if he tried. The NMU sent someone to apologize for the incident before sailing.

When ready to sail from New York on the second trip, we had another crew beef. I had been off doing the coastwise loop and had two weeks at home coming back the day of sailing. We signed foreign articles before the U.S. shipping commissioner at 1300. Sailing time was set for 1800. At 1700 the NMU crew delegate informed the Captain they had not received the new washing machine as promised and they refused to sail without it. The Captain and Chief Engineer both new didn't know anything about it. The Captain tried to call the port captain, but the office was closed and everybody had gone home. The Captain and Chief Engineer offered the crew the officers' washing machine, and a new one would be flown to Barcelona, but they refused to swap. The sailing time was canceled. The Captain called the Port Captain every half an hour without results.

I went on watch at 2000 and the Captain gave me a phone number to call every half an hour. When I called at 2200, I was surprised to hear a man on the other end who turned out to be the port Captain who was surprised to hear we were still in port. I explained to him what had happened, and that we had offered to give the crew our washing machine but they refused to swap. He was not a man of many words but told me don't give them fuck all. I will be down in the morning. The following morning a new wash machine was installed for the crew, and we sailed at 10.00, 14 hours late.

The ports of Karachi, Bombay were always very congested with ships laying at anchor for days and weeks waiting for berth. Singapore we worked cargo at anchor.

To me the two weeks around Japan was the highlight of the trip? Nagoya, the fastest growing area, with manufacturing industry originating from pottery, kimono fabric, furniture textiles and fine china exported out of there. The auto industries were gearing up, looking toward exporting to the USA.

We loaded several small Datsun cars for Los Angeles and San Juan. Many shook their heads and said they would never sell in the U.S. Well they did, and still are.

Kobe and Yokohama were my favored ports. The best nightlife in Yokohama was still in China town. One day I left the ship a little earlier than everybody else to walk around in China Town trying to look for my old apartment from the 1950's. I stopped in a bar where I had never been and ordered a Gin and Tonic. I don't know what they did or what they put in my drink or what happened after drinking it. Eight hours later I woke up in jail, standing behind bars with a couple of guys I had never seen before, pretending we were throwing hand grenades at the Police Guard.

I had no recollection of how, why, or when I got there, and nobody would tell me. The police contacted the ship, and Leroy, the chief mate, showed up to bail me out. In the taxi back to the ship I told him what had happened. The next thing I knew he was telling the taxi driver to turn around and go back to China Town to find that bar and destroy it. I managed to talk him out of it.

We had a rough ride across the Pacific heading for San Francisco with one storm after another, and in addition we had fog and heavy overcast day after day. We never saw the sun or starts and crossed the Pacific on a Dead Reckoning, an estimate of the ship's position on the basis of distance run since the last known position. We were right on with the speed, but when we picked up land we were 20 miles south of our course line, not that bad.

Before sailing Los Angeles for San Juan, a passenger in her mid-30 by the name Karla came onboard to make the trip to New York.

Leroy, the Chief Mate asked her," Are you sure you are on the right ship?" The passengers who travel on these type of ships was mostly retired people in their 60's, making a four moths trip around the world for $2000, a real bargain.

Sailing down the coast of Central America to Panama is very enjoyable and relaxing with an opportunity to get a lot work done on deck, like overhauling cargo gear and painting. There was a daily happy hour in the chief Mates room right next to mine, and Karla was always invited to the parties before Dinner and sometimes it went on long after.

Leroy was a Scotch drinker, Johnnie Walker Black. He kept all his booze in the bottom drawer in his desk. I always remember when the party was over he always held up his glass checking it, before putting it away. I don't ever remember seeing him wash the glass.

I was looking forward to spending 3-4 days in San Juan with my wife coming down from New York. We were scheduled to arrive on my watch around 2200 on a Friday evening.

Ater happy hour I went to dinner and turned in to get a few hours' sleep before going on watch at 2000.

When I went on watch I notice the party in the Chief Mates room was still in full swing and getting unusually laud. It was a routine watch with the Captain on the bridge approaching the Port to pick up the harbor pilot and tug boats to assist us docking. After the ship was all fast, Immigration and customs came onboard to clear the ship before anybody was allowed to come onboard or go ashore. My wife was on the dock waiting until ship was cleared. I wrote up the Deck log and arrival slips before leaving the bridge. When I went below and opened the door to my room I was met by the smell of booze, and guess what? Karla was lying in my bed all passed out. I tried to wake her, but it was impossible to get any kind of life out of her. I knew I needed help and went to get two able bodied seamen from my watch to give me a hand carrying her out of my room and down the passageway to her own room without anybody seeing it and we did.

In San Juan, Leroy won a lot of money in a Casino and took us all out for Dinner the following day. My wife, Carole, and I had a very pleasant stay in in San Juan. I don't know why but I noticed the happy hours were a little shorter between San Juan and New York, and nobody ever mentioned how Karla ended up in my bed.

THE NORTH ATLANTIC
AT ITS WORST

I spent the winter of 1965-66 on the SS Exporter as 3rd mate where I encountered some of the worst weather I have ever experienced day after day, trip after trip.

The SS Exporter was one of the six special built C3-E cargo ships built for American Export Line in 1939. She was on the "Adriatic run" from the U.S. East Coast to Lisbon, Barcelona, Marseille, Genova, Naples, Rijeka, Split, and Venice, our turn around port.

It was a fun ship with nice and interesting people to work with. The Saloon (dining room) was unique with several small round tables. I shared a table with the 8x12 engineer, an unforgettable funny song and dance man and a great story teller. He was also able to imitate several movie stars and politicians.

Since we were both working the same hours we decided to go ashore together after midnight when getting off watch and hit the night clubs in the good ports, Thanks to him we became a big hit with musicians and local entertainers, especial in Rijeka, Yogooslavia.

The Captain was in his mid-50's and had sailed as Chief Mate for many years before, being promoted to Captain, which meant he had not been involved with the ship's navigation for some time. To get back in the swing of navigation he spent a lot of time on the Bridge taking sun and star sight, always smoking a big cigar, dropping ashes all over the charts, and chart table.

He didn't have any faith in Radar. One trip, arriving in Rijeka in heavy fog, he told me to man the radar. He showed me on the chart where he wanted to anchor which was one mile off the port entrance, and wait for the fog to lift before entering the harbor.

As we approached anchorage I kept him informed of the distance off and the course to steer. After dropping anchor, I took several bearings and distance of the breakwater by radar and plotted them on the chart giving our exact position, which met his approval.

After getting off watch, I went down for lunch and went to bed to get some sleep before being called out for docking. A few hours later I was awakened by the Captain who was very excited, telling met the fog had lifted and we were in exactly the position I had said, not even the length of a hatch board off.

The outbound Cargo was heavy machinery, U.S. Mail and military cargo for our bases in Southern Europe, and various kinds of foreign aid.

The homebound cargo to the U.S. included brandy, wine, cheese, salami, silk suits, shoes and French perfume. It was loaded and stowed with special care, case by case.

To eliminate damage, special wooden floors were built between the layers of boxes to protect the merchandize from moving or being crushed during ocean transit. Mats were used for separation, a huge and very time consuming job, but necessary.

Watchmen were hired in all ports to watch the cargo, but pilfering was still a big problem everywhere. One trip in Naples discharging a U.S. Navy PX supply, I was standing on deck looking down #4 lower cargo hull watching the longshoremen breaking open and stealing part of the cutlery. By the time I got down there, the box and the contents had been hidden and were never found and of course the watchman didn't see a thing. When I complained to the walking boss, about the incident, he looked at me with a straight face and said, "Mate, we are not Italian. We are from Sicily, and we don't steal"

On the last trip before I was getting off on vacation we were crossing the Atlantic in a great circle course from Lisbon to New York in hurricane force winds and mounting high seas making the ship roll, yaw, and pitch all at the same time and making it very difficult to stand up straight or to stay in bed. I moved my mattress off the bed and placed it on deck (floor) between the bulk head (wall) and the bed to stop me from sliding or being thrown around. The chair and table in my room were bolted to the deck and I tied myself to the chair when sitting trying to read a book to get my mind off the weather when off duty.

We received several SOS signal from ships in distress taking on water. Each time they were too far away for us to assist, not that we would have been much help to anybody.

After a long and rough ride we finally arrived in New York and tied up at the American Export Line piers in Hoboken. After the ship was cleared by Immigration and customs the longshoremen came onboard to unload the cargo.

Looking at the longshoremen gave me a feeling that we were still in Italy as they were all Italian immigrants and didn't speak must English, even though they had been in the U.S. for many years.

We were all wondering how the cargo had held up during the rough ride across. When the hatches opened we were met with the smell of wine and perfume, however the damage was not as bad as we had expected, a feather in the Chief Mate's hat.

There was no apparent damage to the ship above the waterline but the company decided to dry dock her to inspect the hull below the waterline.

I was happy when I finally got a chance to call my wife and was told the baby was due within a week, exciting news. The second night at home, I woke up around 2 a.m. hearing a strange sound which turned out to be Carole standing out in the hallway in severe pain. She was well prepared and had already a small bag already packed and ready to head for the Hospital. I called a taxi who drove us to the Hospital on the East side.

It was about 4 a.m. when she was all checked in and in good care, which gave me time to get over to Hoboken to shift the ship to the shipyard. When the shift was complete, the Chief Mate told me to disappear, and I headed back to the Hospital. I could come back any time before sailing to get my money and discharge. I went back to the ship the following day to pick up my money from the purser. In addition to my wages, he handed me an envelope from the Captain and Chief Mate with $ 20 inside to start the first Bank account for my daughter. It was a nice gesture and I have never forgotten it and done the same to others. I was very excited when I went to the Hospital to bring back my wife and baby, Karen, for the first time

Sitting in the back of the Taxi with baby Karen on my lab I happened to see the Taxi driver looking at me in the mirror. He smiled when he asked. "Is it this your first child?" He quickly added that he had four of those brats at home and there were time when he was trying to sleep they made so much noise he felt like breaking their necks.

MOVING TO SAN FRANCISCO

New York was my favorite city for many years, but we didn't think it would be a good place to raise a family and decided to move to San Francisco. We already had friends there who were moving to London for three months and offered us their furnished apartment while they were away, giving us time to find something for ourselves.

Before I left New York, I went to the Master, Mates, and Pilots local 88 to have my sea time verified for group "A" status which was very important, because only a group "A" member was able to take a permanent job. I didn't waste any time after we were all settled in our apartment before I went down to the Master, Mates, and Pilots local 90 headquarters on Howard Street to register for shipping. The dispatcher checked my union book and license very carefully before issuing me a shipping card. I was shocked to find a big Group "**B**" stamped on it. I showed him a letter from local 88 in New York stating that I had sufficient sea time to be in group "A". He looked at my letter and discharge and said that is on the East Coast. This is the West Coast, case closed.

Golden Bear

Over the years I always admired the Pacific Far East Line ships and hoped to get started with them. The company was started after WWII by Thomas E. Cuffe and a group of businessmen who saw an opportunity in shipping carrying government, and commercial cargo between the U.S. and Japan, Korea, Okinawa, Taiwan, Hong Kong, Saigon, Philippine, Thailand. Hawaii, Midway, Guam. They also offered Reefer service to Japan, Okinawa, Korea. Later they offered Lash ship service to Japan, Korea, Singapore, Saudi Arabia, Iran, Dubai, and Kuwait

Since I had no chance of getting in permanent with them, I decided to start as vacation or medical relief and get to know my way around the company. My first PFE ship was as 3rd Mate on the "*SS Golden Bear*," a new Mariner cargo liner with a crew of 48 carrying 12 passengers. It was a Cadillac on the 7 Seas with seven cargo hatches twenty fourteen 10 tons cargo booms, with electric winches to move and spot the cargo booms. In addition we had two heavy lift booms. I made two trips to Japan, Okinawa, Hong Kong, Vietnam, and the Philippines and back to Japan and San Francisco. I found the ship to be very professional and great people to work with.

Later I shipped 2nd Mate on the "SS *Canada Bear*" an 8500 HP Victory ship which became one of the more memorable ships I ever sailed on. Nice and fun people to work with. The Captain was a native San Franciscan and so was the chief mate nick named John Sex Pack. Both had been with the company for a long time.

A few days out at sea, John asked me how I liked the Orient. Next he asked me if I went ashore in Keelung and Kaohsiung. I told him "I usually do, why are you asking?" He told me he had a girlfriend in Kaohsiung but she always met him in Keelung and that he needed all the time ashore he could get, so he was wondering, since I had the day watch in port perhaps I would be willing to do his work at the same time?

This meant to be in charge of the cargo operation, signing bill of lading, making sure the cargo was discharged and loaded as per cargo plan. That was Okay with me. A few days later he asked how I liked Korea. I told him I liked Pusan the best. What a coincidence because he liked Inchon the best and always went ashore there. "If you take care of my job there I will stand your watch in Pusan, and you will have time off in San Francisco, good deal all around." John later became Captain on SS Mariposa, a passenger and cruise ship sailing the south Pacific and Europe. He wrote a book *Nothing Can Go Wrong* referring to a trip to Europe on the SS Mariposa.

In American ports the company was required to hire MM&P Port Relief Officers, one from 1600-2400 and one from 0000-0800. However, in addition P F E kept a ship's officer on duty with the PRO, mostly for the purpose of measuring free space available for back loading as the cargo was discharged.

Captain Young started teaching me ship's handling by letting me plan the arrivals, and conning the ship up to the pilot station.

Keelung, located at the northern part of Taiwan Island, can be a difficult port to get into during the North East monsoon with strong winds, heavy seas and swells, and rain 300 days a year, often making it impossible for the pilot boat to come outside the breakwater to allow the pilot to come onboard.

If you were brave enough to enter the harbor through the outer breakwater by yourself without a pilot you might eliminate a long delay at anchor. Captain Young was determined to get inside right away. He offered me the opportunity and challenge to take charge entering the harbor. After counting the ships already at anchor inside the breakwater, I realized there was very little space to maneuver after we got in there.

I explained my plans to him, how I would enter the breakwater on half ahead which would give me good steerage when heading directly for the north breakwater light, expecting the wind and swell to push me in the middle of the breakwater. He told me to go for it.

I called the engine room, telling them my plan and asking for extra stern power if needed. The chief mate and carpenter were standing by the anchors. I made a big turn and headed for the breakwater. Everything went as planned except when inside the breakwater in the outer harbor I put the engine on full astern, which made the ship's bow turn faster than I had expected, clearing a vessel at anchor by just a few feet, but I made it. It was my first real experience in ship handling and later in life I had several close calls which always turned out okay, thanks to Captain Young who taught me self-confidence, and to make your plans and stick to them.

The U.S. spent millions of dollars on foreign aid to Taiwan which sometimes seemed like a lost cause due to shortage of dock and warehouse space.

I recall we discharged a large load of clothing with rolls of khaki material for uniforms placed on the dock in heavy rain. When we returned three months later it was still there in the same spot completely ruined from the rain.

As the economy in Taiwan grew and the U.S. was their best customer PFEL was able to take advantage of the opportunity and carried a lot of general cargo back to U.S. Among it was canned pineapple. The shippers came up with a new idea. Instead of stowing the pineapples case by case, they started bringing them on wooden pallets. A lot of attention was given to this idea, making sure it worked. I was not impressed by the idea but guess everybody else was because they kept on doing it.

SS Pacific Bear a West Coast C-2. Our schedule was San Francisco, Los Angles, Honolulu, Wake Island and Guam. Most of our outbound cargo was military PX supply. By the time the ship was loaded and ready to sail, I felt like I was on a floating liquor store because the cargo was mostly beer, whisky, gin, vodka, and some mixer. All the cargo was loaded and hand stowed into the cargo holds with wooden floors built to eliminate damage.

I believe this was every longshoreman's dream to load a ship like this. The company hired security guards to stay down in the cargo holds to watch the cargo. Since they were outnumbered and out smarted, they often looked the other way. I was never able to understand why the long shore men had to open a new case every time they wanted to take a bottle, instead of just open one case at a time. After the cargo was completed in each port, the mate on duty inspected the shoring to make sure everything was properly secured. On this particular ship I would find bottles put away between the sweat battens and ship's hull, or between the overhead beams. One day out at sea we were sitting talking about the amount of pilfering that had occurred.

I mentioned the amount hidden away during my last cargo hold inspection. Fred, the 3rd mate, said he never noticed or found anything. I told him to bring a flash light and go into # 3 cargo hatch which was empty. I was sure he would find all kinds of bottles hidden away around the sweat battens. An hour later he came back empty handed. I told him to follow me down # 3 hold. When we entered the deck house where the manhole and ladder were down to lower hold, I told him to stop right there and look around. He still didn't see anything unusual until I pointed at a burlap sack hidden away in a corner. Just looking at the sack it was easy to see it was full of bottles, and someone in the crew was waiting for the right time to pick them up.

Wake Island is a small flat tropical Island located at 19.17N long, 166.39 E about 2,300 miles West of Honolulu. It was occupied mostly by U.S. Air Force and some civilian contract workers from the mainland. There were two large steel buoys placed fairly close to the beach for the ships to tie up between when working cargo. On top of the buoys was a mechanical device designed to let all the mooring lines go at once by pulling on a small chain attached to the device for a fast getaway.

The ship's crew discharged the cargo into small landing crafts, shuttling between the ship and the beach. The water around the island was clear and blue with very interesting coral with many colorful fish.

Guam, our last stop before heading home empty, was a beautiful deep-water port. It is the largest and southernmost island of the Mariana Islands, a tropical paradise west of Hawaii

Yes, it happened on my watch
"SS Washington Bear" 1970

I shipped 2nd Mate on the "Washington Bear," another PFE Mariner in the Far East run. At the time there were two sentences often heard on ships, "It didn't happen on my watch" or "This is not my Job" The two sentences were often used after something had gone wrong.

On Voyage # 48 three major events did happen on my 4 x 8 watch. I joined the ship at pier 39 in San Francisco where we stayed a few days before shifting up the river to Stockton

The loading and discharging in Stockton took two days and we sailed Stockton on my evening watch, the company's Pilot Captain Wallace at the conn.

It was a nice calm, clear evening with great visibility. The 8 x 12 3rd mate relieved me at 1945, fifteen minutes early. After writing up the deck log I took a few minutes to listen to the pilot talking to the Antioch Bridge operator who was preparing to stop the bridge traffic and hoist the bridge for us to pass under a few minutes before (8 pm). When I left the wheel house, the ship was lined up to pass in the middle of the bridge, proceeding at slow speed. After saying goodbye to the pilot, I went down to my room located on the boat deck port side. I no sooner got into my room when the ship healed over to starboard, the porthole blew open and it looked like smoke coming through the porthole.

I ran out of my room and entered the inside passage, unable to see anything from what I thought was smoke but turned out to be sand. The ship was still listing heavily to starboard, making it difficult to open the outside door to the boat deck due to strong wind.

After getting out onto the boat deck port side, I had a hard time walking or standing up straight or seeing anything due to sand and dust in the air. I was holding on to the hand rail right next to the smoke stack. When I looked up I saw a small red light which was the center of the bridge.

A few minutes later the wind died down, the visibility improved and the ship went back on an even keel. I looked back and saw the

Antioch Bridge, with the center part still hanging up in the air, thinking to myself, what luck that we made it through without any problems.

I went back up to the bridge and wheel house to see if I could be of any help, but everything was back to normal. The Captain and the Pilot were standing talking and going over what had happened.

When the sand storm came, the ship was lined up to sail through the middle of the opening of the bridge when a very gusty wind came out of nowhere, listing the ship heavily to the starboard, kicking up dust and sand and decreasing the visibility to 0. The pilot decided to get as much speed on the vessel as possible to steer better and to keep going, a very smart decision.

Shortly thereafter we entered San Francisco Bay and sailed under the Golden Gate Bridge

The pilot disembarked and we set course for Los Angeles, a 20 hour voyage.

Antioch Bridge

Next morning on my 4 x 8 watch sailing down the California coast, I turned the radio on to listen to the headline news from San Francisco. I was shocked when I heard that the Antioch Bridge was out of commission after being hit by the Pacific Far East Line freighter "S/S Washington Bear" yesterday shortly before 8 p.m. The bridge operator was stuck hanging up in the air, the fire department was trying to rescue the bridge operator who refused to come down, He was afraid of heights. Later I read that the span was stuck in raised position and the bridge tender was stuck in the control house for two days before the local firemen eventually made their way up to get him down. After he got back down he immediately quit his position.

Upon arrival in Los Angeles we were met by the U.S. Marshall who put a lien against the ship. The coast guard was having a field day, checking out the hull of the good ship "Washington Bear" for damage or paint scrapped off. No evidence was found.

The Coast Guard questioned and took written statements from 19 crew members. Next to the Captain's my statement turned out to be very important because where I stood and looked up at the red light right above my head indicated that the ship was right in the middle of the open bridge where we were supposed to be.

The Captain told me later that he happened to overhear one of the coast guard inspectors telling another that either they did not hit the bridge or we have 19 people telling the same story. Take Pedersen 2nd Mate up on the boat deck one more time to assure that he is telling the same story again.

Later it turned out that everybody agreed we did not hit the bridge, but that the wind had been so strong it pushed the bridge into locked stuck position, a big disappointment for the State of California who was hoping to get a new bridge paid for by Pacific Far East Line.

The Captain was in his late 50's, known for telling some unbelievable stories. Like one day he told me that if he and his wife put their wealth together, it would make the Kennedy's and the Rockefellers look sick. He also said that PFE was leasing the piers in San Francisco from him. At coffee breaks we got around to talking about investing in houses and fixing them up to sell or keep. I happened to mention that I had just fixed up a house and added a patio. He looked at me and said, "That doesn't sound like much of a patio to me." He had just extended his patio which took four truck loads of cement. After listening to all his stories, I started feeling sorry for his wife until I met her. She turned out to be worse than him. One day we got to talk about squirrels and after listening for a while she said, "The squirrels down here are nothing compared to the squirrels we have in Canada, where they grow four feet tall."

At the time there was no local pilot service for entering Tokyo Bay, and the Captain brought the ship all the way up to the port entrance or to the Quarantine Anchorage. Since everybody had their own system when arriving, I asked the Captain where he would like me to place the arrival charts, to which he responded, "What charts? If I have to look at chart to enter Tokyo Bay I should not be here."

A Few years later we both attended a two weeks Radar and all weather navigation course at the MM&P Maritime Institute of Technology & Graduate Studies in Linthicum, Maryland required by the companies and the union.

It's a very nice facility, good food, nice bar open every evening after classes where The Captain spent a lot of time in the bar and slept through most of the classes during the day. I started to worry and became afraid he may be disqualified and send him home, but they didn't and guess what, when the final test was completed he was the only one who passed with a 100%

The Chief Mate was a strange looking man, also in his 50's, with a sharp face and big ears. When he talked his tongue seemed to sit on top of his lower teeth, like a man eating snuff, which changed his voice and made him spit slightly when talking. To top it all off he also had a drinking problem. Among the 12 passengers making the voyage was a cadet from the California Maritime Academy who had won a free trip from San Francisco to Japan on a P F E ship. On the day of sailing, a photographer from the Academy came onboard to take pictures. He asked the captain to have a picture taken of him and the cadet standing under the ship's name on the wing of the bridge. The captain told the photographer to get the chief mate, he was much better looking man than he was. I was in my room when the chief mate came and asked if I had a clean khaki shirt he could borrow. A few minutes later he came back asking if I had a black tie. Five minutes later he was back again asking if I had one of those fancy high pressure hats, which I did. Now I started feeling sorry for the cadet, who was to have his picture taken with him. The chief mate already had a few drinks too many.

Two months later we received a copy of the Academy Magazine with a close up picture of the chief mate and the cadet, and there he stood wearing my shirt, tie, and high pressure hat with a million dollar smile, looking like a movie star.

Three weeks later in Hong Kong we tied up to buoy "A" loading and discharging cargo to and from Chinese Junks and Sampans, when one of my biggest challenges and tests of my seaman's ships experience came up. Buoy "A" is very close to the Ocean and Star ferry Terminal on the Kowloon side. There is always a lot of ferry and other traffic crossing to and from Hong Kong. In addition there were ships moored to every buoy around us.

It was August 4, 1970. Sea Watches were set at midnight, and I was called at 0320 to go on watch at 0400.

The 3rd mate I relieved told me there was only one gang of longshoremen working in hatch # 5 they were almost finished and would properly be off the ship around 0530.

When I went out on deck I had a very strange feeling right away. It was very calm and quiet with high humidity and very dark. The sailing time was set for 1000 so everyone was asleep, except the guys on watch. The day worker was to be called at 0720 as normal.

I went to check with the local shore watchman hired by the company to check people coming on and off the ship. All the watchmen were from India wearing turbans and carrying heavy sticks.

I asked the shore watchman if he had been listening to his portable radio during the night, and if there had been any typhoon warnings. He said no typhoon warning.

I made my rounds of the ship, went up to the bow to check our heavy anchor chain made fast to the buoy, all in good order. When you tie up a large ship like the "Washington Bear" to a buoy you disconnect one anchor making sure the anchor is all the way home and tight in the hawse pipe before you secure the anchor using a heavy wire made fast through the anchor shackle to one of the ship's steel bollards.

When the chain is disconnected from the anchor, the chain is lead thru the bull's eye at the ships center, and lowered down to the water's edge before you approach the buoy. When the ship is in a position close to the buoy, a small boat with 3-4 men is used to pick up the chain and connect the chain to the buoy, using a large shackle.

As I walked back from the bow on the port side, I noticed the main deck was full of small and large pieces of wood, straw mats, and papers used for the separation of the cargo. It all looked like a total mess which was fairly common after a few days in port loading or discharging cargo. When I got back to # 5 hatch the foreman told me they were almost finished loading the cargo.

I looked down at the sampan. It was almost empty and getting ready to get away from our ship. He told me he would let me know when they were finished securing the cargo and for me to inspect the lashing and shoring. I checked the shoring before they left which looked good to me. I signed the papers and shortly thereafter all the workers left in the small boat.

I made an inside inspection of the mid ship house and found everything in good order. I called the engine room and told the engineer on watch that the cargo operation was completed and that we would sail at 1000 as planned. Pacific Far East Line is the only company I ever worked for who carried two engineers to a watch, besides a fire and water tender, and one oiler, so there were already four men on duty in the engine room which turned out later to be another good luck for me.

I went up to the bridge to get the navigation equipment ready for sailing. After getting the course recorder started, I went into the chart room next to the bridge to get all the navigation charts ready for the voyage from Hong Kong to Kaohsiung.

At 0640 while still in the chart room, I was almost knocked off my feet, when a 100 + miles an hour wind came roaring down the hills, blowing the port hole open and heavy rain poured in. The wind also made the vessel list hard to starboard. I ran into the wheel house, looking forward but unable to see anything because of the heavy rain. I watched the course recorder and noticed the ship was swinging violently from side to side.

A few minutes later at 0646 I heard a loud noise sounding like an explosion, the vessel shaking as if we were hit by another vessel. I knew immediately what had happened. The shackle or anchor chain had parted. I was still alone and didn't want to waste any time calling anybody.

I ran down the five set of ladders to the main deck, trying to make my way up to the bow to let go the port anchor, dodging all the junk like straw mats, wood and empty oil drums blowing over the side.

At that time all brass tools had to be locked up while in port because the longshoremen would steal and sell them ashore. I knew where the Bosun kept the large brass wrench used to unlock the brakes on the anchor winch. At 0652 I let go the port anchor, two shots of chain in the water, (180ft), tightened the brakes, and called the engine room using the bow telephone.

I told the engineer on duty what had happened and asked to give me power on the steering engine and 20 RPM ahead on the main engine.

I ran back to the bridge as fast as I could and by that time the captain was there. As I entered the wheel house the phone rang and the engineer told me that the main engine was turning 20 RPM ahead and the power was on the steering engine and to go ahead and use it without testing it.

I grabbed the steering wheel and tried to steer into the gusty wind. The captain looked at the whole situation and said. "No need for me to get involved now. You have already saved the day."

0705 the wind died down just as fast as it came up. The visibility and day light was a happy sight.

The anchor and the 20 RPM on the engine had kept us in a good position between buoy "A" and Ocean terminal. We sailed on time, other ships were not that lucky.

August 17. Vessel moored Starboard side to Pier 4 in Kobe, Japan. Sea watches were set at midnight. As usual I was called at 0320 by the 3rd mate who told me not to rush because there was no cargo work until 0800 and he would meet me for coffee in the salon.

Shortly after 0400 I went out on deck, a beautiful calm morning. I looked up and down the dock to be sure the ship was tight alongside the dock. I looked at the ships lying on the other side of the slip across from us. It was an American President Line ship, with approximately 100 feet between us. I walked back to check the mooring lines on the stern, total of three stern lines, one breast, and a spring line which is a normal tie up for a ship this size. By the first observation everything looked okay but I soon noticed that one line was just lying on deck and not made fast to the bollard. My next shock was that after a closer look, they were all that way. I made two lines fast right away, ran up to the gangway to get a hold of the shore watchman and took him with me up on the bow and found the mooring lines up there the same way, all laying loose on deck without having been made fast to bollards. After making them all fast we walked back to the stern to make the rest of the lines fast.

I asked the shore watchman if he had seen anything or anybody during the night that may have done this. He told me that the bosun had come back around midnight, and it looked like he had been in a fight. Shortly thereafter the three ordinary seamen came back and told the watchman they had been in a fight with the bosun.

During the Viet Nam War there was a shortage of seamen. The three ordinary seamen were San Francisco hippies making their first trip to sea, all antiwar, antiestablishment, anti everything except eating, and that was their way of getting back at the bosun not realizing, that if there was any damage to the ship it would not have been the bosun who got the blame, but the officer on watch, in this case, me.

The Purser went ashore in Yokohama for Lunch and a few drinks. Walking back to the ship, a truck stopped and offered him a ride which he accepted. When the truck reached the Gate he jumped off the truck before it came to a full stop and fell and broke his right arm. He went to the hospital and came back just before sailing with his right arm in a cast. It was bad timing because most of his work was just beginning, making up payroll, typing stores requisitions and shorting out all the cargo bills of Lading for the U.S. Customs arriving in San Francisco. I volunteered to help him with his typing and learned a lot from that experience which benefited me later.

LASH JAPAN BEAR

Our Schedule was San Francisco, Los Angeles, Japan, Korea, Taiwan, Philippines, Hong Kong, Singapore, Saudi Arabia, Dubai, Kuwait, Iraq, Iran, a 120 days voyage.

I had a new experience when I shipped on "Japan Bear" a C-8 Lash Ship which stands for lighter aboard ship. She was 778.8 feet long.105.6 foot beam and 41.6 foot draft. 37,460 Gross Tonnage.

There was 16 large cargo hatches, with clear access to the stern. The gantry crane had a cargo handling capacity of approximately 450 L/T was able to travel the entire length of the ship cargo area, and its function was to convey barges from stowed locations aboard the ship to the stern region and to lower the barges or lighter into the water.

In addition, we also had a container gantry crane for handling containers at hatch # 1-2. The container operation was very slow. When the container was connected to a spreader-bar, it was lifted straight up in the air, then turned slowly, moved across the vessel and over the side where the container was turned again before being lowered down onto the dock or waiting truck. The same steps were taken when loading

The 82 barges, all standard size with a cargo capacity of 385 tons, were towed in ports and inland waterways to various shipping points where they are loaded with cargo, then returned to the ship and hoisted aboard.

The barge was lowered into the cargo hold where it was well secured. The hatch covers were made of heavy steel, strong enough to carry two barges above deck with a very good tie down system.

On the deck forward of the bridge we had two 3 L/T cranes used when taking ship's stores. The stores came in special pre-loaded containers for dry and refrigerated containers. At the end of each voyage the containers were discharged through the hatch on the fore-deck and exchanged with loaded containers with groceries and other supplies for the next voyage. The reefers loaded with chilled or frozen stores were plugged into the ship's power. There was a labor dispute between the long shore men and the sailors union who were to handle the containers.

The big advantage was the ability of lash ships to load and discharge cargo from anchorage, eliminating high dock fees, and the cargo was never delayed by lack of dock facilities or port congestion which was very common in many countries. Lash cargo rarely required transshipment, moving from origin to destination with a single bill of lading.

When anchored outside the port of Manila discharging loaded barges to be towed into port to be discharged and reloaded giving us an extra day in Manila.

It was only a short boat ride from the ship to shore and I decided to go ashore hoping to meet some old friends. After making my rounds, I took a Taxi back to the boat landing to return to the ship. Nobody was waiting at the boat landing so I decided to wait. There were three boats tied up side by side and the third boat out was flying the PFE flag. To get out to my boat I had to step off the pier, jump over to the first boat and walk across.

Each boat had a wooden awning to protect passengers from the rain and sun. As I tried to jump onto the first boat I hit my head on the wooden awning knocking me unconscious for a few seconds, and

I fell into the water between the pier and the boat and started sinking to the bottom. I managed to fight my way back up and grab hold of a safety line connected around the boat until I got my strength to climb into the boat. I was bleeding from a cut in my forehead which I managed to stop by applying pressure using my shirt.

The water around the boat landing was very dirty full of garbage and oil slicks and I looked a mess but otherwise ok. I was happy when the boat operator showed up and brought me back to the ship where I took a shower and got out of dirty clothing.

The lash ships never worked for PFEL on the West Coast due to labor disputes from various organized labor groups. The Longshoremen up and down the coast claimed that the barges had to be loaded by them.

Inland boatmens union claimed that only union tugs were to move the barges to and from the ship. The long shore men in Japan posted a picket line around the ship and refused to work the ship at anchorage. Therefore we wound up paying docking fees in all Japanese and U.S. ports anyway.

The ships were built with Government subsidies with military use in mind. PFEL owned and operated six. All seemed to have problems with the cranes breaking down, as well as engine and propeller problems. One ship discharging in Korea had a barge stuck when lowering it down. The crane was damaged beyond repair. She had to return all the way back to San Francisco to fix the problem.

The mooring winches would often break down. The company who made them down in Mississippi went out of business after the ships were built, so no spare parts were available.

We had another serious problem with the steering engine which would move from the center over to a hard right rudder position and stay there for several minutes before coming back on line and move the rudder as directed by the wheel man. It happened twice while I was there

Once while sailing out of Damman, Saudi Arabia, zig-zagging in between ships lying at anchor, the rudder went over hard right, making the ship swing fast to the right for several minutes before the steerageway came back and the wheel man was able to stop the swing. It was a wonder we didn't collide with other ships. The steering engine would correct itself, so we were never able to find out what the problem was.

In the beginning the barges were all made of steel. Quite often the empty barges would be lying around in choppy water rubbing against one another without anyone taking care of them, and they developed leaks. Later the barges were made of fiber-glass which was not always strong enough and the bottom fell out and the cargo was lost.

I made two trips, for a total of eight months, on the "Japan Bear" which turned out to be my last time working for Pacific Far East Line, one of my all-time favorite companies where I met some real interesting people. The company was then bought and under the control of the Joseph Alioto Family of San Francisco who filed for bankruptcy, and the fleet was liquidated.

THE VIETNAM WAR

always had good memories of Saigon in the 1950's, when it was called French Indochina. Saigon was then known as the Pearl of the Orient. The downtown area looked very much like a southern European city with an oriental atmosphere. The French Foreign Legion was fighting to maintain French control and domination, backed by the U.S., but they lost and left a few years later, leaving a divided country.

The U.S. picked up the pieces where the French left off, but by then Vietnam was a hostile nation just like Laos and Cambodia which claimed the lives of more than 58,000 Americans. Another 304,000 were wounded.

The Vietnam War was a military struggle fought from 1959 to April 1975, involving the north Vietnamese and the National Liberation front in conflict with U.S. forces and the south Vietnamese army. From 1946 until 1954 the Vietnamese had struggled for their independence from France during the first Indochina war. At the end of this war, the country was temporarily divided into North and South Vietnam.

North Vietnam came under the control of the Vietnamese communists who had opposed France and aimed for a unified Vietnam under communist rule. The south was controlled by the Vietnamese who had collaborated with the French.

In 1965 the U.S. sent in troops to prevent the South Vietnamese government from collapsing. Ultimately, however, the United States failed to achieve its goal, and in 1975 the Vietnamese reunified under communist control. In 1976 it officially became the Socialist Republic of Vietnam. Three-four millions Vietnamese on both sides were killed

By 1966 the U.S. military buildup continued with over 300,000 troops there. All war material had to be shipped across the Pacific Ocean on American ships which created a shortage of both ships and crews to sail them.

One hundred and sixty WWII Victory ships were already brought out of mothball from the National Defense Reserve fleet. Each ship had to be completely overhauled in a hurry at a huge cost, and each ship was assigned to private companies for operation to carry ammunition, guns, tanks, trucks, trains, river boats, barges, helicopters food, fuel and medical supplies across the Pacific. Three hundred freighters and tankers supplied the U.S. troops in Vietnam with an average of 75 ships and 3,000 merchant mariners in Vietnamese ports at any time. I sailed on six victory ships and several privately owned ships in the Vietnam War supply trade.

To ease the crew shortage the Coast Guard cut the sea time requirement in half for seamen who wished to become licensed deck or engine officers. If you already had a license you were encouraged to get a waiver and sail one rank higher than the license you had.

Maritime unions waived minimum crew requirements allowing ships to sail with less than the normal union-contracts complement; forced vacation was eliminated allowing you to collect vacation pay while still working.

Retired seamen of all ratings were asked to come out of retirement to help out, but some ships would still lay around for days and weeks waiting for crews.

June 21-1967 I stopped by the union hall on Howard Street in San Francisco, not to ship out but to locate a friend of mine. As I stood there looking at the shipping board with 51 open jobs, I was approached by the President of MM&P local 90, who told me he was under a lot of pressure from the ships owners and the government for not being able to crew up the ships. He pointed at the SS Wayne Victory who needed a Master, and four mates. He asked me to do him a favor and take the Chief Mate job to get the ship moving. She was in Seattle loading ammunition for Vietnam.

The ship was operated by a company called Marine Carrier. General Steamship Corp. was the west coast agent.

The company had a contract with the Master, Mates & Pilot (MM&P) for licensed deck officers and Marine Engineers Beneficial Association (M E BA.) for the licensed engineer, and the Sea fares International Union (S I U) for the unlicensed crew.

SS Wayne Victory before she was painted navy gray

The local agent was very happy to see me. He offered me the Master Job, but I did not have the license yet. I was given a first class airline ticket to Seattle, told to take a taxi from the airport to the ship, which was laying at Bangor Navy Base.

When I walked onboard I didn't know that a 90 day nightmare was about to begin.

I noticed heavy fuel oil had been running down the ship's side and everything looked a mess. When I got up on the ship I was met by the port relief officer (PRO) who was very happy to see me because he was there by himself working 16 hours a day 1600-0800 and nobody else there in the day time.

He helped me up to my room with my two suitcases, and then asked me to follow him into the captain's room. When I entered, I noticed the ship's safe was wide open and empty. He told me $ 20,000 was missing and gave me a copy of the Police report.

The port engineer who represented the company told me that another chief mate had joined the ship a few days earlier, and that he had also been offered the Master Job which he turned down.

Later that evening he called the PRO and told him to open the door to the captain's room because he was moving in and was now the Master. Later he was seen walking down the gangway calling a taxi and giving the driver a $100 bill to get him some beer and booze. A few hours later he was seen walking down the gangway carrying a bag in his hands telling a longshoreman he had all the money in the world in that little bag. That was the last time he was seen. Since it was a government owned ship, the FBI was also working on the case. I never did hear what the outcome was.

The port engineer told me that the crew refused to sign on until the money was replaced, and that another $20,000 would be delivered the following day. I was to sign for it and take care of it, and turn it over to the captain whenever they found one. For two days I kept the money under my pillow and kept the door locked.

Except for a Master 2nd mate and two 3rd mates, there was a full crew and she was loaded and ready to sail. The U.S. shipping commissioner was called onboard to sign the crew on foreign article the following day.

The Bosun was the only man in the entire deck department who had ever sailed on a merchant ship before. We had several retired navy men sailing as Able Body Seamen. The three ordinary seamen were right out of S I U, so called school, at 4th Ave in Brooklyn, where for two months they had been free labor for the union, cleaning windows and floors, then charged $1000 to join the union, which would be taken out of their pay together with the airline ticket to Seattle which the union also collected from the company, a win/win situation for the SIU.

The second day, the port engineer came into my room, closed the door before he sat down, and told me about the chief engineer who in his opinion, should be in a nut house.

He showed me the rap sheet they had on him, fired from and sued every company he ever worked for. He was also known for trying to delay the ship by ordering spare parts, fuel and water just before sailing. A day later a captain showed up with a 2nd and a 3rd mate. The captain had spent most of his life in the Alaska trade, the 3rd mate was a retired tug boat man, and the 2nd mate had never sailed on his license before. He had 18 months sea time as an ordinary seaman and was able to sit and pass the USCG examination for 3rd mate and was given a waiver to sail 2nd mate. He was a local Seattle boy looking like a San Francisco hippie.

Normally the chief mate is a day worker, but due to shortage I was also standing the 4 x 8 sea watches for which I was paid overtime.

Just before sailing, the chief engineer decided he needed more water, which by now had to be brought out by barge from Seattle. He also refused to sail before he received some cement he had ordered. There was a sigh of relief when we finally heaved up the anchor, steaming out the Puget Sound toward Japan for orders.

The first day out at sea, the 3rd mate came into my room with two bottles of Vodka, told me he was an alcoholic and that I would do him a big favor by taking them off his hands.

Celestial navigation and dead reckoning was our only means of navigating, using the sun and stars. Since I was on the 4 x 8 watch I took star sightings each morning and evening weather, permitting. We had a good Sperry Radar and not much else.

We had nice weather and yet speed and revolution per minute (RPM) would vary each day. I called the engineer on my watch, asking why such a difference in the (RPM).He told me the chief engineer would occasionally slow the engine due to some kind of overheating, but didn't know what the problem was. Nobody ever called the Bridge or the Captain telling us about the slowdown.

The radio officer was from Texas and had a good sense of humor. My wife was expecting a baby within a few weeks, and she was to send me a message when the baby was born. Since we already had a daughter we were both hoping for a boy. He promised to check with the RCA station in San Francisco several times a day for personal messages.

A few days out of Yokosuka, Japan, the blower down to the engine room burned out, and it became very hot down below. The chief engineer told the captain he was ordering spare parts to be sent out from New York and that the repair job would take eight days.

By the time we arrived in Yokuska we were twenty hours behind our original ETA, not bad considering. The union rules read that when a ship stayed more than 24 hours in port, sea watches had to be broken and port watches went into effect. My watch hours were from 0800-1600, which was great for me since I ran the deck department.

Yokohama was only an hour away by train or taxi. Some of the crew members preferred to go there. One day the 3rd mate asked me if I would stand his evening watch from 1600-2400 in addition to my own so he could have a day off and go to Yokohama.

It was Okay with me under one condition, that he stopped somewhere to buy me a small ice bucket, which he did, but it took him three days to get back and another two days to sober him up.

Steaming toward Vietnam, we were diverted to Subic Bay in the Philippines. When we arrived, the Bay was full of ships awaiting orders. Subic Bay was just a short run away to the South China Sea a safe holding place away from the Viet Cong who often tried to attack ships at anchor outside Vietnamese Ports.

Subic Bay Naval base was real busy with ships coming and going. Clark air base was the largest military base outside the U.S. with troops stopping to and from Vietnam. The officer's club was always full of people serving 25 cent Gin/Tonic, 15 cents during happy hour.

Outside the gate Olongapo was loaded with people and busy keeping the bars open day and night with people and noise everywhere.

A few days later we received our sailing instructions for Wung Ro, Vietnam with a recommended arrival time. The captain decided to get underway at 2200.

The bosun and I were on the bow heaving up the anchor with an Able Bodied Seaman washing the mud off the anchor chain before the chain entered the chain locker where it was stowed.

No sooner did we get the anchor home and were under way when the electrician came running up deck very upset, yelling that the chief engineer was trying to kill him with a fire axe. I called the captain and told him. He decided to go back into anchorage and cancel our departure. We told the navy control that we had an emergency and requested permission to anchor close to the piers, which was granted.

Now it became my job to go and take the fire axe away from the chief engineer which turned out to be easy. The captain called the company and the U.S. Coast Guard who both happened to have people in Saigon and would come over ASAP. The captain told the company he would not sail with that chief engineer any longer and gave them a choice, either send out a new chief engineer or a new captain, and he would be happy to pay his own way home.

The 2nd and 3rd mates asked my opinion on what would happen when the Coast Guard came onboard. Due to the circumstances, not much. The Coast Guard and company representative would try to talk the whole thing down and get the ship moving. The ship could not sail without a captain or chief engineer but was allowed to sail without an electrician. To eliminate a lawsuit they would try to talk him into staying also. We agreed to back up the captain; if he quit we would all go with him. I suggested that we all pack our suitcases and set them outside our doors to show them we meant business.

I was right. The first thing the U.S. Coast Guard and the company representative looked at was the license rack to see if anybody there had a Master license. A meeting was held in the captain's room, first with the electrician, then with the chief engineer. The Navy got involved, a meeting was held ashore, and pressure was put on everybody to sail the ship.

We were told we had some very important cargo onboard both for Vietnam and Burma. That was the first time anybody ever mention Burma. When I asked about it, a Navy officer told me that the 2000 tons of small arms in the lower hulls was to go to Rangoon, Burma, which would add two more weeks to the trip.

The chief engineer promised to be on good behavior for the rest of the trip, the electrician agreed to stay, and we left Subic Bay for Wung Ro, Vietnam right away.

Wung Ro had one De long pier capable of handling two ships at the time, one on each side but the military preferred to have just one ship discharging cargo to make it easier for the trucks to move the cargo off the pier.

There was no pilot or tugboat to assist us docking; the captain was in charge. We waited for a favorable current before entering the bay and making a big turn toward the pier. I was on the bow with the deck crew ready to get a heaving line on the dock ASAP and get a spring line onto the pier and made fast to a bollard and the ship. When the spring line was made we used the engine and rudder to get alongside. The Army had three men standing on the pier forward waiting for the heaving line to be made fast to the heavy mooring line.

We lowered it into the water for the men to heave it onto the pier which was difficult for the two men pulling the line. I noticed the third soldier just standing there looking at them pulling the heavy rope. I yelled down to him, "Please, give them a hand." He looked up at me and yelled. "I will, but I can only give them one hand because that's all I got." I noticed his right arm was missing. I learned a good lesson; don't ever be too quick to judge your fellow man.

A few days later I was standing by # 1 Hatch watching the cargo operation when the radio officer came running up the deck waving a piece of paper, yelling, "You got him, you got him."

He handed me the message from my wife. I read it several times and didn't know if it was a girl or boy. He got all excited and said," Yes, it is signed Karl, Karl." I asked one of the soldiers if he could get me some beer out of the PX, which he did, and gave us a chance to celebrate.

One day, watching the cargo operation and the soldiers handling the ammunition, I noticed most of them had several stripes on their uniforms, except one who was about ten years older than the rest. I asked one of the soldiers why he didn't have any stripes like everybody else. He looked at me and said, "He happened to get drunk at the wrong time and place."

Our steward and cooks were excellent. On a real hot day the steward and the cooks made a big cold table buffet style which everybody enjoyed, and the steward department was praised for their effort.

A few days later I was told that the chief and first engineer had put in for subsistence in lieu of a hot a meal, as per contract. Nice way to show your appreciation to someone who went out of their way to do extra.

One afternoon, steaming up the Malacca Strait toward Rangoon, I was sitting in my room working on the crew's overtime sheets when the radio officer ran down telling me to come up on the bridge right away because we were about to have a collision.

When I entered the wheelhouse and looked out the portholes I saw a large wooden junk under full sail on our Starboard bow crossing a few hundred feet away. The 2nd mate on watch was standing there looking at it. I told the man at the wheel to come hard left and I gave two short blasts on the whistle. I had to make a complete turn to avoid a collision.

I asked the 2nd mate why he didn't change course and get out of the way. He told me he had the right away and that the junk had to get out of his way. I told him when you get off watch you better take a few minutes to read the Rules of the Road # 15, Crossing Situation, which read when two vessels are crossing so as to risk of collision, the vessel which has the other on her starboard side shall keep out of the way, and shall, if the circumstances of the case permit, avoid crossing ahead of the other vessel. He just walked away.

Docking in Rangoon took a long time. First we did normal mooring using our mooring lines. When that was completed we had to heave a heavy chain onboard for/aft making them fast with heavy wires, called a typhoon mooring.

I assumed the cargo was for the Burmese military and was surprised when two Americans came onboard to receive it.

They told me they operated a mining company and had been there for two years. I did wonder what a mining company would do with 2000 tons of bullets. Looking back, they must have been part of the CIA.

They were very helpful telling us the dos and don'ts while in Burma, which was a closed country completely isolated from the western world and under military rule. Therefore many places were off limit for us.

Taylor, the radio officer, and I went ashore for dinners at the Strand Hotel which is the most historic Hotel in town. Hardly anybody was there. One night there were more people in the band than there were guests.

The longshoremen working the ship were a mix of Indian, Pakistani and Burmese nice and all very good. One day after their lunch break, I was wondering why they all stayed down on the dock looking at the ship instead of coming onboard.

I went down on the dock and asked the foreman if there was a problem. He told me the sailor on the gangway watch was drunk calling them names and as long as he was there, they would not come onboard. I removed the sailor right away, and everything went Okay after that.

Homebound, we stopped in Da Nang, Vietnam to load some damaged military equipment to drop off in Subic Bay. The chief engineer decided he needed a pump which had to be air freighted out from New York to Saigon via Amsterdam. The navy volunteered to bring the pump from Saigon to DaNang by boat. We stayed at anchor waiting.

A few days later, a Navy speed boat came alongside # 4 hatch with a big wooden box. We lowered the cargo hook, hoisted the box up and placed it on deck very carefully. The boat left heading back to Saigon.

The bosun opened the box in front of everybody interested in seeing the new pump. The chief engineer took one look at the pump and said that's not the pump I ordered send it back. Everybody felt like killing the guy.

A lot of messages went back and forth from the company in New York and the ship. A decision was made to sail the ship using the old pump which made it all the way back to San Francisco.

The Chief Engineer was always complaining of something either the mail crew or fuel oil. I invited him down on dock twice.

Crossing the North Pacific to San Francisco was very uneventful except that someone painted a German swastika on the chief engineer's door. His comment was that it was better than the Russian hammer and sickle.

It was late afternoon when we finally pulled into San Francisco with 90 days on the payroll. My wife, Carole, was on the dock with the children Karen, 18 months and Karl who I saw for the first time. He was six weeks old, sitting up straight in a stroller wearing a blue suit looking up at the ship. It was a happy reunion.

The Captain and I made up the payroll together, and it all added up. The money was delivered just before payoff the following day, each crew member receiving the money in an envelope with a wage statement in the presence of a U.S. shipping commissioner.

An hour before the payoff a S. I. U. Patrolman I had never seen before came onboard to collect union dues and a political donation (SPAD) from their members. I was surprised when he came up to see me before seeing the crew he represented. He asked for a copy of the crew list, and a list of crew members who had been logged for failing to perform their duties. He got upset when I told him we had a good crew, and nobody had been logged. I guess he didn't believe me and went to ask the captain who told him the same thing.

He was very upset when he came back and told me that whenever a man got drunk or failed to perform his assigned duties he should be logged for a day's pay. I could not believe a union official would make such a statement about their own members. I know the real reason. Each time a man was logged for a day's pay the S.I U fined him $50.

This had been a frustrating and miserable trip just because of a few idiots, and I started to wonder if I should stay away from Government owned Victory ships or give them another try. I needed the sea time to upgrade my license and union status. I also knew that when the Vietnam conflict ended, shipping would come to a standstill again, so I had to make it when the going was good.

For the next four years I sailed as Chief Mate on West Coast operated Victory ships, carrying booms and booze and other types of military cargo to Viet Nam. And it turned out they were all well running ships and they did not have the people problem the smaller East Coast companies had, mainly because each ship, had a company Captain and Chief Engineer assigned. They also carried a Purser. We always sailed short a 3rd Mate which meant in addition to my regular job as chief mate, I also stood the 4 x 8 sea watches on all of them.

Usually I would know my next ship a few days in advance which gave me a chance to round up some of my friends at the Sailors Union of the Pacific to take the jobs. Having a good deck department made my job easy.

Our main ports in Vietnam were Saigon, Cat Lai, Cam Ranh Bay, DaNang, Na Trang, and Vung Ro. Subic Bay in the Philippines PI, Yokosuka, Japan was our refueling and fresh water stops.

Most of the ammunition was discharged by the military themselves, and the general cargo by the Han Jin Company of Korea, or the Luzon Stevedoring Company of the Philippines. Alaska Barge out of Seattle moved the cargo around from ship to shore.

SS "Nashua Victory" Operated by Weyerhauser Steamship Co. I took the chief mate jobs hanging on the open board. Also hanging was 2nd -3rd Mate jobs. It took several days to get a 2nd and 3rd Mate. After several more days in San Francisco we shifted to Port Chicago to load various types of ammunition for Vietnam. The cargo hatches were clean, the old ammo sheathing had been removed. The USCG inspected the cargo gear before loading. A special gang came aboard to install new lumber sheathing before loading to insure the ammo would never come in contact with the ship's steel hull, or tank tops. Sling after sling of new lumber came aboard to be used to secure the crates of napalm bombs in # 4 cargo hatch. The majority of the ammo was 500/750 lbs bombs.

Some of them loaded were one by one into the ship's holds, with plenty of wooden blocking to keep them in place, making sure they didn't move and rub against one another. The cargo was loaded and secured under USCG supervision.

One of the many requirements while alongside an ammo dock is to have fire wires forward and one aft, secured to the ship with the eye hanging above the water's edge on the offshore side in case of a fire on the dock or aboard the ship. Then a tug boat can come along side and grab the wire and tow the vessel away from the dock in a hurry. The Red bravo "B" flag was flying from sunset to sun down and a red light at night and fire hoses were flecked out on deck.

I inspected the loading progress often. The last night before sailing, I came back at around midnight, and checked with the MM&P port relief officers who told me they were unable to get all the bombs below decks and decided to load them on deck by #2-3 hatches with a wooden box around them which had been approved by the coast guard.

I didn't like the idea of loading bombs on deck, and I didn't like the way they were stowed and secured. I told the longshoremen to stop loading, and to remove the ones already there.

The coast guard officer on duty was a young fellow with a big ego, and he started to tell me how the system worked. If I didn't accept the bombs on deck he would have me fired the following day. When he was finished running off his big mouth, I told him that he had better check with his superior officer which according to him, was the captain of the port. I followed him down to his office from where he called the captain of the port at one o'clock in the morning.

He started out telling him that he had granted the longshoremen permission to load bombs on deck, but the ship's chief mate refused to accept them or sail the ship with them. He also told him that he had explained to me how the system worked and that he would call my company in the morning and have me fired for not obeying a direct order from the USCG. After rattling all that off in a hurry he became very quiet for some time.

The next thing I heard was "Yes sir, no sir, yes sir, yes sir." I will be at your office at 0800 hours, and he hung up. He looked directly at me and said "Mr. Mate you don't have to accept those bombs on deck." The Coast Guard doesn't always understand the day-to-day routine of merchant ships.

Accidents do happen. The SS Badger State, a C-2 freighter operated by States Marine Line left Bangor Naval Ammunition Depot in the State of Washington December 1969 with a load of 8,900 bombs for DaNang, South Vietnam. 550 miles north of midway Island she ran into a storm with 30 foot high seas. The bombs had not been loaded and secured properly and started to roll back and forth with each motion of the ship constantly slamming against each other.

The crew tried unsuccessfully to jam mattresses, lifejackets, mooring lines in between the lose bombs. One bomb exploded and made huge hole in the ship's hull above the waterline and the Captain gave orders to abandon ship before the ship sank. 29 crew members died

One of my many jobs as a chief mate was to check and inspect all cargo lashing and shoring daily. A snap roll can put heavy pressure on the shoring, and sooner or later something will give.

Each time I checked the shoring I found everything in good order, except I noticed that some of the bombs were leaking, and the run off would harden and look like amber.

We never received much direct instruction on the danger posed by the bombs, except to make sure they didn't break loose. I don't know how many times I read the instructions in the manual I had onboard but found nothing about leaks and overflow.

I decided not to say anything about the leak to anybody except to the captain who didn't have a clue either. When we finally arrived and anchored by Cape Saint Jacques close to the entrance to the Saigon River and the port of Cat Lai, a U.S. Air Force Officer and a civilian working for Alaska Tug & Barge Company came out to check our cargo plan.

The officer told me they might need to remove some of the bombs before we docked in Cat Lai. If so, they would be discharged onto a barge and towed in. I asked him about the leaking bomb, which to my big relief was normal as the temperature increased. I wished someone had told me that earlier so I didn't have to worry about it.

I took the man from Alaska Tug and Barge aside and asked if he had PX privileges which he did. He asked what I needed. I told him I would like a couple of cases of beer, if possible. He pointed at another ship at anchor and said. "You see that ship laying there? She is loaded with beer and they don't know what to do with it. I will get you some."

A few days later still at anchor, the 3rd mate on duty came and woke me in the middle of night and told me a huge empty barge was coming alongside and perhaps we were to start cargo operation.

I got dressed and went out on deck, watching the empty barge coming along side with the tug made fast on the starboard side. As the barge came closer, I noticed something sitting in the middle which turned out to be six cases of beer for me. What a nice bunch.

After discharging the cargo at Cat Lai, we sailed to Moji, Japan to load cement back to Vietnam before returning to San Francisco empty.

SS "Morgantown Victory" Shortly before Christmas 1968, the Marine Superintendent from Pacific Far East line called me saying he needed a chief mate on the Morgantown Victory arrival Seattle, and that the Captain had asked for me. The ship would be idle from arrival December 22- to the 30th, and that I should stay home and join after Christmas.

When I joined the ship The Captain showed me a requisition and a letter from the former chief Mate who had ordered a set of new lifeboat davits for # 1 lifeboat, and it didn't go over well with anybody. He told me, I want you to lower the boat in the water, test everything, secure the boat and give me your opinion."

The life boat davits were the gravity-type where the boat is carried in two cradles mounted on rollers. The rollers ride along two parallel tracks at right angles to the ship's side. After the grips are released, you ease the brake to allow the boat and the entire assembly to roll down the tracks by gravity, stopping with the lifeboat suspended over the ship's side. The tracking line is to swing the lifeboat up against the ship's side and hold it in position until a frapping line is passed around the wire falls and secured, holding the boat in position to allow people to step safely onto the lifeboat, before it is lowered into the water. A manila rope called a sea painter is led forward and made fast on the ship to keep the boat alongside when it enters the water.

When everybody is in the lifeboat, the frapping line is released and the boat hangs free away from the ship's side. Then the boat is lowered by easing on the brake, checking the wires and sheaves making sure everything is moving freely. As the lifeboat nears the water, the brake is applied to slow the movement and the boat is eased into the water where the hand releasing gear is tested to free the boat from the davits.

Everything was working well with only one problem. To get the boat back in the original position we had to use a chain fall to pull the boat back two inches before it rested in its right position, something I had seen before, and can be corrected by adjusting the wire falls.

The day we were to shift to the Naval Ammunition Depot in Bangor, a big snow storm set in and Seattle was paralyzed for several days, but with the help of two powerfull tug boats we made it without any problems. Unfortunately, everyone was stuck aboard for several days and nobody was able to go ashore to celebrate New Year's eve. It was a good running ship with nice people to work with.

SS "Loyola Victory: Operated by Matson Steamship Co. While in Cam Ran Bay discharging ammunition onto barges, the Viet Cong attacked some U.S. installations close by, and all hell broke loose. Planes and helicopters started dropping bombs in the hills. When the attack was over, all the helicopters returned to the base, flying over our ship at the same time, the old 1st Engineer came out of the engine room and didn't have a clue what had just taken place. He looked up the skies and saw all the helicopters, looked at his watch and said, "Aha, 12 o'clock everybody heading home for lunch."

We received instruction to leave port and steam the South China Sea at night and return after day light to resume cargo operations. In addition the Navy had frogmen swimming under the ships checking for explosives the Viet Cong may have attached to the vessel below the water line.

SS "Muhlenberg Victory" Also operated by Matson Steamship Co. When I joined she was fully loaded laying at the Oakland Army Base with general military cargo below decks, and lumber on deck. The 2nd and 3rd Mates were two old timers coming out of retirement to help crew up the ships, keeping the supply line to Vietnam moving. Ole, the 2nd mate, was an old Swede, Knud the 3rd mate was an old Dane. Knud had the most unforgettable beautiful handwriting, and a way of mastering the English language making most people jealous. Ole and Knud had sailed together on steam schooners back in the 30's and didn't really like one another which had to do with a bar bill in Goose Bay, Oregon back in 1938.

We were scheduled to sail to Japan for bunkers and proceed to Vietnam, Great Circle course to take advantage of the shortest distance between two points. A great circle course is continuously changing along the track. The number of points is a matter of personal preference, a large number of points providing closer approximation to the great circle requiring more frequent course changes. As a general rule, 5 degrees of longitude is a convenient length. At the time before GPS, a great-circle course was solved by laying out the course on a great circle chart taking the points of that chart and transferring to a plotting sheet, or by using tables in the American Practical Navigator Bowditch.

Shortly after departure, I happened to come up to the bridge to make a log entry when I witnessed something I had never seen before.

Ole and Knud stood with a big plastic ruler turned on its edge over a general chart of the North Pacific Ocean, with Knud holding the ruler over San Francisco and Ole holding the other end over Yokohama, trying to draw a great circle line on the chart.

To me it was hilarious, and I busted out laughing and had to leave. On the way down the ladders I met the Captain who asked me, "What's so funny." After telling him what I'd just seen he looked at me and said, "What's wrong with that?

Later the Purser brought up a big stack of Notice to Mariners, a weekly publication of the U.S. Navy Hydrographic Office, giving information on changes in aids to navigation and all other information a mariner must know.

It is the 2nd Mate's job to read and make all necessary changes to our charts and publications. Ole took one look at the stack, told the Purser to take them back down and don't tell anybody about them.

Next morning on my 4 x 8 watch I was standing out on the wing of the bridge with my sextant ready to take star sight to get a fix and a good position, when the Radio operator came and introduced himself. He took a look at the stars and named four or five, telling me that would give me a good fix. I was surprised at his knowledge of the stars and asked him if he was some kind of porthole navigator, to which he responded, "No, but I was Captain with Pan American flying the China clipper where we had to use everything available."

He had never sailed before, but since he had a license he was asked to take a job to keep the ship moving. He was a very interesting person to talk to.

The sea passes went like clockwork, arriving in Saigon in record time. The military was on the dock ready to start discharging right away and continued around the clock until completed. I was told the lumber shipped out earlier had been stolen and sold on the black market. It was a very enjoyable trip all around.

S.S. *Bucyrus Victory* operated by American President Line. She was built in 1944 and named after a town in Ohio. The ship had received a battle star for service in WWII. She had also sailed during the Korean War. The Chief mate getting off was my old friend Pete the Greek, who clued me in. We stayed alongside the APL piers in San Francisco for two weeks before shifting to Port Chicago, loading ammunition which took a week.

The Captain asked me if I needed any duty free liquor. I ordered a case of Tanqueray gin and a case of tonic water. The first day out at sea, the slop chest was open and the Purser told me to come and pick up the Gin. To my big disappointment, there was no tonic water. Gin and tonic have always been my favorite drink, but I can't drink one without the other.

My only hope was to get some at the PX in Subic Bay PI when we stopped for bunkers and water on our way to Vung Ro.

The chief engineer told the captain he had enough fuel and water, and there was no reason to stop in Subic Bay. There went my dream of getting tonic water, out the window. I started talking loud about my last trip to Vung Ro and that fresh water was not available, and you never knew how long you had to stay there. The old chief engineers always had their fingers on two things, water and fuel. A few days later, the chief engineer told the captain that to be on the safe side it would be better to pull into Subic Bay to top off on both fuel and water. That was Music to my ears.

As we approached the Philippines, a typhoon was coming up from the South China Sea reaching the Philippines at the same time we did.

We dropped anchor in Subic Bay late afternoon. The wind and rain had increased considerably; the sea was getting choppy. The navy notified us that the fuel barge would not be able to come alongside that day.

They also informed us that there would be only one shore launch leaving the ship at 1800 and returning at 2200, and that shore leave was at our own risk. The shore launch was a small navy landing craft which stopped at each ship to pick up seamen who wished to go ashore. Most of the time the boat would be full to the brim, but this day it was empty. The operator had a hard time maneuvering the boat alongside the gangway due to strong wind and choppy seas. He told me over the bullhorn to walk down to the end of the gangway and be ready to jump when he came alongside. No problem.

When I got off the boat at the pier, I flagged down a jeep (taxi) right away, told the driver to take me to the PX. He looked at his watch and said it was closed,

By the time I got to the officer's club, happy hour was over, and very few people were there. I talked to the bartender and told him my problem with the tonic water. He told me he was not allowed to sell anything out of the bar, but under severe circumstances like this he would do it anyway. He agreed to sell me six big bottles of tonic water and put them in two paper bags. I gave him a big tip. Standing on the pier waiting for the boat to bring me back to the ship at 2200 hours, I was a happy camper

When the boat came to pick me up he stayed 10 feet off the pier using his search light and bullhorn. The operator instructed me to come out to the edge of the pier and be ready to jump onto the boat when he told me to.

I set my two bags close to the edge of the pier, and watched the boat make several failed attempts to come close enough for me to jump onto the boat. When he came alongside the third time he told me to be ready.

When he gave me the order to jump, I picked up my two paper bags not realizing that the paper bags had been sitting in the water and when I jumped from the pier into the boat the bottom of one bag broke and three bottles fell in the water. To make sure that it didn't happen to the last three bottles I put both arms around the bag when I jumped into the boat and I landed on my right shoulder on the starboard side, and it hurt;

The seas got choppier the further out we got and closer to the ship. Not taking any chances losing the last three bottles, I called the mate on duty to get a heaving line and lower a bucket and pull them safely onboard.

The boat operator waved so-long and yelled, "I sure hope you enjoy that tonic." The following day the wind died down, we received our fuel and water, and left for Wung Ro. The Viet Cong snipers were known for shooting at the incoming ships from up in the hills.

The military discharged the ammunition themselves, but the Coast Guard had two young men stationed there to oversee the discharging. One came and introduced himself and told me he was there to support the ship, and if I had any problems, let them know.

He told me they were kind of on their own and had a hard time getting groceries, but they could get everything else from the PX. I invited them both to come and eat with me on the ship. We stayed there 10 days. The day before sailing, I told them to give me a grocery list. On top of the grocery list was potatoes, carrots and other vegetables.

I asked the steward but he didn't want to give them anything. Not a problem since I had the keys to the ships Storerooms. And since we were homebound bound we had plenty onboard.

I filled some empty mail sacks with vegetables, canned ham and other goodies.

They told me that we had been the best ship in and they were sorry to see us leave.

After undocking and securing the ship, I was in for a lovely surprise. When I returned to my room I found a mail sack with several bottles of Gin and Tonic standing in my shower with a little thank you note.

SS Steel Director Isthmian States Marine Line. The ship was short a Chief Mate and the job had been hanging open for several days when I took it in February, 1970. She was at the Oakland Army Base ready to sail for Vietnam with another load of military supplies.

When I went to introduce myself to the captain, he asked if I had ever sailed on ships without a purser. He told me he did not have a typewriter and had no intention of getting one, and all the paper work was in my hands. I told him it was not a problem, I could handle it.

Before I left his office he gave me a case a beer. I assumed it came out of the slop chest and that it would me on my bill. He looked at me and told me to go down and look at the cargo plan, which I did, and found the whole ship was loaded with beer except for some steel in the lower holds.

The chief engineer and the 1st engineer did not get along. One reason was the 1st engineer did not like to get dirty and always used gloves when working on machinery.

I gave the chief engineer a crew list with all the names, but he came around several times asking.

What is the name of that 1st engineer again? I kept telling him, His name is Waldorf III." He looked at me and said," Do you mean to tell me there was two of those S O Bs before him."

Don't ask me how the Captain was able to talk the company into stopping in Hong Kong for fuel instead of Subic Bay but we did and stayed for several days.

When we arrived in Da Nang, the U.S. Army officer in charge of the cargo operation came onboard to check the cargo plan. He got very upset when he found out the ship was loaded with beer and told me there was no way he could accept it. He took me for a ride in his jeep and showed me row after row of pallets of beer which had been standing there for a long time. He told me that after one more rainy season they would all have to be destroyed. "The soldiers here are young and only drink pop and we don't have enough for them."

He also told me to help ourselves to the beer. That is how I learned there are 88 cases of beer to a pallet. We moved out to anchorage for further instructions. The Army in Quin Nhon notified Da Nang that if there was any Black Label Beer among the load they would accept it. I had no idea but said, yes, and a few days later we were told to sail to Quin Nhon.

When the cargo was discharged and the hatches cleaned, covered and secured for sea, I decided to make a final inspection of all the cargo holds, climbing down through the inside ladders using a good flashlight. I was in for a big surprise. When I stood down in the bottom of # 4 hatch, I saw daylight through the ship's hull about five feet above the water line.

The sailing time was cancelled and temporary repairs were made by building a cement box inside the ship's hull. It didn't take long to find the cause. The steel barge which had been alongside to load cargo had a sharp steel corner which had been pressing hard against our ship when coming alongside.

We sailed to Saigon for permanent repairs which had to be inspected by the American Bureau of Shipping and the U.S. Coast Guard in Saigon before crossing the Pacific.

We also back loaded cargo to Los Angeles. The Captain hired a large paint gang who painted the entire ship for $ 500, and when the job was finished the foreman of the paint gang gave me two brown elephants made of clay which I placed outside my house in San Francisco and they are still there

THE END OF THE VICTORY SHIPS

By 1970, military supplies shipped to Vietnam started slowing down, and government owned Victory ship's carrying military supplies were no longer needed, returned to the Ready Reserve Fleet (RDF) and some were sold for scrap. I worked as night Mate (PRO) on a few of the Victory ships when they arrived in San Francisco. Various types of shore laborers were hired to strip the ships for everything of value.

Most of the ships returned with a lot of groceries onboard. It broke my heart to see cases of steaks, ham and turkey being taken off the ship to be destroyed, instead of giving it to charity. But the law does not allow U.S. meat to enter the USA after it has been overseas.

Besides the Victory ships, private companies were also scaling down and laying up ships, due to lack of cargo. Some went out of business altogether.

When I walked into the union hall in January, 1971 I realized quickly that I was not the only one looking for a ship. The union hall was full of people. In an addition to the locals, there were members from all over the country who preferred to ship out of San Francisco. I made an effort to talk to as many members as possible to find out what kind of ship they were looking for. Some were only interested in West Coast ships, others preferred tankers.

There were two with old shipping cards looking for permanent jobs with Sea Land. I decided not to wait for any particular ship or company, but take whatever became available to me.

At the time, each ship under the MM&P contract had five permanent deck officers assigned, master chief mate, 2nd and two 3rd mates. The companies had the right to promote or transfer their officers from ship to ship within their fleet. If a 2nd mate was promoted to temporarily to higher rank on another ship, his replacement had to be dispatched through the union hall. If a company had to hire a new permanent man, it was always as 3rd Mate, starting at the bottom of the roster. Shipping cards were issued for 12 months and if you didn't use your shipping card within that time span or fell behind with your union dues, you had to re-register.

Besides the ships mentioned in the book, I had several 3rd mate jobs relieving for vacation, medical or leave of absence. I was on SS Guam Bear Pacific Far East Line, a containership sailing between the West Coast, Honolulu, and Guam and later on the Hawaiian Monarch, a Matson containership on the Hawaiian run, as well as the SS Montana, a States Line freighter on the Far East run. Unfortunately we stopped in Honolulu homebound and had to get off, due to a longshoremen strike.

Subsequently, I got a job on the SS President Jackson, American President Line around the world service from San Francisco, to Japan, Hong Kong, Saigon, Singapore, Penang Karachi, and through the Suez Canal to Genoa, Marseille and New York. Unfortunately the Suez Canal was closed for a long period after the Israel-Egyptian War, which forced us to bypass the Mediterranean ports and sail from Karachi, Pakistan, around South Africa to New York, a 23 days voyage.

Like so many others, I had to look for an extra income in between ships. The only thing I knew was painting.

In the past the painters union in San Francisco had been very powerful, but it ran into trouble in 1966 when one union leader was assassinated by another union leader from the East Bay. At the same time the hippies started painting, for half the price of a union painter.

I purchased a ladder, some paint brushes and a few rollers at Sears. I had 500 business card made calling myself "PETE PEDERSEN PAINT COMPANY." My first customers came through the church, which also meant volunteer work for the church. I was painting a house for a Chinese lady in the Richmond district, and one day she said, "I wish my Dad was alive to see me having a white man painting my house."

The MM&P local 90 had two monthly union meetings, and you had to attend at least one to remain on the shipping list. As the shipping kept decreasing, and more and more members lost their jobs, the rotation came up at every meeting. To get it started, all permanent jobs had to be eliminated, except for the master, which may not be an easy sell with the ship owners.

Our shipping rules were part of the master contract and could not be changed in the middle of the contract. Ninety days before our contract came up for renewal, the members had an opportunity to write in their request for changes. In between I spent a lot of time in the union hall looking for a ship. I volunteered to become the chairman of a committee whose job it was to read and separate the incoming mail from the membership. Most of the requests were about sharing the work. A few requests were completely off the wall. Like one member recommended that each super tanker should have three Captains each working eight hours a day? I managed to lose that letter without anybody noticing.

Another request was to have a barber chair installed on all new construction. Against my recommendation it became item # 29.

The contract negotiation was held in New Orleans. Each port sent a MM&P union official and a rank and file. The Port of San Francisco sent two officials and two rank and files. I was nominated to be one of the rank and files. The president of local 90 told me the whole thing would only take a few days, and not to bring too many clothes. We met our colleagues from coast to coast at the hotel where the negotiation was to take place.

As it turned out, our committee from San Francisco was the only one who had everything ready to present in a binder, with a copy for everyone. When it became time to do the final preparation, a member from Baltimore asked me if I considered item # 29, the barber chair, to be a strike issue.

I happened to be in the hotel lobby when the ship owner's attorney and professional negotiator checked in. He had three suitcases and a lot of suits on hangers, not a good sign. When we met with the ship owners our national president opened the meeting by saying that our organization was faced with huge unemployment, and that he found it necessary to implement some type of rotation shipping for everybody.

The attorney/negotiator on the other side of the table stood, and with a straight face said he was shocked and saddened to hear such a ridiculous request, and that he would not even consider talking about. The meeting was adjourned.

After the ship owners walked out, our president instructed one of the officials to tell the newspapers that the negotiation was coming along smoothly, and that we were close to an agreement. Another good reason not to believe everything you read or hear.

We met again the following day, and after a few days of negotiations we settled for getting the 2nd and 3rd mates shipped out of the union hall for six months duration.

The companies demanded the right to select their master and chief mates from a company select list, which meant a man with a chief mate's license could go to any MM&P contracted company and apply for a job. When the company hired a chief mate, the job would be posted on the MM & P shipping board with his name on it.

I was also elected convention delegate twice. The first one I attended was held in San Diego, California. The second one was in Linthicum Heights Maryland.

Years later, without my knowledge someone placed my name on the alternating convention delegate list. I was surprised to get 1,640 votes which put me on top of the list. When called, I declined.

On Captain Thomas O' Callaghan's watch as President of the MM&P four very important changes were made which benefited the organization tremendously.

A Merged all the MM&P locals into one national union under one roof.

B Against large opposition he had the foresight to build The Maritime Institute of Technology and Graduate Studies (MITAGS), located in Linthicum Heights, Md.

C Stood up for the Rotation shipping system

D Merged the MM&P to become a Marine Division under the International Longshoremen Association.

SS Columbia Wolf a one way voyage ending with a sit down strike at Hong Kong International Airport

As a seaman away from home six or more months out of the year, I always managed to plan my vacation and time off to be home for Christmas and for summer vacation when the kids were out of school. I did lose out on some good jobs by doing so, but to me it was well worth it.

I stopped by the MM&P union hall a few days before Christmas and noticed among the open jobs hanging on the shipping board were three on the SS Columbia Wolf, a one way trip to Vietnam, then Hong Kong for scrap, and the crew was to fly home from there.

The ship was to stay in San Francisco over Christmas and New Years, sailing January 2nd. Since the Chief Mate job was already taken; I decided to take the 2/Mate job. The SS Columbia Wolf was the ex SS Alaska Bear, an 8500 HP Victory ship. Columbia Steamship Company bought the ship from Pacific Far East Line and managed to get a one way military cargo to Vietnam then deliver the ship in Hong Kong for scrap within 90 days

The S I U had a hard time finding a crew. They rounded up all the married China coasters they could find, or men who spent their vacations in Asia, telling them what a great opportunity for them if they took a job on the Colombia Wolf. They were told in detail that when the ship was delivered in Hong Kong they would be paid off, and given money in lieu of a first class ticket back to San Francisco. This would give them an opportunity to purchase their own ticket to any destination in Asia, and still have a lot of cash left over. It sounded like a good deal.

By the time the cargo was loaded at the Oakland Army base, we were still short five men, one of them was the Radio officer. The Coast Guard and the union gave the company a waiver to sail without the four un-licensed crew members, but we were not allowed to sail without a Radio officer.

Shortly thereafter they managed to find a licensed radio officer back in Colorado who agreed to take the job if the company would pay for his excess luggage, which included an old heavy ham radio set in a trunk and several suitcases of tools, all very heavy.

The Captain was an old grumpy man and very unpleasant to everyone. To him, everybody was a bunch of useless S F B. The 3/M was of Mexican descent and new on his license. The Captain drove him to tears daily with racist slander and chewed me out for standing up for him.

Since the ship was heading for the razor blade factory after Vietnam, no maintenance work was going on. Everybody was standing sea watches and doing minimum work on the cargo gear.

We had very good cooks and 90 days' grocery onboard, we were fed well. Can't think of any restaurant doing better?

The military in Da Nang must have been waiting for the cargo, because they started discharging right away and worked nonstop until finished.

We contacted a few charity organizations and gave them all our excess food, bed clothing, soap and other cleaning materials. Kept just enough to get us to Hong Kong.

Since the Captain never talked to anybody, I went to check with the Radio officer the night before arrival in Hong Kong.

He told me we were to pick up the harbor pilot on arrival at 0300 and proceed to Junk Bay anchorage awaiting port clearance at 0600. He also told me a Typhoon might be coming our way to.

When I went on watch at 0400, relieving the 3/M, the ship was dead in the water and the Captain was standing out on the wing of the bridge with his binoculars. I asked the 3/M what was going on. He threw up his hands and told me he didn't have a clue. The Captain had taken over his watch, and he only did what he was told.

Before relieving the 3/M, I took several bearings, visual and by radar, which indicated that we were nine miles away from the pilot station. The barometer was going straight down, and when I walked out on the wing of the bridge I could feel the quiet, high humidity, the still before the storm.

After a while the engineer on watch called and asked when we would be getting under way. I told the captain that the engine room wanted to know when we were moving.

He snapped and said he was waiting for daylight. I told him I had been in and out of Hong Kong many times and would like to show him our present position, and the course to steer plotted on the chart which indicated we were nine miles away from the pilot station. Shortly thereafter he decided to get under way again. I called the Hong Kong signal station which was required at that time to use the

Morse code and a signal lamp. I gave them a new ETA which they passed on to the pilot.

When the harbor pilot came onboard he told the Captain the typhoon was moving directly toward Hong Kong and would be here by midday.

After dropping anchor for the last time in Junk Bay at the end of the runway at Hong Kong International Airport, we waited for the port authority to clear the ship before anybody was allowed ashore or onboard.

The agent hired to represent the company, taking care of all port formalities and getting the crew off the ship, came onboard with instructions from Columbia Steamship Company. It was not what anybody wanted to hear. The Captain was to fly to San Francisco at 1300 (1pm) bringing the payroll with him. Everyone else was to fly out that night and be paid off at the airport in San Francisco.

That was quite a difference in what the crew was told when they took the job. Several crew members felt they had been misled and were very upset. We were told to have our personal belongings ready with name tags by # 4 hatches by 3p.m. A boat was to take us off the ship bringing us into the landing next to star ferry, where a bus would bring us directly to the airport. It all seemed like a great plan, except for the crew members planning to go to on to Thailand, Japan, or the Philippines.

The Captain left the ship around 1100 to fly out at 1300, which turned out to be the last flight out of Hong Kong for the next two days.

At 2 p.m. the Agent came back onboard and told us to be ready to get off the ship while still could. He told us the bad news that the airport was closed, and he was trying to get us to stay overnight at the British Mariners Club downtown Kowloon.

First, an old junk came alongside to pick up our personal belongings. It was very difficult for the operator to stay alongside due to strong wind, rain and choppy seas. The bosun had rigged two booms by #4 hatch to lower our gear down into the junk with a canvas sling. The bad news was the ship's power was already turned off. Our only choice was to lower everything down piece by piece using a heaving line or carry it all down the gangway.

As it turned out, we did both. The Radio officer's trunks were heavy when he came onboard in San Francisco but seemed twice as heavy getting off. I helped him get his trunks down the gangway, which was very difficult since the gangway was straight up and down and very slippery. Shortly thereafter a regular shore launch came to bring us into boat landing next to Star ferry terminal. Sitting in the boat wet and dirty, I looked back at the Columbia Wolf disappearing for the last time.

The Seaman Club was only a few blocks from the boat landing, but a bus was waiting for us when we got there. All our personal belongings went on a truck.

All The bad news got worse when we arrived at the Seamen's Club which could only take 10 of us.

The agent contacted several hotels and managed to get the rest of us into two hotels fairly close. The agent being British said the officers should go to the hotel and the crew stay at the Seamen's Club. That started a big discussion, who was going to stay where and why. It made no difference to me and I agreed to stay at the seamen's club.

Since the Captain and Chief mate had already left, there was nobody to take charge. The agent asked me to help being the spokesman for the crew. He was not going to put up with all the bad mouthing he was getting. I knew when the guys started heading for the bars it would be a complete nightmare, so I agreed to help him. I had a copy of the crew list and made up a list with everybody's name and the name of the hotel and room numbers.

At the same time I made a mistake by giving them my room number because early next morning I was awakened by a phone call from a fire and water tender (FWT) and a wiper. They wanted me to go with them to the American Embassy to file a complaint because as American citizens they should be allowed to go to Manila instead of San Francisco.

I told them since they were on foreign shipping articles they had to be signed off on arrival in San Francisco, and furthermore the Embassy was closed due to the typhoon. Next call was someone running out of money.

Next morning the typhoon was still hanging over Hong Kong with heavy rain and wind but eased in the afternoon. The agent came by with new instructions for us to fly out the following day at 1300. Since the airport was just a short distance away he had made arrangements to have us picked up by bus at 1100.

I told him that would never work. We needed at least three hours to round everybody up and one hour to check in. I explained my past experience dealing with people drinking and he agreed. I wrote down the instructions from the agent, made up 30 copies and handed a copy to each man; the ones not around I slipped under their hotel room doors. In addition, I posted the message on the hotel bulletin board asking everybody to meet for breakfast at 0800.

I was up early and happy to see a nice calm and dry morning. I went around making my first headcount which was not very good. There were eleven which left twenty unaccounted for.

I started calling each man using the hotel phone at the desk and managed to get a few more on their feet. Due to heavy traffic the bus had a hard time getting into the Seamen's Club for the first pick up. By the time we left for the hotel pickups it was close to 1000. Only half the guys were waiting and ready to go. The agent worked the telephone calling their rooms. I went around knocking on the doors, asking the cleaning ladies to unlock a few doors. After getting the last few on their feet and helping them down with their suitcases, some demanded breakfast; two wanted a drink since there was plenty of time according to them. The other guests at the hotel were wondering what the commotion in the lobby was all about.

It was 11:45 a.m. when we arrived at the airport with a good hour to check in. That is when things turned from bad to worse. Some left their suitcases in the line and left for the Bar, some demanded lunch. The Ch/Engineer who was bent out of shape went on a sit -down strike with some of the crew members who did not want to go back to San Francisco. One man demanded to have someone from the Embassy come and stop the flight.

One man sitting at the bar fell off the stool and hit his head and was taken to the hospital. another was lying on the floor calling for help. By 1300 everybody's suitcase was checked in thanks to the porters hired by the agent. However, some still refused to leave. I don't know how or why but the Captain of the TWA flight agreed to delay the flight for 30 minutes to get us all onboard.

At 1335 a TWA spokesman said, "We are closing the door with a total of nineteen aboard." The Agent looked at me like what I am I going to do with those drunks sitting in the bar still on strike? He also told me this was the first and last time he would ever handle an American ship.

You had to be there and see it to believe the circus at the airport. I believe Hollywood would have a hard time recreating that scene.

On the flight back, I had several complaints that the Stewardesses refused to serve them drinks, but I told them it's out of my control, and they were lucky to be on the plane in the first place, and that they should get some sleep and be ready for the shit to hit the fan in San Francisco.

By the time we landed things had calmed down and there were no problems with Immigration and customs. We were met by a US shipping commissionaire to sign off our foreign articles, and a Columbia Steamship Co. paymaster to pay us off.

To my big surprise there were no union patrolmen present to square away complaints and collect dues. Guess they were smart enough to stay away.

SS President Tyler Hong Kong, Jakarta, Singapore

A few years later I had a similar experience when I shipped as 2nd mate on the SS President Tyler known as a Sea-racer cargo liner converted to carry containers in hatches # 3 - 4 using a shipboard crane. On the after deck we carried containers on deck only, using ships booms to load and discharge in ports like Jakarta, Indonesia where there were no shore side cranes available.

After passing my medical checkup I went to the APL office where I was issued a 1st class ticket to fly to Hong Kong with Pan American the following day. I was told that an oiler was flying out with me on the same plane. On West Coast ships it was not just the Captain and Chief Engineer flying 1st class, everybody went first class.

We left on a Boeing 747. Cocktails were served right after take-off and shortly thereafter the stewardess came around asking if I would like to dine in the upstairs dining room or remain in my seat. I chose the upstairs dining room which was very nice with two large tables. Cocktails and wine kept coming, and we were served a nice dinner.

I noticed a man sitting another table getting louder and louder, and half way through the soup he fell off the chair the soup and napkin on top of him. I knew he had to be the oiler.

We went through Custom and Immigration quickly and were picked up by a man from APL who drove us to the ship, just in time for me to go on watch and sail for Jakarta, Indonesia.

Jakarta had not changed much since I was there last; everything was done in slow motion, and we always seemed to stay two or three days regardless of how much or how little cargo we had.

The Stevedore foreman was an interesting person who had spent several years working in San Francisco illegally before the immigration caught up with him and deported him. He told me the frustration he had to deal with daily, and how the system worked.

After the cargo is discharged it may sit on the dock or warehouse for days before being released to the consignee, depending on how much baksheesh (bribe) he was willing to pay the customs and other government bureaucrats.

We never stayed long in Singapore or Hong Kong except when waiting for transshipments from other APL ships. Since we never had more than a few hundred containers onboard it looked like a money losing operation, with crew members coming and going all the time, and I was not surprised when we were told the ship would go into lay-up in Singapore and we were all to be sent home. The Captain posted a detailed itinerary about our port stay stating when we would get off the ship and transfer to a hotel, and that we had two days off before flying home to San Francisco where we would be met by the US shipping commissionaire and paymaster at the airport.

He also took the opportunity to thank the entire crew for a job well done and for making the shuttle service a success. He regretted that he was not able to fly home with us because he was staying with the ship doing the lay-up period, but had appointed Mr. Georg Pedersen 2nd Mate to represent him during our stay in Singapore and flight home. After reading the note, the first thing that came to my mind was my experience in Hong Kong getting off the SS Columbia Wolf.

After the cargo was discharged we shifted to a lay-up pier, and shortly thereafter were picked up and driven to our hotels, both close together. APL had hired porters to help us with our suitcases and had someone there to check and tell us we were entitled to charge three meals a day to our rooms.

If you have never been on a ship, it may not be easy to understand everyday life and living conditions. To some it is a home, to others it is like living in the factory, and to others it is like being in jail with the possibility of drowning. The Captain and officers are considered management.

The unlicensed crew would be classified as semi-skilled workers, all on twenty four hour call. Some came on a ship to work hard and save up their money without ever going ashore or having a drink for months, but after they got off a ship they relaxed and celebrated.

When it was time to leave Singapore it was pretty much the same as the experience getting out of Hong Kong, except we only left two men behind.

After getting on the plane I realized the 2nd Engineer was missing. The flight purser gave me permission to get off the plane to locate him.

After I found him, we walked up the gang plank together and, when I entered the plane I walked forward to our seats. When I turned around to look for him he was not there. I ran back to the entrance door which was already closed and secured. I asked the Stewardess standing by the door if she had seen my friend. "I sure did, half way up the gang blank he stopped to light a cigarette." She had managed to get it away from him and walk him down the ramp. She didn't want him on the plane.

We made a short stop in Hong Kong before proceeding to Honolulu where we had a three hour lay-over. When time came to board, the stewardess stopped two guys from coming onboard for being drunk. I did a lot of talking and explained to the purser how important it was for them to get to San Francisco with the rest of us. To let them come onboard, I had to agree to sit between them which turned out to be a long flight for me, but I survived.

Before Containerization cargo was loaded onto the ships on a wooden pallet or sling, and hand stowed piece by piece. I don't know how many warehouses I walked through in my life to get on/off my ships, looking at the freight sitting in wood or cardboard boxes or bales, stacked up to the ceiling. It was not unusual to see cargo to two

or three different ships with different destinations, and I always wondered how they were able to keep track of it all.

Outside the piers were long lines of trucks waiting to have their freight unloaded onto a wooden pallet before being moved into the warehouse by forklift where it often sat for days waiting for the ship to come in. The weather had a big influence on the cargo operation. When it rained everything came to a stop which delayed the ship's departure.

When the cargo was finally loaded a special gang was hired to lash and shore it to avoid damage during the ocean transit.

It was not unusual for cargo to be handled 4-6 times from the time it left the factory until it reached its destination overseas, all very time consuming and costly. It also left it open to damage, and pilferage.

Remember the movie **On the Waterfront** back in 1954 with Marlon Brando showing the corruption and violence on the docks and what a man had to cope with to make a living?

Just to update you on how a Port operates. The Port Authority operates as a landlord, leasing out their piers to the steamship companies. The bigger companies usually lease several piers long term lease and schedule their ships to assure they always have a berth available, and space to stow their cargo.

Smaller companies often have to wait their turn for a berth. Next, the shipping company hires a local stevedore company to supply labor and equipment to work the ship. The stevedore company then selects a man from the longshoremen's union to represent them. Known as the gang or walking boss, he becomes the man in charge of the cargo operation under the shipping company's supervision.

The walking boss is also responsible for hiring the longshoremen needed to work the ship.

Longshoremen looking for work gather around a large wooden platform twice a day.

The union members stand on one side, and the nonunion men wait for the left overs on the other side of the platform. The system gives the walking boss free hand to hire whoever he wants, which leaves a door open for favoritism and kickbacks. It was changed later.

It was not uncommon for a line haul ship to order up to seven gangs of longshoremen with 22 men to a gang. Do the math. With so many men involved in loading or unloading a ship, the waterfront was a busy and exciting place. There are always bars and restaurants on the waterfront, all doing good business when the ships are in, some with elbow room only.

It was also a good place to purchase cheap merchandise, like Italian suits, shoes, perfume, radios, and other merchandise stolen off the piers. I remember sitting in a bar in Boston when a guy came in trying to sell some new London Fog Coats. When he saw me showing interest he told me they came from a place down the street call pier 66.

Some shoe importer found it necessary to ship the right and left foot shoes on two different ships to avoid pilfering. Ccontainerization stopped most of that.

SS ROSE CITY
SEA LAND SERVICE

"S.S. Rose City, owned and operated by Sea Land service, was my first containership, and my first Sea Land Ship as 2/Mate vacation relief in 1971. In the past, when getting a job off the Rotary shipping board it was customary to go to the company doctor for a complete medical checkup, and get the vaccinations required for the trip before going to the company office to check in with the Port Captain. When I checked my assignment slip, it said go to the doctor and directly to the ship laying at the Sea Land Terminal in Oakland.

When I asked the dispatcher if he had made a mistake? He said, Sea Land have their own system and is not interested in who you are as long as you have the license. It's my responsibility to make sure you have a 2nd Mates license, and the Doctor's responsibility to see you are fit-for-duty.

When I reported on the ship, I was surprise to find the Chief Mate's door locked with a note telling all new crew members to see the 3rd Mate on duty. I found the 3rd Mate out on deck checking the cargo operation.

He took me up to the Chief Mate's office to fill out the routine personnel papers, date and place of birth, Social Security number, license information, and next of kin, and allotment to your wife or Bank.

When the paper work was completed he called the custom broker and gave him my information which had to be placed on the ship's foreign articles and crew list as required by law. When the paper work was completed he told me I could go home and come back one hour before sailing the following day.

He explained that Sea Land kept only one deck officer on duty in all U.S. ports, called the man in the barrel. Other companies I worked for had three men falling over one another all day, and then at the end of the day turned it over to the night mate, who sometimes didn't know the ship. He also gave me a phone number to call giving an update on the posted sailing time.

Instead of going home, I decided to change into working clothes and follow the 3rd Mate around to learn the ship and what my job was all about.

The ship's hull was a C-4 Jr class. The bow and stern was from a World WarII T-2 tanker, with a new mid-body welded to the bow and stern, called Jumbo-sizing. Seamen referred to them as American beauties She was 695 feet long, 72 feet wide, capable of carrying 602-35 foot containers and a crew of 39.

I read the chief mate's standing orders for the man in the barrel and the night mate to follow. It was mostly about the reefer containers, and keeping the reefer log up to date.

If any damage was done to the ship or cargo by longshoremen one was to take pictures using the ships Polaroid camera and make out an S-L damage report.

I visited the main gate and watched as the trucks entered the terminal. Each truck stopped and handed a note to the gate keeper. A scanner read the bar coded SEAU number on the container and the information went into the computer. The man at the gate told the driver where to park the container and chassis, or drive it to the ship's side. The container itself served as a mobile warehouse eliminating the cost of storage in transit and lowered the labor cost and damage.

The Marine Operation or cargo office was manned by a small handful of people sitting in front of computers loading the ship. The ships received a pre loading plan on arrival.

There were 602 container positions on the vessel. Each position had a number on the cargo plan.

When a container was loaded, the SEAU number and weight of the container was entered into the Computer and showed on the final cargo plan. The content of the cargo was only shown on the dangerous cargo and reefer manifest.

The reefer containers were loaded on deck and plugged into the ships power outlet between the cargo hatches. In addition a, 35 foot power plant with a diesel engine was carried on # 2, hatch fully equipped with fuel and spare parts if needed. The marine operation notified the mate on watch when to post the sailing board, which had to be posted eight hours before sailing, as per union contracts. Each crew member had a phone number to call for sailing information which was recorded on a tape with the correct sailing time and reminding each crew member to be back one hour before sailing.

Just before sailing, the Chief Mate received the final cargo plan showing the total amount of containers onboard, with weight, vessel draft and stability.

The IBM computer system made that cargo plan available to the Sea Land Office at the next Port of Call.

In the past the break/bulb ships always took several hours to secure for sea after the cargo operation was complete. Now on container ships, when the last container is loaded, the vessel is secured for sea. The hatch covers were held in place by using the wing nut and bolt system, besides the weight from the container. Sea Land had developed a steel stacking frame system placed between each tier of containers on deck.

Each container was loaded on top of four twist locks connected to a stainless steel rod which turned the twist lock into a locked position by moving a handle. To assure the handle would stay locked, a safety pin was used. The longshoremen would lock each tier during the loading checked by the Mate on watch and later by the chief mate.

For me, it was a new experience sailing under the Golden Gate Bridge with a full load of military cargo in containers heading for Cam Ran Bay, Vietnam, a 21-22 day voyage, depending on the weather. Among the cargo were 120 reefer containers loaded with meat, vegetables, fruit, eggs and ice-cream. Containerization enabled the U.S. military to keep the troops well fed, with a reduction in damaged and lost cargo, particularly t perishable items and PX supplies.

Sea Land had six line haul ships carrying cargo to Cam Ran Bay from the U.S. West Coast, bringing 1,200 containers monthly, with transshipments to Qui Nhon, Danang and Saigon by three smaller C-2 vessels with shipboard cranes.

The watch system was the same as on any other ship. As 2nd Mate I stood the 4 x 8 sea watches which are the navigator's watch, taking morning, and evening star fixes.

It was also my job to make sure that all charts and publications needed for the trip were onboard and corrected through the Notice to Mariners weekly publication from the U.S. Hydrographic Office.

I was responsible for the maintenance of the gyro compass, course recorder, sounding equipment, radio direction finder, and that the chronometer was corrected daily. The weather observation was prepared by the watch officer every six hours and sent in to the weather bureau by the radio officer.

We had very nice and calm weather the first trip across the Pacific with many beautiful sunrises and sunsets. On the second trip we ran into a typhoon in the Luzon Strait, and lost two days, but didn't encounter any damage to the ship or cargo.

We entered the Vietnam War zone a day out of Cam Ran Bay, which increased our pay with a 100% war bonus.

The Sea Land pier and terminal consisted of two 300 x 90 foot floating barges (De Long piers) with holes through the barges where pilings were driven into the harbor floor to keep them in place and jacked up on the pilings to the desired height above the water.

Extra support was placed for the two container cranes and container load. The only problem was that the ship was 95 feet longer than the pier which made it necessary to haul ship to work all the hatches.

Off-loading containers in Cam Ranh Bay, the first Deep-water container terminal in South East Asia

Sea Land was far ahead of the competition having their own pier and terminal and their own civilian employees operating the terminal, driving the trucks behind the war zone. The military was liable for damage to the trucks and equipment caused by enemy fire.

Sea Land carried 10% of the supplies destined for Vietnam. The remaining 90% was on 200 dry cargo ships. Sea-Land's effort proved the effectiveness of container shipping for military support in a war zone.

It took approximately 48 hours working around the clock to discharge and back load as many empties as possible before sailing. The freight rates paid by the military for the westbound voyage covered all costs for the entire voyage.

At the time Japan, was the fastest growing economy in the world. Mr. McLean was trying to break into the commercial Asian market, looking for freight to carry from Asia back across the Pacific. Hong Kong and Japan offered great potential for containerized shipping.

Container ships in Hong Kong were something new, and there were no container facilities or shore cranes available. When we arrived in Hong Kong, we docked down town Kowloon next to the Ocean terminal. The ship was loaded and discharged using cherry pickers, a slow operation giving us 3-4 days in port. We were told that McLean was negotiating with the Hong Kong Port Authority to lease space and build a container terminal in the new territory, which became the Sea Land Kwai-Chung-Terminal, the most advanced terminal in Asia at the time. On our second trip to Hong Kong we went into dry-dock for several days for repairs and hull painting, looked like they were trying to spend some money in town, which paid off big time.

Kobe and Yokohama were building and installing container cranes. Containerization was getting a lot of publicity in Japan, both from the newspapers and TV reporters, which came onboard for interviews. Seamen from foreign ships started coming onboard to see what it was all about. Some were skeptics, and others were fascinated. After just two trips, I knew containerization was here to stay, and next time I was looking for a ship, Sea Land would be on top of my list.

2006 Forbes wrote an article. The box that changed Asia and the world which thanks to Mr. Mclean's vision, created a way in which cargo could be shifted from trucks to ship, trains and shipped all over the world without loss or delay on one bill of lading, which had an enormous impact on the Asian and the world economy.

As the Vietnam War scaled down job opportunities went from bad to worse with very few jobs heading the rotary shipping board. That's why I was happy when I got a call from Sea Land who was looking for a Chief Mate on the S.S.Trenton, and my name had come up.

With the new shipping rules in effect, the job was posted on the MM & P shipping board January 15-1973

She was built as another WWII Troopship and converted to a Sea Land containership capable of carrying 610 - 35 foot containers. The run was the same as the SS Rose City, Long Beach, Oakland, Cam Ranh Bay, Vietnam-Hong Kong-Kobe, Yokohama, Japan.

The cargo operation was well under way when I came onboard loading and discharging empty. The empty containers were driven over to the Oakland Army base to be reloaded. When the reefer containers first arrived inside the terminal but not ready to be loaded on to the ship, they were parked and hooked up to an electrical outlet.

In 1963 Sea Land pioneered the first ocean-going refrigerated containers for frozen products and later for chilled. This was a huge investment and taken very seriously. It became the Chief Mate's responsibility to make sure the reefers were working and operating satisfactorily before sailing from each port. The reefers were stowed on deck and loaded last. The ship's electrician plugged them into the ship's electrical outlets between the cargo hatches. I had three ways of checking the temperature. First by the white tag placed in front of the container, then by the setting, and last by the reefer cargo manifest received from the cargo office in each port. It was important to catch problems right away before sailing and have a reefer mechanic from shore came onboard to correct it. Temperature control was critical, spoiled food, meant big claims.

When the cargo operation was complete, and we were ready to sail, I went down on the dock to take the final draft. I was in for a big surprise when I found the ship was down by the head by 3 feet. I went to check with the cargo office that double checked all the weight, hatch by hatch, and they convinced me their numbers were correct. According to the computer printout the ship should be slightly down by the stern which is always preferable. The Sea Land system required a tank report to be sent ashore to the cargo office before a vessel arrived in port showing the weight of the vessel's fuel oil and ballast water onboard on arrival, and how the vessel would look after taking more fuel. I checked the last tank report with the chief engineer, which agreed with the cargo plan.

As it turned out, the captain had no problem sailing with the ship being down 3 feet by the head, and asked the chief engineer to burn out the oil from the forward tanks first.

Out at sea my day started at 0600, first checking and reading the reefer temperature and logging them in the in the reefer log book. If I noticed any discrepancy or mechanical problem, I reported them to the chief engineer at 0800.

Since we were deep in the water when loaded in stormy weather taking seas over the main deck, the water would accumulate between the cargo hatches and get into the electrical outlet blowing out the brass plug which sounded like a small explosion, killing all the reefers.

The first day out at sea, I had a chance to walk and climb through all the accessible compartments and store rooms. When I came up forward and opened the hatch down to the fore-peak I was shocked to see clean salt water all the way up to the top of the hatch. I checked the vessel's blueprint to see the size of the compartment, which was huge. I asked the Bosun if he kept anything down in the fore-peak, which he didn't and hardly ever went down there.

When I took him up forward and showed him the water, he told me it must have been caused by the bad weather they had encountered homebound the trip before, where one brass plate used to cover the hawse-pipe down to the chain locker had been damaged, and it was possible the water had entered from there.

I inspected the bow area and found a four-foot long crack in the deck above the fore-peak, big enough to allow a lot of water to enter and fill up the compartment, which explained why we were down by the head sailing Oakland/San Francisco. To make things worse, the valve and reach-rod were frozen, which made it impossible to pump out the water.

The weather was in our favor, giving us an opportunity to start siphoning the water out using a fire hose which worked well for several days. By the time the siphoning stopped there was still seven feet of water left at the bottom. The Bosun and I decided to take turns diving under the water to pull on the wrench used to open the valve. After several dives we managed to open the valve and start to pump the water out. The engineers welded a large steel plate over the crack on the deck, and built a cement box on top.

I was still wet and dirty, and before stepping into the shower I noticed a huge lump in my right groin which turned out to be a hernia, not a very good beginning. I waited several days before I told anybody.

The Captain, an old Norwegian-Alaska fisherman told me if it happened while fishing, they would tie a rope around the bulb to keep it in place. I did the same. Later when in Hong Kong I went ashore and bought a hernia support belt, which kept everything under control for the next four months.

I enjoyed working with the Sea Land employees in Cam-Ranh-Bay, discharging the cargo onto the De-Long pier and delivering it to the military bases, or stowing it for transshipment to Saigon, and other ports in Vietnam as required. Two days later we were back out in the South China Sea heading for Hong Kong. This was my first time entering Honk Kong through the Lamma Chanel passing Aberdeen harbor with the famous floating restaurant, picking up the pilot at Green Island, before docking at the new Kwai-Chung Sea Land terminal.

We spent several days in dry-dock for repairs and hull painting. There were several Russian ships in the yard. Like so many other seafaring nations, they still didn't have any containerships.

They took great interest in our ship and came onboard to see for themselves what it was all about. They came in groups with each group having a person speaking English. I found them kind of arrogant and not very friendly.

The container revolution in Japan was well under way with container cranes being installed on the piers. Japan was also manufacturing container cranes, exporting them around the world, and the Japanese shipyard had others from all over the world building containerships.

The customs in Kobe was using American ships to train new customs officers. There would be up to a dozen custom officers coming aboard after arrival. They asked me to go with them before they entered the crew quarters.

The average age on the ship was mid-fifties, and I was surprised to see the amount of pills some of the crew numbers had in their medicine cabinets. Customs spent a lot of time studying the pills people had in their cabinets, but we always passed the inspections.

In the beginning we always stayed two nights in Yokohama loading for the US. The first evening after visiting my old friends at the Copenhagen Bar in China town, I took a taxi back to the ship.

The driver was a man in his mid-fifties who didn't speak a word of English, nor did he have a clue as to where I wanted to go. As we approached the port area and came inside a container yard, I asked him to stop and let me out to walk down to the water's edge to see if my ship was anywhere in sight.

As I walked away from the cab, I heard the engine start up. I turned and saw the cab heading directly toward me. I managed to jump to the side and away from him. He turned the car around and tried to run me down again.

By good luck the space between the rows of the containers was too narrow for the car to drive in between. He jumped out of the car and started chasing me on foot, but I outran him and made it back to the ship without any problem.

The next morning around 10 a.m. the captain told me somebody at the Sea Land office who wished to see me. When I walked into the office, I was surprised to see the taxi driver with the harbor police and the owner of the Taxi Company.

They started out asking me if I recognized the taxi driver, which I did. Then they asked me what happened last night after I got out of the cab. I told them my side of the story, which was the same as the taxi driver had told them.

He had given the Police a written statement saying that when I walked away from the cab, he was afraid I was trying to skip paying the cab fare and got so upset he was willing to run me down and kill me. Guess he was still fighting WWII.

The Police asked me if I wished to file charges against him. The owner of the company was very nervous about the whole thing. I kind of felt sorry for the taxi driver. After all, he was honest about the whole thing, and I had no right to blame him for not being able to speak English, just like I didn't speak Japanese even though I had spent a lot of time in Japan, and after all I was in his country. Therefore I told them no. When I offered to pay the cab fare, the owner of the company said it was not necessary. He also gave me his business card and offered me free Taxi service whenever I was in Yokohama.

After walking around with the hernia for four months, it was time to get off and check in at the Marine Hospital in San Francisco. After the operation, I was told to walk around as much as possible. I met several old shipmates in the hospital with various problems.

One day I walked into a room where two men were lying in bed. One was a tug boat engineer who was nothing but skin and bone and was told to gain weight before his operation. Next to him was a USCG man who was overweight and had his stomach tubes tied to lose weight. Guess life is not always fair.

LABOR DISPUTE

In 1973 a labor dispute came up between the MM&P and Sea Land over the fly-out jobs dispatched to the Asian shuttle ships. In the new contract, the company had the right to select their own Master and Chief Mate; all other replacements had to come off the rotary shipping board from the union hall for six month assignments. The contract also said that all fly-out jobs must come off the shipping board. The company said it was not meant to be for the Master and Chief Mate. The union said that it meant everybody except the Master. The company disagreed and took the dispute to arbitration. Sea Land was operating eight shuttle ships under the American flag in Asia. The chief mates on those ships were notified that they would not be relieved for vacation before the dispute was settled The Chief Mate on the SS San Pedro had been there for four months due to get off to attend school in Florida, and decided to walk off the ship in Yokohama and fly home.

I was on the Sea Land select chief mate list but that didn't always guaranty a job when I was ready to ship. The MM&P allowed us to register on the open board which made it possible for me to throw in my shipping card for other jobs. If Sea Land had a job for me I had to change my shipping card to company select 24 hours before the job was posted.

The San Pedro was now sailing short and the company gave in and ordered a chief mate off the board. I was looking for a job and knew about the situation. When the job came up I threw in my shipping card and got it.

My suitcase was packed, passport up to date. After passing the physical, I rushed up to the Philippines Consulate to get a visa to enter as a seaman. Shortly thereafter I was on my way to Manila.

I stayed in a Hotel in Manila overnight waiting for the ship's arrival. Next morning, sitting at the Hotel's restaurant having breakfast, I saw the biggest rat I have ever seen walking across the restaurant floor, which kind of made me lose my appetite. I called the waiter and told him. He looked at me and said, "Yes, we have rats."

The San Pedro was another C-4 J C and in very good shape with excellent cranes and a crew of 41. The unlicensed deck department had been there for years, most of them lived in Asia shipping out of Yokohama. The cooks were outstanding. Our schedule was Japan, Korea, Okinawa Philippines, later Hong Kong, Subic Bay, Manila or Hong Kong, Singapore, Bangkok.

At that time Singapore did not have a container port. Sea Land leased a pier and space in Sembawang 40 miles north of Singapore, offering door to door service through the Island of Singapore and Malaysia. Bangkok was the same, no container terminals. Sea Land used the U.S. military piers in Sattahip 112 miles south of Bangkok, offering door to door service throughout Thailand, and to the U.S. military.

Reefers coming out of Bangkok were a headache and took a lot of attention. They had often been on the road for hours by the time they reached Sattahip. The reefer containers were able to run on gas when in transit on the road, but the big question was always, did they?

It was very important to plug them into the ship's power making sure the temperature went down to the required degrees right away.

Once we loaded a reefer for Los Angeles via Hong Kong which manifested dry fish at+ 29 degrees. I had never heard of dry fish being carried at +29. I broke the SL seal, opened the container and found it loaded with frozen Shrimp which are carried at -5. I didn't wait for instructions, just lowered the temperature to -5, and made out an exception.

The Bosun was an old timer who had spent his entire life at sea. He was a former National Maritime Union (NMU) goon from the 1930s. He was a walking library when it came to labor and union history. I always enjoyed sitting down talking to him. The deck department wanted to get as much time off in ports as possible. I made a deal with them that benefited everybody. In Pusan Korea, and in Manila, Philippines, I hired shore labor to paint and clean when the crew was off in Pusan. I had the ship's hull, entire amidships house and smoke stack painted for $300. To pay for the work, the sailors added $300 on their overtime sheet, and turned the money over to me to pay the labor bill. In addition I had them add the amount to their OT sheet as working OT out at sea. A good deal for everybody, the ship always shined and the sailors had all the time off they wanted. They still made the same amount of money, and the company saved money.

On arrival before entering port, the Bosun and I cleared the anchors taking the lashing off getting them ready to drop in an emergency. We were always notified before arrival which side to the dock.

If starboard side to the dock as safety precaution we would lower the port anchor to the water's edge before approaching, making sure it would run out quickly if needed.

Communication between the bow and the Captain on the bridge was done by telephone, which didn't always work due to moisture inside the box where the telephone was stowed.

In addition we used Walkie - Talkies the size of a brick and not reliable either. The battery always seemed to be down when it was needed most. In some ports our conversations were blocked by taxi drivers talking to the dispatcher or someone placing an order at a drive-in restaurant.

Harbor pilots worked on many different types of ships and sometimes forgot that a steam powered vessel doesn't have the same backing power as a diesel ship. Twice I had to make a quick decision on my own and let the anchors go to avoid a disaster.

On a clear, calm sunny day in Sembawang when approaching the berth, the pilot had way too much speed on when trying to make a turn. By the time he ordered the engine on full astern we were close and getting closer fast to a big empty tanker laying at a repair yard. Several men were hanging over the side painting the tanker hull, all watching us approach fast. They dropped the paint in the water, climbed onboard the tanker and ran. I called the bridge to inform them we would not swing clear and waited for instruction to let the anchor go. No response.

I gave the bosun the order to drop the port anchor two shots (180 feet of chain in the water.) Thanks to having good brake ban, the anchor held, turning us away from the tanker and avoiding hitting it.

Later, on a rainy and windy night in Hong Kong approaching our berth between two Sea Land ships, the pilot was coming in way too fast and unable to stop by coming full astern. I tried unsuccessfully to make contact with the captain on the bridge, however it was obvious something had to be done to avoid a disaster, and I made a decision to drop both anchors, which turned out to be the right decision. A few weeks later out at sea I met the Captain taking a walk around the main deck. I suggested that when he walked by the anchor winch to make sure to tip his hat twice. He agreed.

I always tried to make friends with the chief cook, praising him when doing something extra, or letting him know if he needed any repairs or items from deck department, just let me know. On this ship, I shared the table in the mess hall with the Captain and Chief Engineer. The dinner menu on Sunday and Thursday usually included steak or prime rib. I could not help but notice that my steak or cut of beef was larger and better than anyone elses. One night the Captain told the order to the server to get him a rare steak, "and by the way tell the cook it's for the Chief Mate."

After six months I went home on vacation, returned again for another six months, and was happy to see most of the unlicensed crew was still there.

Laying alongside the Sea Land terminal in Yokohama, a Sea Land SL-7 came in to tie-up behind us. I never found out why, but after she was all tied up, she moved ahead and knocked off our flag pole and did some damage to our permanent wooden awnings. However, the big question was did she do any damage under the water line to our rudder and propeller? A diver was hired to inspect our propeller and rudder and the bulb on the SL-7. No damage was found.

The chief Engineer tested and operated our rudder, and turning the propeller he found all in apparent good order. The trouble started the following day sailing out of Yokohama. In the beginning maneuvering on slow speed was no problem, but as we increased speed the vessel started to shake followed by a grinding sound coming from the propeller shaft. The ship vibrated like a washing machine on spin cycle. The company hired various experts to ride the ship to come up with a solution, but they never did. Later we returned to San Francisco for dry docking to correct the problem.

After dry-docking we entered the Inter Coastal trade sailing between Oakland-Long Beach through the Panama Canal to Elizabeth, New Jersey, and back.

While in New Jersey I experienced something I often think about. At the time all, new crew members had to sign on in front of the

U.S. shipping commissioner, and in this case he was located in lower Manhattan.

Sea Land had made arrangements for a Taxi to pick up the Captain at 0700 and drive him to the Custom House in Manhattan with the ships articles to sign on two new crew members and have them return with him. The Captain didn't feel like making the trip and asked me to go.

The security guard at the gate called me in the morning saying a Taxi was waiting for me.

I jumped in the back seat of the cab, and the lady driver asked me, "Before I turn the meter on, do you have any problem driving with a female driver?" As we drove off she told me that a few weeks earlier she had been down to pick up a Captain from another Sea Land ship and he refused to ride with a female driver.

"San Pedro" was a good ship and after a great year, my finances were back in good shape which allowed me to purchase a nice piece of income property in the City by the Bay.

MY LAST LABOR DAY PARADE

When I signed up to participate in the 1974 Labor Day Parade in San Francisco, I didn't know it would be my last. I asked my seventeen year old son, Karl, to come along, telling him it would be fun and a great experience. I was shocked when he told me "HELL NO," and don't you go either, making a fool of yourself. Can't you see you will be walking up Market Street with the same guys who have been crossing your picket line, taking your jobs away? When you get to the city hall, politicians will be making political speeches promising you the world and giving you nothing. The unions will be passing out beer and hot dogs. It is nothing but a photo op for the politicians & the union officials. Don't go"

Labor Day came and as I was walking up Market Street with my MM&P colleagues I took a good look at the other unions participating in the parade. The group ahead of me was the Marine Engineer (MEBA) who a year earlier had walked through our picket line and sailed the Prudential Line Lash ships using their own deck officer. Had it not been for the longshoremen in New Orleans, we would have lost those jobs forever.

The groups behind me was the Seafarers International Union (SIU) and the American Maritime Officers Union (AMO) also knowing as MEBA district 2, both known for undercutting everybody.

The parade ended in front of city hall, where we were met by a few politicians making politically speeches. Beer and hot dogs were passed around, lots of pictures taken just like Karl had said, but how did he know that? After all he had never been out in the work force, and I had always spoken highly of the unions and the health plan MM&P provided for us, and I never sailed on a non-union ship.

It made me look back thinking of my past union experience and the politics involved, starting with all the union papers I read over the years. On the front page would be a picture of some politician, usually a Democrat standing with his fists up in the air in support of a strong US merchant marine and the Jones act. In the meantime we went from 2200 ships down to less than 400, half of them government-owned laying idle in the Ready Reserve Fleet (RRF). It also made me think that politicians don't buy ships, Corporations and private investors buy ships hoping to make a profit on their investment.

Keystone Shipping, Marine Transport Line, Maritime Overseas and Moore McCormack Bulk, who between them operated 54 tankers, using MM&P licensed Deck Officers, and MEBA for the licensed Engineers, and NMU/SIU for the unlicensed crew. A few years later when the MM&P contracts came up for renewal, the companies decided to gamble the safety of their vessels and crews by hiring all new non-union Deck officers, rather than continue to provide union scale wages and benefit to the masters and mates who had served them well and faithfully for years.

MM&P sent out a message to all involved telling the members to remain on the ships to protect their jobs, which led to some of the Masters and Mates being taken off their ships in handcuffs by the U.S. Marshall while the other unions MEBA, NMU and SIU remained on the ships, and did not support us.

I stood in several picket lines in the Bay Area watching members from
other unions drive through my picket line. One guy even gave me the finger.

I happened to hear a SIU union official telling their members that the strike was about getting rid of the fat cats, meaning the MM&P, and by getting rid of them it would benefit others who were willing to work for less. You have to wonder how a man like that could become a union official if he had not been the President's nephew. On the bright side, the same guy is still in jail for child molestation, and child pornography.

"SS Gateway City" the ship there changed ocean shipping for ever

In late 1957 when sailing as an Able-Bodied Seaman on the "S.S. John Weyerhaeuser", a WW II liberty ship docked in Port Newark discharging lumber piece by piece from the Pacific Northwest, I watched "S.S. Gateway City," the world's first fully cellular containership come in and dock across the water way from us. When she was all fast, a handful of longshoremen started discharging and loading containers using the ship's cranes. 12 hours later she left with a full load. The "S.S. Gateway City" became the big talk around the coffee and dinner table on our ship. Some said it would never work because the longshoremen's union would give them a hard time and run them out of business. Others said containerized shipping was just a fad with no real future. They were all wrong.

She made her maiden voyage on October 4th 1957 the same day the Russians sent the first sputnik into orbit which got a lot more publicity. She was built as a C-2 dry cargo ship for Waterman Steamship in 1943 by Gulf Shipbuilding Corp, Chickasaw, Alabama, and named the "SS Iberville." The U.S. Navy purchased the vessel before she was launched, and converted her into an APA-52 attack transport vessel sailing under the name the "USS Sumter." She received six battle stars for her service in the Pacific during WW II.

In 1946 the Navy returned the vessel to the US Maritime Commission who sold it back to Waterman Steamship Company where she sailed under its original name her "SS Iberville" from 1946-56.

Among seafarers she was known as a Waterman C-2. The difference between a Waterman C-2 and a standard maritime commission C-2 cargo vessel was that the amidships structure was rounded and looking more attractive, and the interior was nicer.

The cargo and mooring winches were steam, preferred in the lumber trade, and the unlicensed deck and Engine department quarters where aft on the fan tail.

Twenty years later I joined her in Hong Kong as Chief Mate. She looked old, rusty, and tired. She came out to Vietnam to carry military cargo up and down the coast during the war. When the war ended she stayed in Asia and became a shuttle ship building up a new inter-Asia trade for Sea Land at the same time working as a feeder ship supporting the line hauling ships coming from California.

The hull dimensions after the conversion were 450 x 72 x 25 and a total of 9,014 GRT capable of carrying 226, 35 x 8 x 8 foot fully loaded containers. 35 foot containers were the maximum size allowed on the freeways in some states. The ship's engine, the 6000 HP General Electric drive turbine gave her a speed of 16.5 knots

The sponsons added on each side of the hull gave her nine feet more beam, which improved her cargo capacity and stability.

The two ship cranes were able to move freely on rail tracks welded on top of heavy steel beams next to the cargo hatches. Each crane was powered by a diesel engine capable of lifting 25 L/T.

When working cargo, the crane driver sat in a cap well above decks with a clear view of the length of his track in front of him. He also had an electrical panel with instruments giving him full control of the crane. A thirty-five foot spreader-bar was connected to four runners (wires) which were connected to a self-stowing drums controlled by the driver to lower or hoist the container. The spreader-bar had four mechanical cones and flippers on each corner.

After the first row of containers was discharged, the ship could be loaded simultaneously. Each time a crane traveled to the dock with a load to a waiting chassis, it would pick up an outgoing container and place it in an empty cell. Under normal operations each crane would load and unload 15-18 containers per hour, which could cut the total port time down to 10-12 hours. The containers below decks were carefully lowered inside a heavy steel cell guide stacked four high. The cell guide kept them well secured.

On deck, the containers were stacked two-high secured with twist locks, wires and turnbuckles. When the cargo operation was complete, the ship's crew moved the crane to its stowing position forward and aft of the amidships house, with the arms lowered against the crane and secured with chain. Heavy pad-eyes were welded to the main deck connected to special designed turnbuckles to the cranes. Out at sea in bad weather the turnbuckles were tightened every four to six hours.

It was a well-designed operation all around for its time, but twenty years of wear and tear was taking its toll. It was a full time job to keep the cranes working, basically putting a Band-Aid on top of another Band-Aid. We carried two unlicensed crane electricians, who, in addition to keeping the cranes running, also worked in the engine room, plugged and unplugged reefer containers. We used our own cranes in every port except Hong Kong. The deck department maintained the cranes, and the engine department did all the repairs.

The ship was managed by Sea Land Oakland office with a total crew of 41. The Deck and Engine Officer where dispatched out of San Francisco from for a four to six month period. The unlicensed crew was China coasters shipping out of the Seafarers International Union halls in Yokohama and San Francisco.

A sailor known as a China Coaster is a man who likes the Orient and the Asian way of living. He is often married to an Oriental and lives somewhere in Asia. I enjoyed sailing with them

Our schedule (a) Hong Kong, Subic Bay, Manila, Hong Kong a 7 days turn around. (b) Hong Kong, Singapore, Bangkok Hong Kong a 14 days turn around.

We stayed 24-30 hours in each port except in Hong Kong where the Sea Land Kwai-Chung terminal had two ships alongside the dock working cargo 24/7 using shore cranes. When one ship pulled out, another slid in behind. Containers were stacked everywhere in the yard, and in addition to handling our own ships they also did stevedoring work for other companies and operated the largest and most efficient freight consolidation center in Asia. Sea Land developed a round garage type stowage facility where the containers and chassis were handy to get to, a great system which was copied later by the Hong Kong Port Authority.

My job as Chief Mate was the same as on any other Sea Land ship, in charge of the vessel maintenance, cargo, safety equipment, medical, clerical work and dealing with port officials.

Since this was before PCs or Xerox machines, onboard ship my only tools were a typewriter and plenty of whiteout. The cargo office in Hong Kong was open 24/7 and I took advantage of using the Xerox machines making the required copies in each port for the voyage. In addition to paper work, it took 3-4 cartons of cigarettes for a speedy clearance in the Philippines, and in Bangkok six cartons and a box of Washington State apples.

Every sixty days we received stores in Hong Kong brought out from Oakland on the SL-7. It came in three containers, frozen, chilled and dry, loaded onboard into number four hatch and emptied out at sea by the ship's crew. The Steward Department worked hard to maintain the S I U standard and we were well feed.

The Chief Engineer was an unforgettable character and a pain in the ass. He walked around in a white builder suit with special made Sea Land logos all over it, like he was Mr. Sea Land himself. He liked to tell anybody willing to listen that without him and his supervision the ship would not move because the whole Engine department were a bunch of useless idiots unable to fix or repair anything and therefore he had to do it himself.

It may seem strange, but a ship's Chief Engineer was not supposed to work with tools without being paid overtime and therefore he was the highest paid man on the ship.

The shipping articles were broken every 12 months in Hong Kong and each crew member had to sign off the foreign article and receive a discharge and money due to him in cash or check, his choice. If you wanted to get off you received an Airline ticket back to your port of engagement. If you wished to stay on you went to another table and signed on the new shipping article as required by law.

The way the Sea Land system worked at the time was that everybody's overtime sheet was turned into the Captain from each department and approved by him. After that he made up a message with everybody's total hours due, and money advanced against his wages and wired the information to the Pay Master in Oakland who then made up the final payroll sending it to Hong Kong.

When the captain checked the Chief Engineer's overtime sheet which read like a novel, he called him up to his office and told him, "I will give you two choices. Go down and rewrite your overtime sheet and come up with $ 10,000 less, or I will dispute your pay-off and you can take it up with the union. The Chief Engineer decided to rewrite it.

Unfortunately for me I had to sit at the same table in the mess hall during meal hour listen to all his bull shit stories. He told me he was a member of the Yacht Club in Manila where he met all the important politicians and business people from around the Philippines, and they often asked him for advice.

One trip in Manila I made a deal with one of the local shore watchmen to follow him ashore to see where he went and stayed. The following day I got a full report. The watchman had followed him by taxi to some flea bitten Hotel where he was shacking up with a prostitute. He followed them to a bar where he had the opportunity to talk to the woman who told him she had only known him for a short period.

It was a big relief for everybody, especially the Engine department, when he finally got off and a new chief engineer came onboard, but guess what? We kind of missed him because now we didn't have anybody to be mad at.

With all the containers stacked in the yard to be shipped around the world, mistakes happen. One trip two hours out of Hong Kong toward Manila the Captain received a message from the Hong Kong cargo office to return to Hong Kong to unload some containers loaded by a mistake. It happened the cargo belonged to a new important customer, and a decision was made to correct the mistake at any cost,

We had several rough rides out in the South China Sea. One trip between Bangkok and Hong Kong we ran into a typhoon moving through the South China Sea and were forced to stay hove-to for a day and a half, rolling and pitching heavily in rough seas.

The Captain sent in an ETA indicating that we would be two days late arriving in Hong Kong. Shortly thereafter he received a nasty message from the Port Captain demanding an explanation why we would be two days late and to see him in his office with the deck and engine logs on arrival. When we finally arrived without any damage to the ship or cargo we never heard a word from the Port Captain's office.

Guess he must have read the newspaper and learned that several ships were lost in the South China Sea.

Later that same Port Captain got mad at me for posting the final schedule on the bulletin board in the crew mess hall. There was a rumor going around that the "Gateway City" together with five other American flag feeder ships were to be sold for scrap and replaced by new Korean ships and Korean crews.

We had arrived in Hong Kong early in the morning. I went to the cargo office to get a cargo plan for the next voyage and to do my clerical work using their Xerox machine. The cargo office always had an up to date schedule posted on their bulletin board which I used to copy and post onboard ship. When I picked up the latest schedule hot off the wire I can't say I was shocked when I read that the Gate

Way City (GW) was making her final voyage to Singapore, Bangkok, returning to Hong Kong for scrap.

When I went back onboard I gave a copy of the schedule to the Captain and Chief Engineer and posted a copy in the crew mess hall, as always.

At 0730 the Port Captain came onboard to have breakfast with us as he often did. The Sailor at the Gangway greeted him saying, "You sure did us in this time" The Port Captain asked what he was talking about. The sailor told him he was referring to the ship being scrapped in two weeks. The Port Captain assured him there was nothing behind all those rumors.

The Sailor took him into the mess hall and showed him the schedule. The Port Captain blew his stack and asked who had posted this. "The Chief Mate did." He got very angry and told him to go get that fucking Square head down here right away. When I entered the crew mess hall he was standing there with the schedule in hand asking where I got it from. I told him I picked it up at the cargo office which I did every trip. He got madder and madder and told me that I had no fucking business posting crap like this, and stormed off the ship. Guess he went back to the office to check his latest correspondence.

It was with mixed feelings that I posted the sailing board for the last time

Before sailing Bangkok for the last time I had the longshoremen load two empty containers on number one cargo hatch with doors facing forward next to the ship's stores room. We had three full work days preparing for the layup, taking inventory and moving all useable items out of the store rooms and into empty containers, items like new mooring lines, wires, tools and paint which could be used on other Sea Land ships.

The Sea Land's office in Oakland requested to have the ship's binnacle shipped to them. (A binnacle is a wooden stand in which the magnetic compass is mounted on the flying bridge above the wheel house). The Captain was not interested in taking any mementos home from the ship, but told me to take whatever I wanted before it all disappeared. I am now donating them to the Gulf Quest Museum in Mobile Alabama.

Vietnamese boat people

The second day out at 1640 hours in Latitude 07.36 N – Longitude 106.48 E we spotted a boat at a distance waving a large white flag heading directly toward us. We stopped to let the boat come alongside. As we expected, it was full of Vietnamese refugees. The Captain told me to lower the gangway and go down and tell them they could have all the food, water, and fuel oil they needed, but we could not take them onboard.

All eyes were on me when I entered the boat with men, women and children jammed in a small space with unsanitary conditions. The spokesman, Nguyen, a 32 year old educated man who spoke very good English, told me they had been sailing around for five days, dodging the Thai fishermen known for robbing refugees of everything they owned and raping the women. They were completely out of water and food. He also told me that several large ships had passed them by.

I went back onboard and told the captain that we could not leave them there, and he agreed. He told me to take charge and get them onboard one at the time, and get their names, passport numbers or whatever kind of ID they had. I asked Nguyen and one more to come up first to help me get the necessary information from each one. When everybody was safely onboard the tally, showed 22 men, 11 women, and 18 children a total of 51.

We had no choice but to let the boat drift away hoping it would sink or be picked up by some fishermen to avoid being a danger to other vessels. If I understood correctly, each family had paid $2000 in gold for that old rotten boat, not seaworthy for any kind of journey.

After a good meal and a chance to shower, the women and children were given the spare rooms, and the men slept in empty containers on deck. Next morning the men helped us with the work we had to do before arrival. One of them was good behind the typewriter, typing all the refuge's names making it very formal, and also typing up the inventory list for items going ashore in Hong Kong.

Arriving in Hong Kong, the port authority kept us at the Quarantine anchorage for 24 hours before allowing us to dock at our terminal in Kwai Chung. Sea Land had made arrangements to transport the refuges by bus to the refugee camp in downtown Kowloon where they would be kept for several years before Red cross gave them an opportunity to settle in various parts of the world. I often wonder what happened to them and where they are today. I hope they are all living happily, and I would love to hear from them some day! I passed the pictures and names around in the Vietnamese community here in Seattle, but so far no luck. My dentist and her parents were among some of the last ones getting out of Saigon by helicopter. My local barber shop is run by two Vietnamese sisters who were boat people and made it to Indonesia where they stayed in camp for two years before coming here.

After the cargo was discharged and everybody was paid off and issued airline tickets to the port of engagement or cash in lieu thereof, a wrecking gang came aboard and killed the plant and towed her away to her final resting place. It is fitting that a ship like the "SS Gateway City" on her final journey to the graveyard became the instrument of new life rescuing the Vietnamese boat people and giving adults and children a chance for new life.

The "SS Gateway City" in war and peace time did a great service to our nation and the world which should never be forgotten. The Economist May 18th 2013 wrote that the containers have been more important for globalization than free trade.

SS RAPHAEL SEMMES

The Gateway City being old and tired looked like a yacht in comparison to her sister ship SS Raphael Semmes. When I came aboard in Hong Kong, the captain told me to make sure the not under command signals, which were two all-around red lights, by night, and two black balls in a vertical line by day, were they would best be seen ready at all times when out at sea. The chief engineer sleep in his lazy boy chair fully dress and ready to run below, when called.

Thanks to radar, we were one step ahead of Columbus when he crossed the Atlantic on the Santa Maria. All our navigation was done by celestial navigation when available. During the monsoon season with heavy rain and overcast skies, everything was done by dead reckoning (DR) where you advance a previous known position on the course line to estimate speed, allowing for current and wind direction.

The first time I went down to the engine room I stopped half way down. The steam and smell of oil was everywhere. The fire and water tender (FWT), all china coasters didn't seem to mind it. They had been there for years.

On one trip a new second engineer came out from San Francisco and decided to check out the engine room before signing on. Guess he didn't like what he saw because he turned right around and went home. I never even got his name.

We had a lot of crane problems, mostly caused by wreckless and careless longshoremen in Taiwan and the Philippines. One trip in

Keelung, Taiwan during daylight hours the driver was hoisting a loaded container from # 4 lower hull using excessive speed which made the container move violently from side to side with a fast upward movement.

By the time the limit switch kicked in, the damage was already done. All four runners parted and the container and spreader-bar fell back down into the lower hatch standing on one end.

A floating crane came alongside and hoisted the container out of the hatch and reach across the ship to place it on the dock, where the deck department replaced the broken wire and repaired the damage to the spreader-bar.

To make things worse, a typhoon was moving toward Taiwan. The port authority notified us that the port would close at 2200, and we had to be out of the harbor by then or stay alongside the dock. Talk about bad luck. The engineer had one boiler off line for repairs, and they might not be able to get back on the line for a 2200 sailing.

I told the Bosun to get all the spare mooring lines out and have them ready before the typhoon hit, just in case we didn't get out.

Bad news travels fast. The Captain of an American President Line ship lying behind us came over asking if we needed any help or spare parts or extra mooring lines. He was getting underway at 1800. I was very impressed with his concern and thanked him for his offer, but I felt we were okay with what we had onboard.

Rain and wind picked up considerably as the day went by. Large swells entered the harbor making the ship pitch and roll alongside the dock, slowing down the cargo operation. By good luck we finished the cargo operation at 2100. The chief engineer informed the captain that he would not be able to get both boilers on line before sailing, which meant sailing on one boiler on a reduced speed.

Shortly after 2100 when we started taking in the mooring lines to get underway, we faced another problem, not enough steam to run both winches at the same time.

We decided to take in all the mooring lines aft first to assure the rudder and propeller were clear and ready, and to keep one tug boat aft to keep us alongside the dock.

A powerful tugboat was made fast forward to pull us away from the dock and turn us around against the wind. Even though it was a brand new mooring line it parted, and the ship started to swing back toward the dock. By good luck the tug managed to get around on the starboard bow and push us away from the dock avoiding a disaster. Finally when the vessel was turned around and the pilot was off, we headed for the breakwater on 45 RPM which was all the speed the engine could do on one boiler. The seas started coming over the bow and the bosun and I ducked behind the anchor winch, watching for what seemed to be forever before we cleared the breakwater and harbor. It was a big relief when we cleared and entered the East China Sea with room to maneuver.

It was a long slow and rough ride across the Taiwan Straits to Hong Kong. As we approached the pilot station, I happened to see a large flash in the sky not far away. Shortly thereafter we saw a lot of debris falling from the sky into the water. As we came closer we found a lot of cardboard boxes, and three dead men floating in the water. We stopped the ship and called MARDEP, the Hong Kong Marine Department, and told them what we had seen. Soon several rescue boats came out and picked up the dead bodies. Later we were interviewed by the Kai Tak Airport investigators who told us it was a British cargo plane that had exploded in front of our eyes. The plane had caught fire in one engine during takeoff. The pilot decided to get out over the water and dump the fuel before making an emergency landing, but it failed. The South China newspaper mentions the "Raphael Semmes" as the first ship on the scene.

The next day we sailed out of Hong Kong for Singapore and Bangkok with a big load of cargo including new Sea Land chassis shipped out from the States to be used in Singapore and Malaysia for the fast growing business there.

Unfortunately, we didn't get very far before the engine broke down. After drifting for several hours the engineers managed to get us moving again with just enough speed to make steerage heading back to Hong Kong. The chief engineer convinced the company that we would have to switch from temporary to permanent repairs, which would include dry-docking.

The cargo was discharged and transferred to a charter ship. Two tug boats towed us from the Kwai-Chung Terminal to the ship yard where we entered dry-dock right away. It would be a two week repair job. Since we had power and water from shore we all stayed onboard. Seven days later with the engine all taken apart, Sea Land scheduling decided they needed the ship. We were towed back to Kwai-Chung-Terminal where we loaded containers for Singapore and Bangkok.

When the cargo operation was complete we were towed out to anchorage to finish the repair work before sailing. I was suspicious and wondering about the repair job because it took a half hour to get the anchor up due to lack of steam.

While in the shipyard a huge wild house cat came onboard and made his home on the fore-deck. We were never able to get close to him. We put out food and water for him. I had seen him ashore in Subic Bay once, but he returned before sailing, except this one trip he didn't make it back. I saw him sitting on the dock looking at the ship as we were pulling away. I felt sad for him.

One trip steaming up the Mekong river to Bangkok, we were boarded by pirates who came alongside in a speed boat, climbed onboard and ran for a container on # 2 hatch port side. They broke the lock and seal, opened the container, and stole a bunch of Japanese made speed bikes, dumped them into the boat and disappeared. I often wondered if it was a coincidence, or if they knew what was in that container.

The Mekong River was very dirty and polluted. There were always a lot of small boats coming alongside the ship, selling food, tea and fruit to the Longshoremen. The cooking was done on the boats and handed up to the workers. Later the dirty plates were washed in the river water, the same water people up stream would take a dump in. In addition to selling food they also sold tea and soft drinks served in small plastic bags.

When the bag was empty it was dumped into the river where it would float for a while before it got caught on the screen to the vessels water intake below the water line. Before sailing it became necessary to hire a diver to clean the screen for plastic bags.

One of the AB's got caught in Bangkok buying marijuana and ended up in jail. The bail was set for $500. The captain, against everybody's advice, bailed him out. Since he was not allowed to come back to Thailand anymore he had to get off in Hong Kong and fly home. With no money on the books the Captain was out the $500.

Big Al, the Bosun, was a longtime friend and my right hand man. I don't know what I would have done without him. He was always there and ready to go to work, rain or shine, day or night. The only place he went ashore was in Hong Kong where he would go across the street to the Seamen Club and drink beer. He always came back onboard two hours before sailing, stopping by and checking if there were any special instructions before securing the ship for sea.

I was on the Bridge undocking, sailing out of Hong Kong and after the last line was gone, and the tug boats were pulling us away from the dock, the second mate called me on the walkie-talkie from the bow asking me if I knew the bosun was sitting down on the dock.

Looking through the binoculars, I saw Al sitting on a bollard smoking a cigar. I asked the captain to get the pilot to have the tugs push us back alongside the dock. I ran down on the main deck and lowered a Jacobs's ladder over the side to get down on the dock. When I asked Al what happened, he told me he was mad at the Day-man who he had given a special job to do. It was not done, and he was afraid he would beat him up. Big Al was already accused of killing a man in a bar fight in San Francisco, and he didn't want any more trouble and would rather jump ship.

I told him, "I am not sailing without you," and that I would get rid of the day-man in Manila. I told him, "Come back onboard and I will lock you up for the night, and tomorrow when you're sober we will come up with a solution." It worked and he followed me onboard.

When I came back up on the bridge I told the captain everything was taken care off, he never asked me what the problem was. Guess he had a lot of faith in me.

A few days later, in the middle of undocking in Subic Bay sailing for Manila, the same day-man walked off the bow and went back on the stern. He took his shoes off, jumped overboard and swam ashore. He came onboard in Manila the following day to pick up his gear and money due, problem solved.

Delayed sailing was mostly caused by cargo coming late. Each department had its own delegate representing them. It was usually a job nobody wanted, and the one who got stuck with the job was not always the brightest guy in the bunch.

The deck delegate was an AB named Harry, a heavy drinker. He looked very respectable going ashore at each port carrying an umbrella, but looked like an unmade bed when returning. One trip in Sembawang/Singapore the cargo was late, and the sailing time had to be moved back. Since I didn't know how late it would be, I told the bosun to have the sailors stand by.

Guess Harry wanted to go back ashore because he came up to my office telling me that I was not allowed to keep them onboard without changing the sailing board. I explained to him how the system and union contract worked, but he was not listening. Since he didn't go away, I finally told him, "Harry, I am not allowed to punch you in the nose onboard the ship, but come down on the dock and tell me all that crap again." Half way down the gangway he changed his mind, and went back onboard in front of the whole deck department watching. Harry was no longer the deck delegate.

Guess the word was out around the union hall that the Raphael Semmes was also on her last leg and would soon be scrapped, because when the steward got off, it took over a month to get a new steward. Normally the chief cook would take over the job getting double salary but, in this case it didn't work because he was unable to read or write.

I told the cooks I would help them and do the Steward work and they would split the steward salary as per union contract. I started out by copying the old menus. Later I added my own favorite meals, always checking with the cook first before typing up the menus, or ordering fresh provisions. I took a complete inventory, kept the steward departments overtime sheets up to date. It was a fun experience, and it worked for everybody.

When the foreign article was broken and each man was paid off in front of the U.S. Consul in Hong Kong, my time was up and my replacement was already there.

Big Al was also getting off and decided to fly home with me. He took his entire payoff in cash which had me worried.

Shortly after we checked in at the Mariner Club downtown Kowloon, I went to the bar where Big Al was sitting buying drinks for everybody and giving money away. I managed to get the money away from him except for a few hundred dollars.

I sealed his money in an envelope and asked the manager to keep it in his safe, and not to give him any cash unless I was there. It took me two days to get him away from the bar and on a plane for San Francisco.

Sadly enough that was the end of the American flag shuttle ships which were replaced by new ships flying the Korean flag, and crewed by Koreans

SEA-LAND
IN
ALASKA

December 16,1964, the Sea land vessel SS Anchorage broke the ice, so to speak, by making her historic Cook Inlet passage unescorted by an icebreaker, which was the beginning of year round service to the port of Anchorage, and the beginning of door -to -door trucking service throughout Alaska, which benefited the Alaskan consumers tremendously.

In February 1979 I was asked to fly to Seattle and make a ten day medical relief on the SS Portland. The ship was docked at the Sea Land terminal in West Seattle, loading containers for Anchorage,

Alaska. The ship was very much like the other Sea Land converted C-4 except she was still the original size, 523 ft. long, 72 ft. beam, and now capable of carrying 366-35 foot containers. She had heavy steel reinforced on the bow and along the water line to better stand up to the ice in Cook Inlet.

We had a rough ride heading north past Vancouver and Queen Charlotte Island through the Gulf of Alaska, rolling and pitching all the way. I went out on deck twice a day to check the reefers. Otherwise we stayed indoors. An Alaska license is required when transiting Cook Inlet. I was used the pilot coming onboard by boat, but in this case he came onboard by helicopter from Kenai, half way up the Cook Inlet. We had a small landing pad aft on top of the deck house extending out over the fantail. Each corner of the pad had a white light. The way it was explained to me sounded very exciting, like something out of a John Wayne movie. However, the excitement disappeared quickly when I was called out at 0300 in a cold windy snow storm to stand by the landing pad with a Walkie-Talkie to keep the captain informed about the helicopter and pilot coming onboard. Visibility was no more than forty-fifty feet, drift ice banging against the ship's hull. The helicopter had a hard time spotting the ship, circled twice before setting down on the small landing pad. When the pilot stepped off the helicopter with his bag, I thought he must need a job real bad.

Most of the ice in Cook Inlet remains broken because of the large tidal range and wind variation which creates a continuously changing distribution of flow and thickness of the ice. The closer we got to the dock the heavier the ice pack.

Under normal conditions, preparing for docking didn't take more than a half hour, but in this case we had to knock off the ice covering the forward winch before operating it to bring up the mooring lines from below decks. We crossed the shoal at Fire Island on a flood with four feet of water under the keel.

Docking on a flood meant port side too. We had to dock against the current, getting a spring line out forward and using the engine to keep the bow against the dock to stop the ice from moving between the ship and dock. All this while waiting for the ice already there to drift away, which took three hours from the first line to all fast.

There can be up to a twenty eight foot tide twice a day which meant the ship would be high above the dock with the gangway straight up and down. The mooring lines had to be tended at all the time. The longshoremen used a torch to melt the ice before getting the wire lashing off the containers before they were able to open the cargo hatches.

Since I had never been in Anchorage and didn't expect to come back, I decided to go uptown to look around. After walking around in the snow and ice for a while, I stopped at the Scandinavian bar on 4th Avenue for a beer. I got to sit next to an Alaska Eskimo who was drunk and very hard to understand. He told me he lived 100 miles north of Anchorage and came into town once a month to collect his check from the State of Alaska. The bartender told me later that he and others would call a taxi from Anchorage to drive up to pick them up and drive them into Anchorage to collect their monthly checks, and a few days later when the money was gone, they would take a bus or catch a ride home.

Sailing from Anchorage with nothing but empty containers made the ship very stiff, rolling violently all the way back to Seattle. Out at sea the captain communicated with the Sea land Seattle office twice a day. He told me the man I had relieved was not coming back, and the job was mine, if I wanted it? Four months later the ship went into lay-up in Seattle due to a teamster strike in Alaska. Before I went home, the Seattle vessel manager told me the reason he had hired me for ten days only was that he wanted to make sure I would fit in.

Guess I did fit in because he called me after my vacation and offered me a job on the SS Newark, another C-4 just like the Portland, and on the same run. Like so many other WWII built ships there was a lot of history behind the ship. She had been built as a troop transport in 1944 by the US Maritime Commission and named SS General H. B. Freeman, capable of carrying 3000 troops during two wars. After the Korean War she went into lay-up as a part of the National Defense Reserve fleet where she remained until sold to Sea Land Service who converted her to a container ship in 1968.

I came to the conclusion that the people in Alaska must be the biggest consumers in the world with two large container ships and two large Ro/Ro ships leaving Seattle/Tacoma weekly, including tugs and barges bringing loads of cargo north bound with bread, ice-cream, vegetables, meat, building materials, hardware, clothing, cars, boats and more. Thanks to the containers there was no storage fee to pay. When a container was unloaded it was driven directly to the customer where it was unloaded and returned to the ship before sailing the same day.

The Merchant Marine act of 1920, better known as the Jones Act, requires that all goods transported by water between U.S. Ports be carried in US flag ships, constructed in the U.S. owned by U.S. citizens, and crewed by U.S. citizen. It also states that the U.S. shall have a Merchant Marine capable of serving as a Naval and Military auxiliary in time of War.

People in Alaska complain about their high cost of groceries because of the Jones act but never mention the high cost of labor in Alaska where the low man on the longshoremen's payroll was making $120,000 a year. There are also people in Alaska upset that the oil has to be shipped down to the lower 48 on American ships, because it cuts into their profits. In other words fuck you, we are okay.

The summers in Alaska were beautiful, and it opened my eyes to nature and wildlife, and at the same time the people were very friendly. I stayed on the Newark for six years, working three months on/off, and commuted to San Francisco

We had a good crew which made my job easy, but we also had our share of bad weather. North bound in bad weather with a heavy load, shipping water over decks and containers became a challenge for the chief engineer and electrician to repair reefers.

We had a homemade wooden platform for them to stand on, tying themselves and their tools to the containers using rope and safety belts. It took team work to replace a burnt out compressor, first getting the old one down on deck from the second tier, then moving it back to the engine room, get the new one out of the engine room and up on deck, and hoist it into place.

On a trip coming back empty in bad weather, we took a 54 degree violent snap roll. The sailor standing behind the wheel steering the ship was knocked off his feet, slid across the deck and hit his head against the starboard side of the wheel house, then slid all the way back across the wheel house to the port side where he hit his shoulder, slid back again and hit his head on the water cooler making a big dent in the water cooler, but he managed to hang on and pulled himself back up on his feet, grabbing the wheel and resumed steering without any comment. Later he asked for two aspirins.

There are not very many cities in the world where you can stand down town fishing for King salmon, or just watch the salmon returning to their birth place after a journey of thousands of miles out in the open ocean navigating up stream by memory around every bend. It is fascinating to watch. The Sunday brunch at Captain Cook's Hotel is also a great experience.

I consider myself very lucky being in Anchorage on the right day to witness the excitement of the famous dog sleigh race across Alaska starting on 4th Avenue, which was closed off for all traffic and transformed into a sleigh dog track.

You could hear the dogs barking with excitement long before they arrived with their owners by trucks. When all the sleighs were lined up at the starting point waiting for the signal to get under way, I can still see one lead dog that kept turning his head looking back, as if making sure everybody was pulling their share.

It is important to know and watch the tide before docking in Anchorage. I was told that one ship miscalculated the tide, docking starboard side to the pier on what they thought was the end of ebb, but it turned out to be the beginning of a flood. When they approached the dock and realized their mistake, it was too late and the crew ran off the bow for safety and down the main deck on the offshore side.

The ship hit the dock several times before the outboard containers got hooked up to a crane belonging to the port, dragging it along the dock causing severe damage to both the crane and ship. When the ship finally was freed from the crane and bounced off the dock, they managed to steer away from the dock and got out into open water to turn the ship around.

The Sea Land always had a man on the dock to spot the ship calling the ship several times asking if anybody was hurt, but no response. He kept calling. "This is the Sea Land dock calling the ship. "Please let me know if anybody got hurt." Finally after a while the chief mate came on the air saying, "No, nobody is hurt yet, but we are going to try one more time."

One trip lying alongside the dock in Anchorage, I heard what felt like an explosion in the engine room. I ran down and found everything to be Okay. The longshoremen told me it was an earth quake. It happened during low tide and the vessel was either sitting on or very close to the bottom floor when the earth quake hit. I documented everything in the log book with letters to back it up for insurance purposes.

A diver went down in Kodiak the following day and found some damage to the bottom in various places.

The ship was still seaworthy and we sailed directly to Todd shipyard in Seattle for dry docking and repairs.

On the Alaska ships each crew member was issued a nice warm blue insulated jacket with the Sea Land logo. I never expected the logo would get me in trouble in Seattle. There were two bars close to Sea Land terminal, the Blue Eagle and the Chelan. One evening at the Chelan I was sitting drinking a beer minding my own business when a longshoreman came up to me, calling me all kinds of names and knocked me off the bar stool. Later I was told the longshoremen had a dispute among themselves.

The scallywags out of the union hall didn't like the steady Sea Land longshoremen gang bosses and crane drivers, and he had taken me for one of them.

My friend, big Al, was on the ship at that time. We decided to go back to the Chelan looking for that longshoreman the following evening to give him something to remember me by. When we walked in, the bar was full of people and smoke, but he was not there. Since there was no room at the bar, we sat down at a booth against the wall. A few beers later the whole wall caved in around us. Some guy in a pick-up truck forgot to put the break on when parking outside.

During the fishing season we stopped in Kodiak every trip bringing in regular supplies, and back loaded Salmon, both frozen and in cans. It was not always an easy port to get in and out of, entering between two reefs, often in poor visibility, strong winds and long swells. When clear of the reefs and rocks you made a 90 degree course change toward the port, passing the City Sea Land dock and entering a small basin just big enough for us to turn around in, often against a strong wind, and with the help of the tug, Kodiak King.

The ship was 100 feet longer than the pier, which was no problem. During stormy weather the vessel would roll and surge alongside the dock. One night we parted four mooring lines which we re-spliced right away and used them again. Empty containers sitting on the dock were blowing in all directions.

Growing up in a small fishing village by the Baltic Sea, I never miss an opportunity to walk around the harbor looking at the boats, watching them unloading their catch, or bringing the fish to the cannery. There was an old liberty ship Star of Kodiak, laying in a fill area and no longer floating, now used as a fish cannery. There were lots of seals, sea lions, eagles, and sea gulls all around us. Sometimes bears were standing on top of a hill looking down at us.

Crab fishing off the ship was great and it didn't take long to fill up a pot. We used a clean oil drum as a steamer. However, later it became illegal to fish off the ship. There was lots of activity in the bars when the fishing was good and everybody had money in their pocket, and it was always fun to sit and watch and listen. There were a heated toilet and showers close to the boat harbor. I walked in one cold winter day and was hit with a smell and hot air, which made me turn around to leave in a hurry, but as I was turning around to get out I noticed two guys sitting on the floor drinking beer and eating Kentucky Fried Chicken.

A few years later the ship started to lose speed when steaming, usually a sign of a dirty bottom. A diver was hired to clean the bottom alongside the dock in Seattle. When the diver was finished cleaning, he informed the Sea Land manager that the bottom looked like an accordion in very bad shape. Underwater photos were taken but not shown to anyone.

The only reason we found out about the bad bottom was because the diver sat in the bar laughing and telling everybody about the bad bottom on the Newark, and that everybody better buy a survival suit before sailing, and some did.

Shortly thereafter we went into dry-dock in Seattle. It was late evening as we all stood around waiting for the water to be pumped out, and for the ship to sit high and dry on the wooden blocks, high enough for people to walk underneath to inspect the bottom. Among them was a surveyor from the American Bureau of Shipping, USCG surveyors from the insurance company, and a Sea Land port engineer with the vessel manager, and the shipyard foreman.

It was sad to watch the water dripping out of the double bottom and from the rudder. I didn't know who was trying to blame who, but I remember the insurance company representative telling the port engineer, "Look, I don't want to hear any more about the earthquake in Anchorage three years ago."

Next morning we were refloated and shifted to a lay-up pier in west Seattle, awaiting instructions from higher up to either replace the bad sections of the bottom, or scrap the ship. In the meantime the whole crew was paid off and went home. Several weeks later she went back into dry-dock for repairs. A few months later we were back in service, and I stayed until 1985.

Sea Land updated their company seniority where some people were bumped by higher senior licensed deck officers. At the same time they established a system on their vessel whereby the Chief Mate was required to hold a Master license which made me attend the Maritime Institute of Technology & Graduate Studies license advancement program. I successfully completed the USCG examination and was issued an unlimited Master license.

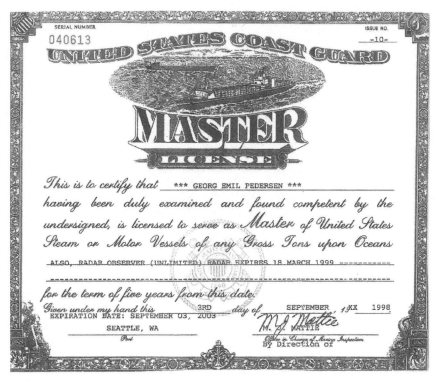

Copy of Master license

In addition I have satisfactorily completed the following noncompulsory education at the Maritime Institute of Technology and Graduate Studies, International Organization of Masters, Mates and Pilots.

1975   Advance Training-Maritime Liquid Cargo Operation
1978   Radar, Collision Avoidance & All Weather Navigation
1981   Advance Training - Shipboard Medical Care
1985   Advance Training - Ships Simulator Course
1985   Advance Training - Dry Cargo/Vessel Stability
1988/ 92   Basic and Advanced Marine Fire Fighting
1993   Advance Training - Vessel Personnel Management

1994   Oceanography/Heavy Weather Avoidance
1994   Advanced Electronic Navigation Systems
1994   Advance Bridge Resource Management
1994   Diesel Control Systems

In 1985 Sea Land moved their operation from Seattle to Tacoma to get more space and easy access to the railroad. Tacoma added one hour steaming time to the schedule.

One trip passing Brown's point, I witnessed a sight I had never seen before. Four killer whales trapped a sea lion, throwing him out of the water and up in the air several times, killing him before eating. At the same time I noticed a small seal sitting on top of a buoy looking very alert and safe watching the activity at a distance, as it saying, "Don't look at me, I am part of the buoy."

Just before getting off and going home on vacation, word came down from the office to call the captain in charge of fleet operation back east, which I did. He offered me a Masters job on one of the eight SL-7which Sea Land had sold to the US Navy and converted them from containerships to roll on/ roll off cargo ships capable of rapidly deploying military ground force around the world if needed. Sea Land had been asked by the Navy to operate the ships. The ships often stayed in port for months at a time with a skeleton crew ready to sail on short notice if needed. Not very exciting, and less pay and vacation. I told him over the phone I was going home on vacation and would think about it.

After being home only a few days, he called me telling me to fly to Norfolk to join the USNS Regulus the former S-L Commerce as Master. He got angry when I told him I had just started my vacation and was not ready to ship.

PEDERSEN SHALL NEVER SAIL IN ANY CAPACITY HIGHER THAN CHIEF MATE

When I returned to Seattle to rejoin the Newark, the vessel manager told me he had assigned me as Master on one of the other Alaska ships and ran it through the Captain in charge of fleet operation back East. Shortly after he received a message that Pedersen shall never sail in any capacity higher than chief mate. I had no problem with that because that was my favored job anyhow, and since I never met the man, I had no reason to be mad at him, and I considered myself lucky that I never had to sail with him.

When he retired, and a new man took over, I started sailing Master relief on various ships before being assigned as permanent Master.

In 1980 Sea land built 12 new Diesel powered Containerships in Japan and Korea, with a container capacity of 1,678 TEU. Five years later they returned to Mitsubishi Heavy Industries ship yards in Japan to be extended by 100 feet to 845 feet which added two more cargo hatches and increased the cargo capacity to 2,472 TEU. After the conversion they were classified as an automated D-9J with a crew reduction to 21.

In 1986 it became apparent that the old C-4 was on its last leg and would soon be scrapped. The Seattle manager offered me an opportunity to transfer to the "Sea Land Independence" which became my new home away from home for the next three years. It was a Cadillac in comparison to some of the old clunkers I had sailed on in the past.

She was due to arrive in Tacoma on a Sunday morning, paying off the crew on arrival. My assignment slip had me starting at 0800 Monday 2-2-86.

Schedule: Yokohama, Kobe, Singapore, Hong Kong,
Kaohsiung, Kobe, Yokohama, Tacoma

Since I had never been on a D-9, I decided to fly to Seattle a day early to meet the ship a few hours after arrival with a list of questions to ask the Chief Mate getting off. To my surprise, he had already left and so had everybody else. I found a note in the chief mate's office welcoming me aboard, telling me about the cargo operation. He also mentioned that the deck department making the next trip had Monday off, and that 11 new crew members would join Monday. Voyage bunkers and stores would be delivered and handled by the Sea Land shore gang.

P.S. there will be a U.S. Coast Guard annual inspection starting at 0900 tomorrow. I don't think you will have any problems.

After reading that note, I started wondering what kind of ship was this and who was in charge and what did I get myself into?

I checked with the shore-gang bosun who was a friend of mine, and he gave me the bad news that nothing was ready for the USCG inspection, but his gang would take the voyage stores first and then start preparing for tomorrow's inspection. The wire falls had to be replaced on # 1 lifeboat which meant the boat had to be weight tested before tomorrows Fire and boat drill which is part of a USCG inspection.

I didn't get much sleep and started early signing on new crew members as they came aboard in the morning. I knew I was in trouble when the Coast Guard deck inspector stepped into my office asking if I was ready for the inspection. If not, he was leaving. He also told me he didn't want to hear me asking him what's next, but for me to follow the blue book and tell him what was next. The problem was I didn't have a blue book.

The Sea Land shore gang worked hard and was a great help with everything. The Fire & Boat drill was scheduled for 1300 with only ship crew making the next trip. The crew was mustered at their fire station with the hoses led out under full pressure. Everything worked in good order.

Next was the life boat drill where the crew was mustered with their life jackets properly worn and ready to lower the boat into the water and sail around using the motor first, and later the crew had to show their expertise in rowing.

The new 2nd Mate was in charge of the boat, and everything went great, getting the engine started and sailing around close to the ship.

I was standing on the bridge wing watching the boat crew start rowing. It looked like a total disaster, and I had to look the other way.

After the life boat was safely back onboard in stowage position, I didn't know how I would be able to talk myself out of what I called a total disaster. So I was surprised when the inspector was satisfied, saying it went very well. That's when I realized the guy didn't have a clue what to look for.

Sometimes the quality of the inspection left a lot to be desired due to lack of experience on the part of men who conducted the inspection. The USCG safety manual 46 CFR had a paragraph stating that nothing shall limit an inspector from making such tests or inspections as he deemed necessary to assure the safety and sea worthiness of a vessel.

That paragraph is often abused and costly if the inspector didn't like you or the company. Most inspectors were very professional and reasonable, but like the old saying there has to be one in every crowd. At the end of the day, I was relieved when I watch the USCG team walking down the gangway, and I was finally able to concentrate on the ship and the Cargo operation.

By the time we sailed out of Puget Sound with a full load of cargo heading for Japan, I had been on my feet for about 36 hours and was looking forward to getting some sea time where my day started and ended on the bridge standing the 4 x 8 sea watch. Thanks to the Global Position System (GPS), invented by the U.S. Department of defense the sextant and dead reckoning navigation were eliminated by the push of a button giving me the exact position, course, and speed.

By another push of a button, we had the course to steer, with time of arrival. We often met ships sailing without (GPS) who called us on the HVF asking for a position to check against their own dead reckoning position. I made sure I would never forget how to use a sextant, chipping hammer or how to splice a wire or rope

In the 1950-60s the U.S. Maritime Administration built several classes of new and faster ships with new technology. One of those new technologies was the bridge to engine control which had proved effective and reliable on both steam and diesel ships worldwide.

The MEBA claimed it was their jurisdiction and that a licensed engineer should be on the bridge pushing the handle to control the Engine, and not the captain. That marked the beginning of a 74 day strike costing the companies involved over $50 million in lost revenue. Companies suffered longer-term damage that for many proved fatal, and convinced shippers throughout the world that American lines provided less reliable service than their foreign competitors. The Bloomfield Steamship company never resumed operation after the strike.

Now, twenty years later the system was finally put to use. The powerful 9-cyl Sulzer diesel was controlled directly from the bridge. In addition, the engine room was unmanned from 5 p.m. to 8 a.m. Sensors monitored the main engine and other machinery with engine room alarm panels in various locations. Whenever a sensor triggered an alarm, a buzzer would go off and didn't stop unless silenced by the duty engineer.

Each night in rotation engineers who had already put in a full day's work in the engineer's room were assigned to respond when problems came up, which happened quite often. Two hours before arrival, the duty Engineer was called to get ready to maneuver.

We still had some of its original 35 foot containers in use, therefore adjustable cell guides were installed in several cargo hatches. Hinge frames system used to secure the containers on deck worked Okay in the beginning, but later became a big problem.

The large wheel house/bridge had a good layout with big windows with a great view. The steering stand was in the middle, radars to the right, and the console, the brain center, to the left. The large chart table was in the back with curtains all around to eliminate light from distracting the mate on watch, eliminated the chartroom

The radar and Collision Avoidance System/ Automatic Radar Plotting Aid (ARPA) eliminated radar plotting as I knew it in the past. No more plotting sheets or grease pencil. The ARPA gave you a quick picture of approaching ships by the true motion radar presentation with digital read-out of other ship's course, speed, bearing, distance off, and time of closest point of approach, and course changes to make to avoid collision. When a new target entered the radar screen, a buzzer went off notifying the officer on watch.

No system is completely reliable or perfect. I encountered two situations where the ARPA didn't warn me or pick up targets. The first time was during a very heavy rain squall on the east coast of Taiwan.

The radar showed a lot of sea clutter which I was not able to eliminate. By good luck the rain eased for a few seconds, long enough for me to see a large fishing vessel close on the starboard bow and crossing. I managed to change course by coming hard right and avoided a collision.

A year later coming home over the Pacific Ocean on a great circle course from Japan with strong wind and high seas and swells, I happened to see a fishing vessel close by. Each time our radar antenna turned toward the fishing vessel, the vessel was hidden between two large waves and the radar never showed the target.

Our outbound great circle course took us north of the Alaska Aleutian chain, south of the chain homebound to advantage of the Kuroshio Current, which gave us a good push.

In addition to standing the 4 x 8 watched I was still accountable for the care of the cargo, making sure it was well secured. The system had not changed as far as reading the reefers logging the temperature in a reefer book. The contents of the reefer cargo on this run were very valuable, frozen beef, fish, chicken, Dryer Ice Cream and apples, oranges, grapes, vegetables.

Some shippers had started placing their own monitors inside the reefer containers for their own record.

My average work day was 12-14 hours each day, seven days a week. Six hours uninterrupted sleep was a luxury.

The Bosun, Joe, was one of the last real characters I sailed with. He had a way with words, knowing every swear word in the book and using them all the time. If you didn't talk back to him the same way, he didn't hear you. The first day out at sea I noticed a bunch of container twist locks lying on deck by number two hatch. I told him to pick them up and put them back in the bend where they belonged. Next day they were still lying in the same place. I tried a new approach, telling him to get those f------ twist locks off the deck before some stupid SOB falls and bust his ass. That got his attention and they were moved right away.

While in Tacoma he had been thrown out from a bar for telling the owner to get rid of those old hay bags working behind the bar, and hire some decent looking broads instead.

He had a habit of calling me on the phone telling me what he was doing, or going to do. One morning after sailing Kaohsiung where I had been on my feet for over 30 hours, I told him before I went to bed not to call me. I no sooner got in bed before he called telling me what he was going to do for the rest of the day. I told him to listen very carefully. If you call me one more time today I will come down and tear your f------ phone of the bulkhead (wall) and shove it up your ass.

Shortly thereafter he walked into the crew mess hall where everybody was having lunch, telling them that if they saw him walking around with a f------ phone sticking out his ass, it was because the chief mate had shoved it up there. To him that was another feather in his hat.

Joe had been active in union activity back in New York in the 1950-60's. When the SIU President attended maritime meetings, he often brought a bunch of rank and file members with him to show strength and support. During his speeches he would give sudden signs which meant start clapping.

Women were barred from entering the US Maritime Academies prior to 1974. Several sex discrimination cases had been filed against the academies. The Maritime Administration together with other politicians were holding meetings on what action to take. Maritime unions were invited to come and give their opinions. Joe went to Washington as part of Poul Hall's clapping gang.

During the meeting, one of the politicians pointed at Joe asking for his opinion of women onboard ships, to which he responded." Those f------broads don't belong on ship." That was the last time Joe was invited along in the clapping gang.

Joe was paying the highest taxes required by law. Yet he was in big trouble with the IRS for not filing. If he had, he would have been getting money back. The IRS slapped a huge fine which was taken out of his salary. At the same time we had a man on a green card from Yemen who claimed 9 dependents and didn't pay any taxes at all, very unfair.

Once in Tacoma, I overheard a conversation he had with his mother back in Boston telling her that of course he would like to come home to see her, but how can I as long as those rotten S F B at the IRS toke all his money. "But don't worry mom, I will make it home before you croke."

I was happy being back in Asia again. The economy was booming in Japan with ships from all over the world. It was not unusual to have 40-50 ships on the radar screen when approaching Tokyo or Kobe bay. Shipping lanes had been established for all vessels to follow, however the small coasters and fishing vessels were crossing the lanes in all directions.

I always enjoyed working with the Japanese longshoremen who often started before the ship was all fast. Instead of waiting for the gangway to be lowered down, they came onboard with the crane and rode the cranes spreader-bar, to be lowered onboard, where they took the lashings off the containers before we were moored.

Kaohsiung was the biggest and fastest growing container port in Taiwan with new container cranes springing up everywhere and an incredible amount of cargo moving in/out.

The population of Kaohsiung had grown to 1.5 million, and the air pollution had grown with it from all the heavy industries surrounding the area. Kaohsiung was still selling knock-off books, Rolex watches and blue Jeans.

Hong Kong, the city that never sleeps, kept expanding its port. New construction was going up everywhere. Nathan Road was full of shoppers from all over the world buying clothing, jewelry, cameras. The Mass Transit Railroad ran over 80 km underground through 43 stations, always packed with people, moving over two million people daily.

At the time stowaways out of Hong Kong were a problem. Before sailing each department head in addition to conducting preliminary crew check making sure everybody was aboard after the ship moved several feet off the dock a stowaway inspection was conducted throughout the vessel.

Singapore was on the way to becoming the busiest port in the world. No government anywhere was more aggressive in preparing for the container age than Singapore, which became the commercial hub of South East Asia, moving containers to and from Malaysia, Thailand, or Indonesia. Approximately 800 ships transited the 65 mile long Singapore Straight daily, the main highway to and from Asia to Europe, Persian Gulf, India, and Africa.

It was also a breeding ground for pirates, mostly coming from Indonesia and getting more aggressive using bigger and faster boats. The long knives had been replaced with modern weapons. They operated after dark in long narrow speed boats approaching from the stern coming alongside ahead of the propeller. If they successfully managed to come alongside unnoticed and throw up a rope with hook at the end which would catch on to the uprights, or hand rail, they would then quickly climb onboard and head for the captain's room where the money was. We took various precautions keeping the ship well lit with strong lights shining down the ship's side, fire hoses spraying water over the sides making it a little more difficult to come alongside.

Extra lookouts were placed on the wing of the bridge, and all outside doors were locked. The Sea Land Voyager while in route from Singapore to Hong Kong was boarded by five pirates 150 miles east of Singapore. The ship's safe was raided, but no one got hurt.

One Captain on Seas Land vessel got killed in the port of Huston, Texas by two gunmen during day light hours, when refusing to open the safe.

Another Captain got robbed in the Port of Oakland California. After the robbers made him open the safe and took all his cash, they locked him in his closest where he stayed overnight. I guess ships are easy targets.

I sailed Tacoma with around $ 20,000 Cash in the safe. I ordered a lot of one dollar bills and rolled them tightly together using rubber bands with a few $100 bills showing on top and bottom making it look like rolls of $100s bills and hid the bulk of the cash in a safe placed in the slop chest which is always locked and sealed in port. I consider myself lucky I never had any problems.

THE ECON-SHIPS

Unites States Lines was a prestigious Government subsidized company operating over 50 ships under the American flag, including the great passenger ships, the SS United States, and the S.S. America.

In 1984 the company took a big risk when they built a dozen large containerships in Korea known as Econ-ships. The ships were 950 ft. long x 106 ft. wide with a draft of 38 feet, total 57,000 gross tonnages with a container capacity of 4,600 TEU which made them the largest post Panama container ships in the world at that time. The propulsion was a 7-cyl Sulzer diesel which gave them a speed of only 18 knots, one of the downfalls.

Unfortunately the company went into Bankruptcy in 1986, and the ships were arrested in ports around the world, and the crew was stuck for weeks on the ships without money or transportation home. A year later the banks holding the mortgage chose to sell the ships.

Since the ships had been built with U.S. subsidy they had to be purchased by an American company. Sea Land bought all twelve at garage sale prices. To make sure there was enough cargo for all the ships, they started a joint venture and space sharing program with Nedlloyd, a Dutch company, and P & O Lines, a British company. When a big company like United States Lines goes out of business it becomes a hardship for the maritime unions involved. In this case both companies had a contract with the Masters, Mates & Pilots for the Licensed Deck Officers. The company and the union agreed to keep one U.S. Line Master or a Chief Mate on each ship.

I was home on vacation when I received a call from a vessel manager back East telling me he was looking for a Chief Mate who was not afraid to get dirty and that my name had come up. The job was on the M/V American New York laying in Singapore. I agreed to take the job but made it clear that I would be able to return to my permanent ship the Sea Land Independence at a later date. The union confirmed it on my assignment slip.

When I arrived in Singapore I checked into the popular luxury Oriental Hotel located in the Marina Square along the Marian Bay. I was impressed when I entered my room with an unforgettable view overlooking the city skyline, harbor, and Singapore Strait. That became my home away from home for seven weeks. I met the Sea Land manager, a former US Line manager, and the Captain assigned to the ship. The rest of the Deck and Engine officers showed up one by one. Each day we were brought to and from the ship by a mini bus.

Out of the twelve ships, two had been arrested in Singapore and kept at anchor in the Straits of Johor on the other side of Singapore Island. We went out to make a survey of the ship the following day and were shocked to see how dirty the ship was from dust and bird droppings. When we unlocked the galley the smell was unbelievable. Rotten food had been standing around for a year, and the galley was alive with white maggots everywhere.

I was hoping the ship had been pressure washed before entering the Jurong shipyard to eliminate carrying the bird droppings inside the living quarters, but that was not on anybody's agenda. A few days later the inside was just as dirty as the outside.

At the time there was a shortage of labor in Singapore, and the shipyard had to hire laborers from Malaysia. The women hired to clean had to leave home each morning at 0500 by bus to get to the ship by eight, and didn't show much interest in the job. The technicians from Korea and Japan took the main engine and generators apart to clean and repair as necessary.

The bridge to engine room console, radars, and communication equipment completely overhauled by Siemens technicians from Germany. The outlet for the reefer containers on deck had to be changed to fit the Sea Land, Nedlloyd, and P&O reefers containers which turned out to be a difficult task.

All fire and lifesaving equipment had to be replaced, together with lifeboat wire falls, and to be inspected by the USCG who came out from Honolulu. I worked with the American Bureau of Shipping to inspect the ship hull, double bottom and ballast tanks. The entire ship was painted, using Nedlloyd's color scheme.

The Banks holding the mortgage on the ships changed the name from "American New York" to "Catherine K" and later "Nedlloyd Holland"

The unlicensed crew came out from New York a week before sailing. Fresh provision were purchased from the local ship's chandlers. We found several cases of old dry and stale cigarettes full of brown spots unfit for human consumption.

The Captain ordered fresh cigarettes, and we decided to keep the old stale ones, and use them as baksheesh when transiting the Suez Canal.

We left Singapore in ballast for Germany, seven days ahead of schedule. Had nice weather across the Indian ocean, through the Gulf of Aden and up through the Red Sea to Port Suez, where we arrived on schedule 12 days later.

The Suez Canal, also known as the Marlboro Canal among seafarers, is one of the world's most important waterways and brings in over 3 billion dollars in fees annually. You would think the Canal Authority would be able to pay their workers a decent salary and stop them from harassing the ship's crew from the time they come onboard until they get off.

I always dread having to deal with the bureaucrats who are constantly bumming us for cigarettes, coffee, peanut butter, shaving lotion, and pens for their daughter in school, and canned milk for their children. Unfortunately, bribing is necessary to get the ship through the canal without delays. Most companies allow their captains to pass out 25 cartons of cigarettes to the officials each transit. This was my chance to get even with them by passing out old and stale cigarettes.

As soon as we dropped anchor at Port Suez and lowered down the gangway, an army of port officials in uniforms came onboard with the Canal transit agent. The Suez Canal special tonnage certificate, ship's registry certificate, original safety construction certificate, previous name of vessel, engine room plan, crew list, oil and ballast tanks certificate, were all part of the necessary routine certificates presented to them. An agent was hired by the company to bring the certificates ashore, to clear the ship and to make sure the canal transit fee was paid. He rides the train alongside the canal and brings the certificates and port clearance back to the ship before leaving the canal at the other end. By the time the ship was cleared I had already passed out over 25 cartons of cigarettes, and everybody went ashore happy.

The Canal is around 100 miles long and takes 10-12 hours from start to finish. At the time there were two convoys a day, one south bound, and one north bound. The canal is not wide enough for two large ships to pass; therefore we sometimes had to anchor in the Bitter Lake waiting for the other convoys. The Canal Authority notified us that we were vessel # 4 and to be ready to get under way at 0400 the following morning. The Canal crew came alongside with their boats and hoisted them up to the level of the main deck where they were secured hanging ready to be lowered into the water in case we had to stop and tie up alongside the Canal during transit. The pilot came onboard on time and we were on our way. The Canal crew set up their souvenir shop selling Egyptian handicrafts, tools, knock-off watches, and jewelry. They preferred cigarettes rather than cash. Next they wanted to know when breakfast was served. One guy told me he did not eat pork, but American bacon and eggs was Okay.

Since I had over 100 cartons of old stale cigarettes to get rid of, I pretended to be on their side and bought a lot of small tools for the ship. If they asked for three cartons, I gave them four. By the time the boat crew got off in Port Said I had used all the cigarettes, and everybody was happy telling me that this was a number one ship, number one Captain and number one Chief Mate.

I wonder how they felt when they tried to sell those stale cigarettes ashore.

The transit went okay and the Agent came out in a small boat as we were passing Port Said at slow speed. I had a large bucket which I lowered down onto the boat for him to put the large envelope in with all the ships certificates and Canal clearance. He also told me he had a present for me, which turned out to be a box of chocolate. Guess what? The chocolate was stale just like the cigarettes. Guess he was the only one who got wise to me.

When we docked in Bremerhaven, Germany I saw something new and very clever. Instead of having 3-4 men standing on the dock pulling in the heavy mooring lines, there was one man with a specially designed truck parked next to the bollard. It had a power winch which made it easy for him to heave the line on to the dock and slip the eye onto the bollard. Wonder why the rest of the world is not doing it that way? We stayed in Bremerhaven one week to get on the regular schedule and also stopped in the port of Felix Stove, England and Rotterdam before crossing the Atlantic to Boston, New York and Savanna, Georgia, where I got off and went home on vacation. It was a good and interesting experience.

Snug Harbor for Old tired Containerships

Early in 1989 Sea Land Service was awarded a new three-year contract to deliver military cargo to Subic Bay Navy Base and Clark Air Force base in the Philippines, which all had to be carried on American vessels. The transpacific line hauling ships coming from the

U.S. West Coast did not stop in the Philippines, but discharged the cargo in Kaohsiung, Taiwan for trans-shipment to the Philippines. Sea land found themselves in need of a ship for that service.

They had four older D-6 class ships, the Sea Land Leader, Pacer, Pioneer, and Adventure all laying idle in Setubal, Portugal.

The Sea Land Pacer was picked out of the four. There was one big problem. They were all fitted for 35 foot containers and had to be converted to 20-40 footers before entering service to meet the new world standard.

I was offered a Master Job on the "Sea Land Pacer" to sail her from Setubal to Singapore and stay with her throughout the shipyard conversion. As always everything happened in a hurry. I left for Lisbon via New York right away. At the New York Airport I met Jack, the Chief Mate, assigned to the ship, and together we flew TWA directly to Lisbon. In Lisbon we were met by the local agent who drove us to a hotel in Setubal, and later to the ship. The Port Engineer was already there. He told me he would be able to get us out of there in about a week. I called the ship's manager in New York the following morning for instruction. I was told that it was very important for us to be in Singapore no later than January 30. The engineers assigned to the ship arrived right away and the rest of the crew would arrive two days before sailing. To save time, the groceries and other stores would be bought locally. I contacted the local ship chandler to supply new navigation publications and charts for the voyage.

The Sea Land Pacer was another American beauty, built in 1942 as a T-3 tanker, for Standard oil. In 1962 she was converted to a Sea Land container ship, with a new and larger amidships section fitted to carry 476 thirty-five footer containers. The old bow and stern section with the original steam engine intact was spliced to the new amidships body, and named the "SS San Juan."

In 1978 she was converted again, this time in Japan. The old bow and stern section was cut off and scrapped. New bow and stern sections were spliced to the amidships section.

A new six cylinder Sulzer diesel and bow thruster was installed, and she was renamed the "Sea Land Pacer" Her final dimensions were 662 x 78 x 39. 17,618 gross tons. 1,345 TEU speed 18 knots.

Jack and I commuted to and from the ship by taxi daily. One evening at the hotel after a long day's work we sat at the bar having a few drinks when the lights went out. Guess it didn't happen too often because they didn't have any back up lighting of any kind. I took out my small flashlight and shined the light on to the bar, pushed Jack's drink over in front of him and told him to hang on to it. I can still see his face when he asked "Do you always carry a flashlight?" "Yes, I do."

He looked at me again and said "Guess that's why you are the Captain and I am the Mate."

When the crew arrived from New York, the bosun came up telling me they would not be able to work that day because of jet lag. I asked him if he had met the chief mate yet. If not, go and take a good look at that man, he has suffered jet lag for the last 20 years, but that never stopped him from working. They started taking stores right away, and prepared for sea.

The next day the chief engineer told me he was ready for a trial run. I ordered a local pilot and tug boat. Unfortunately, we didn't get very far before the engine died. The second try was better and the chief engineer was satisfied, except for one item. The bridge/engine control was out of order and could not be fixed before sailing which was Okay with me as long as the engine telegraph was working.

When we started out on our 7,250 miles voyage to Singapore the 2nd Mate and I worked out a ETA allowing for stopping in Algeciras, Spain for bunkers, and allowing for the Suez Canal transit, I sent in our ETA for Singapore for 10 a.m. local time January 28th.

The ship was high in the water and very stiff and rolling violently for several days sailing through the Mediterranean. A large refrigerator in the mess hall bolted to the deck broke loose and smashed several chairs and a bulkhead.

Except for the usual harassment, the Suez Canal transit went smoothly with very nice weather down the Red Sea and a lot of traffic. By the time we crossed the Indian Ocean, burning 55 tons of fuel a day, the ship started to shake more and more each day. The global position antenna located on the radar mast was shaking so much it was impossible to pick up a signal or a position. We reduced speed twice a day, long enough to get a position.

Even today I can't believe we actually arrived at 10 a.m. 20 days later on January 28th. I don't think I would be able to do that again. We went directly to Jurong shipyard and tied up next to a large tanker for two days before entering the dry dock which was big enough for two ships.

The crew was hired for a one way trip. When paying them off, I gave everyone a choice between an airline ticket back to New York, or cash to buy their own in case they wished to stop somewhere on the way home.

The ships engineers would stay through the conversion and dry-docking. I arranged for us to stay at the Oriental Hotel where I got my old room back and spent two pleasant months, commuting to and from the ship daily through the conversion.

After a complete overhaul and a $300,000 paint job, the SL Pacer entered the Far East weekly shuttling service between Kaohsiung, Taiwan, Subic Bay, and Manila in the Philippines, carrying military cargo to and from Subic Bay, and commercial cargo to and from Manila. Kaohsiung was in and out, but we always stayed 12-18 hours in Subic Bay and two full days in Manila, a very nice run.

It was disappointing to see that the living standards for the average Filipino had not improved since the first time I was there some thirty years ago, mostly due to over population. It seemed like every family had four or six kids, and could only afford one. A man from the Manila office was assigned to assist me dealing with the port officials, like customs, immigration, public health, and other government bureaucrats involved for a vessel to enter and leave port. If it's not done correctly, it can cost delay and money. However, several cartons of cigarettes would take care of most problems. I became very good friends with him and visited his home several times. His day started at 5 a.m. first by making sure the wife had enough water for the day, if not he had to go out and buy it. He also helped his wife get the four children ready for school before he was able to leave for work in the office.

One of his many jobs was to assure a berth was available each time we arrived in Manila, and ordering the harbor pilot, tug boats, repair workers, fresh stores, and laundry service.

He also took crew members to the doctor and picked up new crew members at the airport bringing them to the ship or hotel, he worked long hours, but never complained.

I had the opportunity to go with him to visit some of our customers outside Manila where he made sure they were happy with our service. He took me to a small village where everyone was involved in making baskets for the U.S. Christmas market, shipping one or two containers at the time. The lady in charge was very proud of their business and the quality of their products.

Sometimes small simple things can become complicated. All our curtains for the port holes and windows were falling apart and looked torn and worn and needed to be replaced.

Ships curtains have to have a black layer on the back side to prevent light from interfering with the ships navigation. The ship's manager in Los Angeles insisted she would have them made and ship them which would take two months at a cost of $ 6,200. I did not want to wait that long. I contacted a lady taylor in Manila who gave me a bid of $1100 with two weeks delivery. The manager agreed. The lady making the curtains was grateful for the job, which would help pay for her daughter's education that year. In addition each time she came onboard she brought me a lot of good Mangos.

Manila has an abundance of taxi and jitneys, a jeep-style vehicle carrying 18 or more passengers normally sitting facing each other. During the rush hour people would be standing on top of each other. The jitneys are very nicely painted in bright colors with interesting decorations. One evening heading back to the ship I found myself out on the street with no taxis or jitney in sight, which was very unusual.

Finally, I saw a lot of black smoke coming around the corner which turned out to be a taxi that stopped to pick me up. As I tried to open the back door, the driver told me to wait.

The door and window were held in place with rope and wire. It took him some time to get the door open and closed after I got in.

As we started the bumpy ride back to the ship me sitting in the back almost choking to death from the strong smell of oil and smoke, I wondered if we would ever get there. When we pulled up in front of the gate and ship, I asked him how much I owed him. He asked for $2. When I gave him $5, telling him to keep the change, his face lit up and he shook my hand wishing me good luck.

As I stood there watching him drive away covered in a cloud of black smoke, I was thinking he was the one who needed the good luck. This is one of the many memories I have of working with people struggling to make a living around the world.

One nice calm evening out at sea heading for Kaohsiung, the 2nd Mate went out to walk the main deck after dinner and noticed a stowaway standing in between the containers.

It turned out to be a Vietnamese refugee named Nguyen Chinh Thanh who had been in a refugee camp in Manila for two years and decided to run away from the camp hoping to stow away on a ship. He told me he had walked the docks in Manila looking for a ship to stowaway on, and saw the American flag on our ship and assumed we would be heading for the USA.

He had watched the ship and cargo operation from a distance, saw the Filipino longshoremen all dressed alike in blue working clothes walking up and off the ship without being stopped by the watchman at the gangway. He made a deal with one of the longshoremen, bought his blue work cloths and walked onboard the ship without any problem. When safely onboard the Pacer he entered # 3 cargo hatch where he had stayed for ten days without food, or water. He had survived on a jungle survival stick which he had made for himself while in the camp.

Each cargo hatch has an emergency escape trunk with a cover which can be opened from the inside, which he had done to get fresh air. He had become aware that the first port had been Kaohsiung, and the second port was Subic Bay. The big disappointment for him came when he realized that the third port was Manila where he had started from. But he decided to stay onboard. He had no identification, but memorized his ID number. He also memorized a phone number of his brother in Los Angeles. I contacted Sea Land in Los Angeles and told them my situation and gave them his brother's phone number, which had been disconnected.

A letter was sent to his brother's last known address in Los Angeles, with a forwarding request. The Immigration in Kaohsiung demanded he be locked up and a security guard stationed outside his room while in port. On the way back to Manila he told me he would rather jump overboard than return to the camp.

I tried to give him encouragement, telling him I was working on locating his brother, and that we would locate him one way or another, but that it would take time.

I felt bad when the immigration and the person in charge of the refugee camp came onboard and took him back to the camp.

One evening in Manila two trips later I heard a slight tap on my door. When I opened the door I was shocked to see Nguyen standing there again dressed like a longshoremen. He had taken another chance getting away from the camp to come down to check if I had any news locating his brother. I assured him that I was still working on it, and that I would succeed, and that I would not give up on him. I walked him off the ship and out through the main gate, gave him some money for a taxi and told him to be careful getting back to the camp, and that I would visit him when I had news. I became very attached to him and was impressed with his determination to get on with his life somewhere in the world.

By good luck shortly afterward I received a long distance phone call from Nguyen's brother who had moved to Atlantic City, New Jersey. I told him that his brother was in a camp and needed his help. I got his new address and phone number, which I hand delivered to Nguyen in Manila.

I made several visits to the camp to follow up on the progress before I went home, but never knew the outcome.

The pirates around the Philippines were still small scale chiefs in comparison to the ones around Indonesia and Malacca Strait. Around the Philippines they would be looking for ships proceeding at slow speed, approaching from the stern using a rope with a hook at the end which would connect to the ship's hand rail given a man a chance to haul himself onboard, hoping to find a new mooring line and quickly lower the eye of the line down to the water edge, where the men in the boat would tie it to the boat and run with it, and the man who was on the ship would quickly jump in the water and swim away. The mooring line was very valuable, approximately $1000 each;

it would float for a while and was easy to steal. If a ship was lying at anchor they would climb up the anchor chain and do the same thing.

On each trip in Manila we had the same six watchmen which didn't stop the pirates from stealing a new mooring line right in front of them. The first thing that came to my mind was to fire the watchmen; at the same time I knew the other companies would not be any better. The owner of the security company came onboard to apologize and said it would not happen again. I suggested that he should go out and try to buy the mooring line back from the thief, but he told me it would be impossible.

I told him that I would give him and his watchman enterprise one more chance, but to do so he would have to give me a car with a driver each time I was in Manila, which he did.

When it was time for me to get off after two assignments on the "Pacer" I managed to get bad food poisoning dinning at a Seafood restaurant in down town Manila.

I am sure it was from the tartar sauce which had mayonnaise in it. In the Philippines where it is hot the mayonnaise often sits out on the table for hours, and even if it is in the freezer it goes bad because the power is often off for several hours at the time. I have had food poisoning twice in my life and each time I tracked it back to the mayonnaise, but that doesn't stop me from using it at the right places.

At the camp bringing Nguyen his brothers new address and Phone #

Sea Land Developer 1990 - 1993

We started out in the Trans Pacific service. A year later we entered the inter Asia service carrying cargo between Japan, Hong Kong, and Taiwan, three countries with booming economies which kept the ocean's highway around them busy with ships from all over the world.

The three watch standing officers are the Master's representatives and their primary responsibility is the safe navigation of the vessel. I have been lucky and always sailed with highly qualified deck officers. But even the best of men can get into a dangerous situation without realizing it.

One clear morning in heavy traffic between Yokohama and Kobe I was sitting in the captain's chair watching the ships and fishing boats around us. I kept my eyes on a small loaded coastwise tanker on the starboard bow proceeding on the same course but slower than us. On the port side was a huge fleet of fishing boats, the type and size with only one man onboard who is for the most part busy fishing and doesn't always look out for the oncoming traffic, or be aware that he may be inside the shipping lanes.

As we came closer to the tanker who was now cutting in on us, I noticed the Mate on watch was getting nervous. I asked him what he was going to do. When he didn't answer, I took the Conn and ordered the sailor behind the wheel to come hard left.

The ship responded, quickly moving away from the tanker toward the fishing fleet. I blew the ship's whistle to let the fishermen know we were coming their way. By good luck they all got out of the way in a hurry. I managed to navigate my way out between the huge fleet without hitting anyone.

Later I asked the Mate why he didn't take action earlier when it became obvious the tanker was on a collision course. He told me he got confused and didn't see any way out without hitting someone.

I based my decision on whether I would prefer running down a fishing boat or have a collision with a tanker. If you have never been on a ship you may say, why not just slow down or stop? It's not that easy. It takes too long

I don't know how many times I have heard that the safest place for a ship is in port safely moored to a dock. That's not always true, because the only mishap I ever had was when the good ship Sea Land Developer was safely moored Starboard side to Honmoku Pier A-6 in Yokohama, Japan on March 21-92.

At 0748 I was sitting in my office, when I felt the ship shake and heard a loud crashing noise coming from the forward deck. I ran up to the bridge where I saw the Liberian freighter T. A. Navigator pulling away from our vessel after she had struck at # 8 - 9 cargo hatches. The crashing sound came from the damaged steel hinge frames used to secure and keep the containers in place above deck.

The T. A. Navigator was moving past us, assisted by two powerful tugs and preparing to make a 90 degree turn toward the dock across the waterway. The harbor pilot miscalculated the distance between the ships, and failed to use the two powerful tugboats properly.

The rest of my day was spent making out the damage report and notice of claims. Even though a local licensed pilot is in charge of the movement of the vessel when docking, the ships master is the one who bears the responsibility when something goes wrong.

NOTICE OF CLAIM

The owner, operator of the M/V Sea Land Developer on behalf of the Master, hereby place the owner Master operator and its agent of the T.A. Navigator on notice of claim for any and all damage sustained and the partial loss resulting from the collision with the M/V Sea Land Developer on March 21, 1992 at 0748 hours local time while vessel is lying afloat at Honmoku Pier A-6 since 3/29/1992.

The vessel Sea Land Developer now in Yokohama will receive full survey of damages including complete damage to the hinge frames, containers and cargo.

We have full right to reserve our claim for your full responsibility in this regard to cover our loss and damage including fabrication of hinge frames and towers to be as original.

I hand delivered the letter Notice of Claim to the Master of the T.A. Navigator, the Tokyo Bay licensed Pilot Association, and to the Kawaski Tug-Boat Company, whose tugboats were assisting the T. A. Navigator while proceeding down the waterway.

The harbor pilot in charge of the T.A. Navigator when the collision occurred was a man up in years with many years of maritime experience. I can still see him standing in my office as a broken man bowing and apologies for his mistake.

A repair gang with a large floating crane was hired and went to work cutting off all the damaged hinge frames. As it turned out all the damage was well above the water line and the good ship Sea Land Developer was still sea worthy.

Since we were never sailing fully loaded on this shuttle service we were still able to maintain our regular schedule. A month later we went off schedule in Kaohsiung and left for Kobe completely empty to enter dry docking, and to replace the missing hinge frames. The timing was bad because we ran into a Typhoon and had a rough ride rolling all the way to Kobe.

SL Developer

Routine dry docking includeshull inspection, Bottom survey, propeller and shaft, rudder, Stern tupe, sea valves, anchor chain and chain locker.

The bottom is sand blasted and painted. The U.S.C.G. and American Bureau of Shipping came out from Hawaii to participate in the inspection and renewed our certificates. After all repairs were done and the ship's hull Freshly painted from the keel up, we left for Kaohsiung in ballast anxious to get back on The regular schedule.

Would you believe we ran into tropical storm "Polly "with strong winds, heavy rain and rough seas which lasted two days. When the weather moderated, I made an inspection of the vessel to check for damage. When I looked over the side to check the anchors I noticed the new paint on the port side below the water line had started peeling off.

When we arrived in Kaohsiung, the port was closed for 24 hours due to the tropical storm Polly. After docking I made a survey of the port side and found that approx. 25-30 % of the red paint had peeled off, some places all the way down to bare steel below the water line. The red paint was sticky and rolling right off.

I was told later that the shipyard had two outside contractors to clean and paint the ship's hull. The contractor who did the starboard side did everything right, but something had gone wrong on the port side. I still don't know what caused the mishaps on the port side. The job was done over shortly thereafter when the ship returned to dry-dock.

Among the crew was an AB who was an alcoholic. Each trip in Kobe he attend AA meetings. Five days later in Hong Kong he would go ashore and get drunk and come back looking like a total mess. The AA lecture may work on some but didn't do much for him.

When entering the first Japanese port coming from a foreign port we were met by a man from the Husbanding who is hired to do the clerical work like bringing the ship certificates and crew list to the custom's house with a clearance from the last port. They also bring the shore passes back to the ship, allowing the crew members permission to go ashore. Before sailing they bring everything back with a Port Clearance and collect the shore passes.

The gentlemen who handle the Sea Land ships served us loyally over the years, and I was always impressed with their politeness, knocking and bowing before entering my office, and then bowing again after entering.

That is why I was surprised one trip in Kobe. Instead of one of the old gentlemen standing outside my door bowing saying' "Good morning Captain, three times before entering, a young man knocked on my door, entered, and in perfect English said, Good morning Cap how are you? He placed his brief case on the spare table and in hurry took out the necessary documents requiring my signature and placed them in front of me to sign. As I looked at him, I politely asked if he had been educated in the States, to which he responded, "Yep, three years at the University of Puget Sound in Tacoma." After he left, I realized I had just witnessed a generational change in Japan.

Mr. McLean, the man who put his money where his mouth was and standardized the container shipping without government subsidy, is my hero. He had the same philosophy as President Reagan who said the Government is not the solution to our problem, the Government is the problem. That is definitely true for the U.S. Merchant Marine where the American ship operators have so many handicaps against them.

In our situation for well over a year we made our revenue overseas carrying freight between three foreign countries, yet the company was obligated to pay the same taxes on our earnings as if it was made in domestic trade. In addition, the customs collects 50% duty on all repairs we had done overseas.

I guess that's why I was not too surprised when we return to Tacoma and the vessel's manager gave me the bad news that the Developer may be one of the twelve ships the company had decided to re-flag under the Marshall Island registry, using foreign crew to reduce the operation cost and eliminate the unfair taxes the U.S. Government impose on them.

He offered me an opportunity to transfer to the "Sea Land Tacoma" sailing in the Alaska trade covered by the Jones Act

During my twenty four years with Sea Land I dealt with the vessels operations, as well, as marine operations in charge of loading and unloading the containers on and off the ships but had very little knowledge on how the rest of the company functioned until I attended two Quality Management Seminars where all departments were present to explain their daily operation.

I learned from the sales department that there are 42 steps and approximately 120 people involved in the life cycle of a shipment from the first phone call or email from a customer to the cargo delivered at its destination overseas. The bean counters explained that 83% of the expenses came from shore side operation, and 17% from the vessel's operation.

The biggest bit of the operation cost comes from Stevedoring, terminal, and delivering the container. Then the Banks holding the mortgage, fuel oil, insurance, railroads, trucking repairs, sales, maintenance, stuffing the containers, Fringe benefits, paid vacation, pension and medicals, attorney fees, Pilots, tugs and other port costs, and documentation.

SEA LAND HISTORY OF INNOVATION IS VERY IMPRESSIVE

Sea-Land has built an impressive record of innovation since it invented Containerized ocean shipping in 1956 which benefitted the World.

Over the next several years Sea-Land turns its patents on container design and construction over to the industry, allowing, free of charges, the development of the ISO standards containers and widespread growth and acceptance of containization.

1962   Pioneered design for open top containers.

1962   Patented shipboard crane design

1963   Pioneered the first ocean going "marinzed" refrigerated containers

1963   Panted corner castings and chassis concept & design. Released these for free to use of the industry. This patent is the heart of containization. Without its release the industry wouldn't have happened.

1964   The S.S. Anchorage breaks through the ice-clogged Cook Inlet. The beginning of year around service to the port of Anchorage.

1967   Sea-Land sets up container port facilities in Saigon, Cam Rahn Bay, Da Nang and Que Nhon Vietnam.

1969   Developed and patented the first "Flippers" for container handling equipment (cranes). These greatly decreased the cycle time for engaging containers with the cranes spreader bar.

1970   Introduced the first "power" container.

1972   Pioneered the first "reefer" container designed for chill as opposed to frozen cargo

1972   Developed and patented the double and frame container design that has enabled the industry to intermix 45ft containers in their 20-40 foot operations.

1980   Developed and deployed the industry's only mobile research laboratory dedicated to developing methods and means to enable the containerized movement of perishable commodities.

1980   Introduced the industry's first bottom discharge reefer making carriage of sensitive chill cargo possible.

1980   Patented power line transmission of data technology. Released same to the industry
This became the basis for ISO development of its remote reefer monitoring standards and monitoring standard and for a number of the monitoring diagnostic systems use today on container cranes.

1986   Pioneered a robotic based high density container yard concept that has become a basis for a number of operating, partially automated systems.

1988   Took a leadership role in the development effort that has led to ISO standardization of radio frequency identification devices for the automatic identification containers.

1989   Pioneered the use of voice technology to enable direct voice into computers by container inspection and inventor control personnel

1991   Pioneered the use of expert systems technology to improve the efficiency of container yard operation 1991 Pioneered use of Pen-Point computers for real tie inventorying of containers in a marine yard.

1993   The automated Delta Terminal in Rotterdam begins operation.

1996   Sea-Land celebrates 40 Years of Transportation Creativity

Reunion

Dennis Manning, Albert Ringuette (Big Al), and Arnold Eckert
Don't even think about messing with any one of these guys.

Bosun, Bos'n' both short for Boatswain is an experienced seaman, and the senior man in the unlicensed deck department who supervises the deck crew under the chief mate's supervision. On SIU ships he is also the unlicensed crew union chairman. This picture is from a get-together in 1991 in Tacoma with three of my friends and Sea-Land bosun's who made my job as Chief Mate easy and enjoyable.

"Sea Land Tacoma" a D-7 class vessel built in Sturgeon Bay, Wisconsin in 1987 for the Alaska trade capable of carrying 800 -40 footers of which 280 can be refrigerated containers. She was powered by a 22,500 hp Burmeister & Wain diesel engine giving us a top speed of 21 knots. The bow area had ice banded to reinforce their hull plating to fight the ice in Cook Inlet.

Our schedule and transit times between ports

Tacoma to Anchorage	3 days 6 hours
Anchorage to Kodiak	0 days 14 hours
Kodiak to Tacoma	2 days 21 hours
Kodiak to Dutch Harbor	1 day 9 hours
Dutch Harbor to Tacoma	3 days 21 hours.

Anchorage and Kodiak looked the same to me. The big change in the service was Dutch Harbor located in the Aleutians Chain with some of the world's richest fishing grounds outside its doors, which had been added to the service. Everything in Dutch Harbor was centered on fishing, my kind of town. In addition to the crab and Pollack the Bristol Bay Salmon catch was shipped down to the lower 48 or Japan through Dutch Harbor. It was not uncommon to load over 200 reefer containers of frozen fish.

It was a great place during the summer months but a harsh place in the winter. Sea Land had its own dock and container crane. The tug assisting us docking remained alongside the vessel in case a severe wind came roaring down the mountains. When the wind reached 25-30 mph the cargo operation would cease because the crane operator was not able to keep the containers steady to lower onto the ship. It was not unusual to see empty containers blowing around on the dock both in Dutch Harbor and Kodiak.

The airport is located between the harbor and town with the runway crossing the road which had to be closed for all traffic each time a plane came in for landing or take off. I take my hat off to the pilots coming in between the mountains to land on the small landing strip, sometimes in gale-force winds with rain or snow.

The "Elbow Room" was by far the best known establishment in town and had become world famous when Playboy Magazine voted it to be the second-most dangerous bar in the entire United States.

In the 1980's when fishing was booming, the bar was full of people with money in their pocket which sometimes led to a fistfight both inside and outside the bar.

Now years later things were a lot quieter. The owners must have decided to add some class to the joint when he cut a hole in the structure facing the bay and installed a round window providing a nice view over the harbor.

In my spare time I took every opportunity to go fishing for Halibut.
Some times on a tug boat taking a spin outside the harbor and sometimes
on a charter if I had a good catch we had fish and chips on the menu for days.

I never got tired of being around the harbor watching the activity. Fishing in Alaska is a great experience. Sailing out to your favored fishing spot passing some of the most beautiful sights you will ever see anywhere in the world, with deer and bears standing on the beach looking at you when sailing by, eagles, seagulls, whales and sea lions all around you.

For me halibut are the most exciting fish to catch; the tremendous strength of a halibut must be experienced to believe. A halibut, like any other fish, frantically struggles to escape the hook and to avoid being pulled onboard your boat.

A large halibut is a once in a lifetime catch, and you will remember every detail and never get tired of telling the story over and over. Everybody always has their favorite spot to fish. Some of those spots are deeper than others and make a big difference in the work and fun involved. Once fishing for halibut in 400 feet of water, I felt one nipping on my bait.

It would nip eat, and stop, nip eat and stop which seems to be the pattern of a halibut. Finally, after what seemed forever he took the rest of the bait and the hook. I started to reel him in. I knew I had a big and powerful halibut. I was able to pull him up 20-30 feet off the bottom turning my reel the best I could, when he started fighting to get back down to the bottom again and I would start out fresh and pull him up 40-50 feet off the bottom before he went down again. After working him for about a half an hour I had him up 50-60 feet off the bottom when he used all his power to get back down again, and I was unable to hold him. When he headed for the bottom he gave 3-4 strong jerks and broke the line by the lead sinker. The line was tested for 280 lbs. Fish can be bigger and tougher than me and my equipment.

Another time fishing for halibut, spending a lot of time getting the bait on right before lowering my hook down to the ocean floor, I no sooner hit bottom when I felt a fish start eating my bait. Same routine I had experienced before. He would eat a little, stop and keep me wondering if he had left my bait for something better, but he came back repeating the same pattern for a while before he took the hook. I knew he was big and powerful but not anywhere near as powerful as the one that broke my line before. It took me 20-25 minutes to get him up the 400 feet from the ocean floor to the waters edge. I had a lot off help to get him into the boat. He was 5'9" and weighed 175 lbs.

After putting fresh bait on my hook before letting it out again, I don't think my hook was on the ocean floor for more than 5 minutes before another halibut started eating my bait, same routine all over again. The second halibut weighed 150 lbs.

What luck? Within one hour I had two large Halibuts in the boat, total of 325 lbs. of my favorite fish. The Skipper on the boat marked the spot on the chart as Georg's hole.

Fishing for salmon is another exciting challenge when reeling him home shining like a diamond. A large king can often take 20-25 minutes to haul in. Unless you have caught a large King salmon it is hard to describe the sensation. When trolling for kings, it's important the bait is on the hook correctly so it will spin in the water. Then comes the question, how far down do you want the hook. Even with a fish finder yours is just as good as the next man's, because salmon move fast. Sometimes you can sit around waiting for what seems forever and nothing is happening. Other times you feel something is chasing your bait and hook, and then it will be quiet again for a while. A salmon can chase the bait and sometimes snap the bait without you feeling it, it's important that you pull your hook home and change your bait often.

You have to be alert when hauling in a salmon. One minute he is heading right toward you, next he is under your boat or changing course 180 degrees or jumping up in the air fighting to get off the hook. Many times he can be right next to the boat before he takes off again. When that brute of a silver scale beauty first leaves the water all colors of the rainbow are shown, and getting the fish into the boat is an unforgettable experience. The biggest King I ever reeled home weighed 38 lb. White King is my favorite eating salmon.

I enjoyed listening to the fishing boats communicating with one another on the VHF radio in the daytime. One day in Dutch I happened to hear the Police calling an outbound fishing vessel. The Police told the skipper that they had one of his men in jail, and bail had been set.

After a long pause the skipper asked for the man's name. When the Police officer gave him the name of the crewmember in jail, the skipper responded quickly, by saying he is an ex-crew member, over and out.

Two years later on a winter night out in the Gulf of Alaska heading north toward Anchorage in bad weather, the ship took a heavy roll to starboard and stayed there long enough to stop the flow of fuel to the main engine, and the engine died. The engine alarm went off, sending the duty engineer running down into the engine room to restart, which only takes 5-10 minutes.

I ran up to the bridge where the 3rd mate was on watch, asking him if we had any ships nearby. He told me he had a southbound fishing vessel close by, and that he had already talked to him for a starboard to starboard passage. I told the 3rd mate to call him again and inform him we were dead in the water, and to give us an extra wide berth. As my eyes adjusted to the dark, I was able to see the light on the fishing vessel bouncing up and down. We were rolling heavy, but nothing compared to what he had to cope with. I was standing there watching when the skipper of the fishing vessel called us and in a strong, sincere voice asked." Hi, do you guys need some help over there?" I thanked him for his offer, and told him we would be Okay and underway shortly. As I kept watching him being thrown around, I thought to myself, if anybody needs help, it's him.

In most storms the wind and seas come from the same direction, and sometimes swells come from another direction from a previous storm. The Gulf of Alaska can be different with the wind and seas from one direction and the swells from several other directions.

One such night northbound with a full load of cargo, I was keeping in mind the schedule is flexible but the ship is not. I tried to ease the rolling by reducing speed and course changes which in most cases will ease the movement of the ship, but in this case it didn't do much. After falling out of bed several times, I decided to stay on the floor between my bed and the bulk head.

As I was lying there being tossed around unable to sleep, I asked myself, why I am I here? With 48 good years at sea behind me, a good MM&P pension to look forward to, I decided to call it quits and retire.

Since I was only 60, I had to wait two years to collect Social Security. I applied a few months before my 62nd birthday. When I went for my final interview, a very efficient and polite gentleman told me that everything was in order, but to make sure the numbers added up he said he had to ask a few questions. First, how much money did you make the last year you worked? I told him, and the year before that? I told him. He looked up at me and asked, "Why did you quit?"

Finish with Engine for the last time

I always felt I had a great and exciting job in the best of times in a diminishing industry. It gave me an opportunity to see the world, meeting many interesting people from different cultures and traditions, sometimes under strange circumstances which gave me a wealth of knowledge. I also had an opportunity to dine and party in some of the world's best known bars and restaurants, and some of the worst, and I lived to tell it.

When I listen to people talking about their two weeks' vacation in Hawaii or a cruise to somewhere, I look the other way and try not to make any comments, but say to myself what luck that I didn't have to settle for that.

The world and its people have been a great and grand host to me, and I am forever grateful.

BRIEF RESUME OF GEORG E. PEDERSEN

I was born during a snow storm in 1934 in Rodvig, a small fishing village in Denmark. Despite the German occupation I had a great childhood. I had my own row boat at an early age, making money fishing, hunting and trapping minks, and dreaming about having my own large fishing vessel someday.

When I turned 14 and with no further education available to me my father gave me two choices: "Stay Home Fishing or Ship Out." I chose the latter. For the next 48 years I sailed the seven seas on 62 merchant ships working my way up from Deck Boy in Denmark to Captain in America. The ships became my home and floating work place. Regardless of where I went in the world, I was never more than a taxi ride away from home - the ship. I had the opportunity to meet and work with many interesting people from different cultures and traditions, sometimes under strange circumstances which gave me a wealth of knowledge.

My 14 years as an Unlicensed Sailor in the foc'sle from 1948 to 1962 on 23 different ships were by far the most exciting time of my life. It was the Golden Age after penicillin, and before the SS Exxon Valdez oil spill in Alaska which changed the industry forever. I saw countries in Europe and Asia in ruins after World War Two with a shortage of food and everything else, whereas on the ships the food was plentiful. American cigarettes were king. Going ashore with just a few packs in your pocket, you were a millionaire for the night. It was a great time to be young and adventurous. It was a time that can never be repeated or recreated by Hollywood.

I sailed as a Licensed Officer from 1962 to 1996, working my way up to Master. I was a member of the "Danish Sailors Union," "The Sailors Union of the Pacific," and I am still a member in good standing of the "Masters, Mates and Pilots," since 1962.

APPRECIATION

My heartfelt thanks go to Christopher W. Fraser, Computer Scientist and Neighbor, who gallantly crossed the street to help me whenever I had a computer problem. And to Kathryn Jordan, Novelist and Editor, who did a fabulous job editing the manuscript as well as supported my effort.

Made in the USA
Middletown, DE
10 August 2015